Lecture Notes in Economics and Mathematical Systems 554

Reto Foellmi

Consumption Structure and Macroeconomics

Structural Change and the Relationship Between Inequality and Growth

Springer

Reto Foellmi
MIT, Department of Economics
E52–251D
50 Memorial Drive
Cambridge MA, 02142
USA
foellmi@mit.edu
rfoellmi@iew.unizh.ch

Library of Congress Control Number: 2005928610

ISSN 0075-8442
ISBN-10 3-540-25991-0 Springer Berlin Heidelberg New York
ISBN-13 978-3-540-25991-6 Springer Berlin Heidelberg New York

Springer is a part of Springer Science+Business Media

springeronline.com

Printed in Germany

Typesetting: Camera ready by author
Cover design: *Erich Kirchner*, Heidelberg

Printed on acid-free paper 42/3130Di 5 4 3 2 1 0

Preface

Institutions are a key determinant for growth. I am very happy to have pursued my research at a very good and stimulating institution, namely at the institute for Empirical Research in Economics (IEW). My special thanks go to my thesis-supervisor, Josef Zweimueller. With great enthusiasm, he pointed me towards interesting research subjects. It was a very fruitful collaboration, which allowed me to start quickly my dissertation. Josef Falkinger, my co-advisor, was always an excellent discussant - not only in economics - and I profited from his useful comments on earlier versions of this dissertation. Daron Acemoglu, Philippe Aghion, Marios Angeletos, Giuseppe Bertola, Oded Galor, Omer Moav, and Gilles Saint-Paul provided very valuable comments and suggestions to topics related to this dissertation. I gratefully acknowledge the support and numerous discussions with my colleagues, especially with Zava Aydemir, Men-Andri Benz, Johannes Binswanger, Markus Knell, Volker Grossmann, Urs Meister, Manuel Oechslin, and Niels Zilkens. Furthermore, my research also profited much from the interplay between teaching and research, as it was a very satisfactory task to guide ambitious students to macroeconomic problems.

Finally, I want to thank my parents, Marcel and Rosemarie Foellmi-Kuster, for their great support. As entrepreneurs, they provided me, early on, with a critical view on economic problems and puzzles.

Jede Forschungsarbeit profitiert ungemein von einem anregenden Umfeld. Ich hatte das Glück, am Institut für Empirische Wirtschaftsforschung (IEW) solche idealen Bedingungen vorzufinden. Mein erster Dank gilt dem Betreuer meiner Doktorarbeit, Josef Zweimüller. In einer für mich sehr fruchtbaren Zusammenarbeit wurde ich an äußerst interessante Forschungsfragen herangeführt. Dies alles erleichterte mir den Start in die Dissertation außerordentlich. Als zweites bin ich meinem Koreferenten, Josef Falkinger, zu Dank verpflichtet. Josef Falkinger ist in allen Bereichen der Ökonomie und darüber hinaus ein äußerst engagierter und wertvoller Gesprächspartner. Wertvolle Hinweise zu Themen meiner Dissertation verdanke ich überdies Daron Acemoglu, Philippe Aghion, Marios Angeletos, Giuseppe Bertola, Oded Galor, Omer Moav und Gilles Saint-Paul. Viele Anregungen und vor allem Unterstützung habe ich auch von meinen Kolleginnen und Kollegen erhalten, allen voran von Zava Aydemir, Men-Andri Benz, Johannes Binswanger, Volker Grossmann, Markus Knell, Urs Meister, Manuel Oechslin und Niels Zilkens. Zusätzlich hat mir das Zusammenspiel zwischen Forschung und Lehre, da ich bei letzterer stark engagiert war, auch immer wieder neue Forschungsideen gebracht. Es war überdies eine sehr befriedigende Aufgabe, ambitionierte Studentinnen und Studenten für die Probleme der Makroökonomie zu begeistern.

Schließlich möchte ich meinen Eltern, Marcel und Rosemarie Föllmi-Kuster, für ihre Unterstützung danken. Aus einer Unternehmerfamilie stammend, hatte ich das Privileg, schon früh einen kritischen Blick für wirtschaftliche Zusammenhänge erhalten zu haben.

Cambridge MA, im Mai 2005 Reto Föllmi

Contents

1 Introduction

’Αλλὰ μὴν πρώτη γε καὶ μεγίστη τῶν χρειῶν ἡ της τροφῆς παρασκευὴ τοῦ εἶναί τε καὶ ζην ’ένεκα. Δευτέρα δὴ οἰκήσεως, τρίτη δὲ ἐσθῆτος καὶ τῶν τοιούτων.

Now the first and greatest need is the provision of food for existence and life. The second is housing, and the third is clothing and related things.

(Plato, Politeia, II. 369d)

In a market economy, the individual needs and desires determine which goods are developed and finally produced. *A priori,* the value of a product does not hinge on the costs incurred to produce it; the value only depends on the consumer's willingness to pay. The chain from needs to desires, from desires to demand, and finally to consumption determines all economic activity. The founder of economics as a discipline states this in the following way: "Consumption is the sole end of all production" (Smith, 1776). He continues, "the maxim is so perfectly self-evident, that it would be absurd to attempt to prove it."

In fact, macroeconomics has analyzed extensively the determinants of the size of aggregate consumption. To take an example, one of the main modern developments in macroeconomics, the microfoundation of macroeconomic theories, starts with the "Theory of the Consumption Function" by Milton Friedman (1957). The purpose of microfoundations is to explain macroeconomic phenomena by individual decisions which are in turn governed by the individuals' preferences and restrictions. If we think about consumption it would therefore be natural to start with a specification of the agents' preferences over different goods. However, (macroeconomic) consumption theory only tries to explain total consumption of a consumer (if this is possible without referring to an agents' preferences over single goods). Thus, it seems that consumption theory has stopped at half way in the microfoundation of consumption behavior. In particular, the theory has been almost silent about the question of how the consumption *structure* looks, i.e. *which* goods are consumed. When different goods are taken into account, it is normally assumed - following Dixit and Stiglitz (1977) - that there exists a non-changing "composite commodity", a consumption basket where the ingredients do not change.[1] Therefore, the previous theory is unable to judge how macroeconomic consumption structure changes over time or how it is affected by the distribution of wealth across consumers. One reason for these assumptions is their analytical simplicity. For issues where the time dimension or the inequality of agents plays no role, this seems innocuous. However, as soon as we are interested in the long run behavior of an economy or in questions dealing with inequality, the validity of analysis will be - possibly strongly - affected.[2] The modest purpose of the present book is the analysis of these questions when we take the changing consumption structure into account. Further, we discuss in what sense one should rethink many important macroeconomic problems.

Given the large empirical literature on the behavior of the consumption structure, the little role that the consumption structure has paid in macroeconomic theory is very surprising. Already 150 years ago, the German statistician Engel (1857) stated that the share for food is decreasing in income: "*Je ärmer eine Familie ist, einen desto grösseren Antheil von der Gesammtausgabe muss zur Beschaffung der Nahrung aufgewendet werden (p. 28)*". This relationship has since been called "Engel's law". The subsequent empirical studies impressively

---

[1]A composite commodity can only be constructed if the different wants may be reduced to a single one. (Which can be measured by a cardinal number, namely "utility".) Even in economic science, this claim is not shared unanimously. Georgescu-Roegen (1966, p. 196f.) argues that there is a "Irreducibiliby of Wants": The consumption of bread presents no substitute for the satisfaction of thirst, for example. We will take up parts of this argument indirectly in chapter 2 below. We argue that individual preferences are characterized by relative satiation in consumption of a single good. Formally, the elasticity of substitution declines with consumption.

[2]A broad critique of the representative consumer approach in macroeconomics is provided by Kirman (1992). Applied to consumption theory, Carroll (2000) argues that "*the representative consumer should be abandoned in favor of a model which matches key microeconomic facts* (p.110)."

confirmed Engel's result.[3] Houthakker (1987) even concluded that Engel's law is one the most robust empirical findings in economics. In particular, many writers since Engel have emphasized that Engel's law holds not only for food, but is a more general law of consumption. In their influential book, Deaton and Muellbauer (1980) conclude that the vast majority of studies obtains the result that the expenditure share of a product changes systematically with income. This observed consumer behavior rejects the hypothesis of homothetic preferences, i.e. that the expenditure share of a product does not vary with income. Based on the solid empirical evidence, Kindleberger (1989, p. 9) summarizes these results as follows: *"Engel's law applies to more than food, it is a general law of consumption. With growth, demand for some one or more products - but only a few at a time - starts off with high income elasticity, and then declines as income rises. (...) A given item may go through the Engel's consumption cycle of a luxury, with high income elasticity, to a necessity with low income elasticity."* Thus, the empirical evidence leaves no doubt that the structure of consumption changes in a systematic way. It changes *across individuals*, as we compare a rich and a poor individual, and it changes *over time*, as all agents get richer.

Those overwhelming empirical results suggest that the underlying needs must be ordered according to some hierarchy. "Elementary" goods, such as food, basic clothing and housing, are fulfilled first. As income rises, the consumer moves on to needs of a lower priority, for example culture, health expenditures or travel. To give an additional example, Jackson (1984) presents pervasive empirical evidence that the number of commodities purchased - being a proxy for the "number " of needs satisfied - increases with income. He explains this pattern as a "hierarchy of purchases". As we observe such an ordering of purchase there must be - as we will call it - a "*hierarchy of needs.*" Many writers from various directions have already emphasized that such a hierarchy must exist. We already cited Plato (360 BC).[4] Georgescu-Roegen (1966, p. 193ff.) extensively argues why wants are structured, and he points out that the hierarchy of needs was a key proposition of the theory of consumption of early neoclassical economists such as Menger, Jevons, and - less obviously - Pareto. In particular, Georgescu-Roegen states that there exists the "*Principle of the Subordination of Wants*" in referring to Banfield and Jevons: "*the satisfaction of a lower want (...) merely permits the higher*

[3]Classical examples include Clark (1940), Taylor and Houthakker (1970), and Houthakker (1987).

[4]Plato argues that the satisfaction of the several needs builds a principal reason to found a πόλις. It would be too time-consuming (because there are advantages from specialization) for a single person to produce all goods himself to cover his needs (Plato, Politeia, II. 369b - 370b).

want to manifest itself."[5] Engel (1857) himself concluded directly from his empirical observations that the needs must be structured: *"Nunmehr (ist) gleichsam eine Scala der Bedürfnisse des Lebens zu Tage gefördert. Es unterliegt nicht dem mindesten Zweifel, dass die Nahrung das Bedürfniss erster Ordnung ist, ihm folgt das der Kleidung, darauf folgt das der Wohnung und alsdann das der Heizung und Beleuchtung (p. 27)."*[6] The idea of a structure of wants is not restricted to economic science. In his famous article "theory of human motivation" the psychologist Maslow (1943) formulated a "hierarchy of basic needs" and emphasized that one need must be satisfied (at least relatively) before another emerges: "*But when a need is fairly well satisfied, the next prepotent ('higher') need emerges. (...) The hierarchy principle is usually empirically observed in terms of increasing percentages of non-satisfaction as we go up the hierarchy* (p. 395)."

In pure - or modern - economic terms, the hierarchy of needs is - in principle - nothing more than the well known law of declining marginal utility. In fact, if we consider an economy with many goods satisfying different needs, a hierarchy of needs and the declining marginal utility of income are two sides of the same coin. If incomes rise, individuals move on to needs of lower priority. In utility measure, the satisfaction of these needs gives less utility value than the basic needs, hence the marginal utility is falling.

In the light of these arguments, our aim is to analyze which goods will be consumed and produced at which prices depending on the (distribution) of income per capita. To do so, we must bring the afore mentioned arguments into a coherent and tractable model and discuss its implications. As we allow the consumption structure to vary both over time and across poor and rich individuals, there are two key implications. First, if the consumption structure changes over time, there will be structural change, second, with inequality determining the structure of demand, there will be relationship between inequality and prices, profits, and growth. This gives the principal outline of the book.

In the introductory chapter 2 we develop a general framework of non-homothetic and hierarchic preferences. Different special cases of this framework will be used throughout the book. Given the empirical evidence on income elasticities of demand, we derive the critical functional assumptions needed to generate these

[5]Georgescu-Roegen (p. 195) adds a "Principle of the Growth of Wants" because the "number of wants seems to know no end". This proposition is central for answering the question whether the growth process will last infinitely or come to an end. In chapter 3 below we will come back to this point.

[6]The reader may note that Engel switches the order of needs stated by Plato. Clothing and housing have changed their places.

"stylized facts". We then discuss how aggregate demand depends on inequality in a static setting. In the second part, we turn to the dynamic problem and show how the notion of a composite commodity, i.e. an aggregator for a bundle of consumption goods, can be reintroduced into a setting with non-homothetic preferences where the structure of the consumption bundle changes over time.

Chapter 3, then, is devoted to the interaction between endogenous growth and (demand driven) structural change. With innovation-driven growth, a successful innovation increases productivity and real income. When preferences are hierarchic, higher incomes lead to a change in the demand structure towards the innovative goods: Having covered the basic needs, the individuals put their additional income primarily into the new goods covering needs of lower priority.[7] This demand shift implies that R&D for new goods becomes profitable. These new innovative goods again raise the productivity level and the virtuous circle is closed. Therefore, the demand channel working via hierarchic preferences gives an intuitive argument why there is structural change. The preferences imply that individuals in a richer society will demand other goods and more goods. As production equals demand, the production structure must mirror the consumption structure. Hence, in a richer society the fraction of labor employed in sectors which primarily satisfy basic needs (e.g. agriculture) will be low, whereas the share of labor in "sophisticated" sectors, e.g. information technology, health sciences will be high.[8] Second, as mentioned in the beginning of the introduction, the needs, manifested in demand, determine where the economy grows. As it makes no sense to develop products for which there is no demand, the development of products must follow the hierarchy of needs. In standard R&D models with horizontal product differentiation (e.g. Romer, 1990), it is completely random where a new good comes from due to an innovation because all potentially producible goods offer

[7]Already the classical writers emphasized that the growth process will not result primarily in a growth of consumption quantities. Eventually, an individual will get saturated if he consumes more and more of the same product. Or, to use the words of Adam Smith in his Wealth of Nations, "*the desire for food is limited by [the] narrow capacity of the human stomach*". The growth process rather results in new (and better) products. Thinking in terms of the hierarchy described above, many needs were not satisfied at all in earlier times, such as mobility (by cars, air planes etc.), telecommunications or health care for infectious diseases. Or, only a tiny part of population could afford to satisfy it, e.g. cars, vacuum cleaners, or TVs in the first half of the 20th century.

[8]Colin Clark (1940) saw this point very clear from his empirical observations on the change in the demand structure: "*With these universal forces constantly changing the structure of demand, it is not hard to find the basic reason for the steady shift of the working population from primary to secondary, and from secondary to tertiary industries* (p.446)."

the same utility.[9] In contrast, we argue that growth is not a technological hazard, but it follows the individuals' desires.

The last point, however, opens up a new question.[10] The whole growth process is maintained through demand only. The research for new products will be undertaken only if there are still needs to satisfy. As the needs become less and less important, the growth process might come to an end. Again, it is interesting to consider the arguments of the classical economists.[11] For them, the answer to this question seemed much more uncertain than it does for us because they could not look back to long sustained growth in the past. In fact, Malthus argues "*The savage would slumber for ever under his tree, unless he were roused from his torpor by the cravings of hunger, or the pinchings of cold.*[12]" Put in other terms, after the individuals cover their basic needs thanks to technological progress, they will be saturated, and do no effort to develop new products or techniques. On the other hand, Ricardo (1810ff) takes a "modern" position. He states "*I believe them [sc. the needs] to be unlimited. Give men but the means of purchasing and their wants are insatiable*." Our analysis (and the history) shows that Ricardo is right. Although the needs still unsatiated in a rich economy are less important - in *absolute* terms - than the basic needs still unsatiated in a poor economy, the desire to develop new products to satisfy more needs will not vanish. The reason lies in the fact that individuals in richer economies exhibit a higher willingness pay (their marginal utility of income is lower) for new products. Put differently, in *relative* terms, the uncovered needs are as urgent for rich individuals as for poor individuals. This is just another variant of the observation that necessities and luxuries are relative terms. As we explained above, many durable consumption goods, e.g. cars, vacuum cleaners etc. were luxuries at the time they were developed, but now they are bought by a large share of the population. The task of chapter 3 below is to develop a model which tries to match these facts.

In chapter 4 the relationship between inequality and demand structure is analyzed in an endogenous growth model. According to Engel's law, modeled with hierarchic preferences, the rich consume more goods than the poor, and they will

---

[9]Note that these models explain growth by the introduction of new products. However, only the range of intermediate goods increases. The (final) consumption good does not change.

[10]Of course, it is a very *old* question in economics whether growth will last infinitely or come to an end.

[11]I owe parts of this overview to A. Victor Walser, who summarized the opinions of the classics about consumption structures in his student thesis in 2002 ("Semesterarbeit") under supervision of mine.

[12]Malthus (1798), p. 357, First Essay on Population cit. by Falkinger (1986), p. 53.

spend relatively little on goods covering basic needs. Naturally, this opens a new channel for inequality to affect growth. If inequality affects aggregate demand (the exact technical conditions will have to be shown), the profits and the research incentives of an innovator are affected by income distribution. If the distribution is very unequal, there will be people who will exhibit a high willingness to pay for innovative products, hence, an innovator will be able to sell his product early and to set high prices. On the other hand, the market size will remain small over a long period of time because a large part of the population is very poor. It is the purpose of chapter 4 below to explore this trade-off.

Again, this analysis opens up a new question. With non-homothetic preferences, the pricing decisions of firms with market power depend on the income distribution. For example, as outlined in the paragraph above, the innovators may set higher prices at the introduction of the products when the richest group in the population gets even richer. However, these decisions determine whether or not certain groups are *excluded* from the consumption of certain products. By exclusion we mean that an agent cannot buy a product although his marginal willingness to pay is above marginal costs. To maximize profits, the monopolist may choose to set the price higher than the reservation price of a poor group and to sell to the rich part in the population only.

In chapter 4 the demand function on the single product market was assumed to be very simple such that the exposition of the dynamic model could be made as easy as possible. To study the interesting relationship between inequality and product market power in detail, we develop in chapter 5 a static model in which we put less restrictions on product market demands. It will turn out that more inequality leads to more exclusion of the poor, even when preferences are symmetric. In addition, a more unequal income distribution is associated with higher markups and a higher profit share. This implies that the marginal revenue product of labor is lower which may lead to unemployment even when wages are flexible. The usefulness of this static framework lies in the fact that it allows us to study how imperfections in one market lead to imperfections / inefficiencies in other markets. Even more importantly, the model in chapter 5 explains that inequality affects factor prices when markets are imperfect[13] and it presents empirically testable hypotheses about the relationship between inequality and (macro)economic performance.

[13]In this setting, we focused on imperfections in the product market. However, we could also focus on imperfect capital markets, as in Foellmi and Oechslin (2003), or on imperfect labor markets.

2

Hierarchic Preferences

2.1 Basic Set-up

In this chapter we propose a general formulation of non-homothetic hierarchic preferences. The purpose is to develop functional forms which are still tractable for macro models but which are general enough to match the empirical facts about the income dependent structure of demand. To start from general notion of preferences has the advantage that it allows us to identify the critical assumptions on the curvature of the utility function needed to match the empirical facts. In the first part of the chapter we focus on a static set-up which allows us to remain fairly general in our choice of the utility function. The second part of the chapter shows which additional assumptions on the utility function and on the price structure are needed to deal with dynamic problems. When the hierarchy function is a power function and the supply side satisfies certain symmetry conditions, we obtain a result wherein the indirect utility function takes a constant relative risk aversion (CRRA) form which is compatible with steady states. This result is very helpful. Although the composition of the consumption basket changes over time we can find a consumption aggregator that has the same properties (i.e. CRRA) as the composite commodity in standard monopolistic competition models. We will make use of this result in the following chapters 3 and 4. At the end of this chapter, we compare our hierarchic utility function to different functional forms suggested in the previous literature.

Consider an economy with an infinite number of potentially producible goods ranked by an index j. A certain need j can be satisfied by consuming the corresponding good j. Put in other terms, a good represents a "technology" which satisfies a given need. A meaningful specification of hierarchic preferences then has to take account of three facts.

(i) Needs are ordered.

(ii) Some goods may not be consumed, i.e. some needs remain unsatisfied, because the consumers cannot afford it. Technically speaking, marginal utility at zero must be finite, at least for goods of lower priority.

(iii) If a consumer has additional income, he should spend it primarily on goods that have lower priority because the needs of higher priority are already saturated (at least in relative terms).

Therefore, we study the structure of consumption that is generated by preferences of the form[1]

$$u(\{c(j)\}) = \int_0^\infty \xi(j)v(c(j))dj \tag{2.1}$$

where $v(c(j))$ is an indicator for the utility derived from consuming good j in quantity c. The 'baseline' utility $v(c(j))$ satisfies the usual assumptions $v' > 0$ and $v'' < 0$; and the *'hierarchy' function* $\xi(j)$ is monotonically decreasing in j, $\xi'(j) \leq 0$, hence low-j goods get a higher weight than high-j goods. It is important to note that we make three important assumptions or restrictions, respectively, at this stage. First, the marginal utility of good j only depends on $c(j)$ but does not depend on the consumption level of other goods. Thus, utility is assumed to be *additively separable.* This assumption seems rather innocuous for the questions we want to study. In addition, a deviation from this usual assumption would cause analytical complexity since the goods space is modelled as a continuum (the number of goods is infinite). As a consequence, this utility function defined over different goods is formally analogous to additively separable intertemporal preferences defined over consumption at different points in time. Second, the utility of the goods only differs in the multiplicative factor $\xi(j)$. We will see below that this formulation is flexible enough to derive the patterns mentioned above. Third, all consumers have the same preferences. Hence, all differences in demand come from differences in endowments and not from differences in tastes. This assump-

[1]Earlier versions of hierarchic preferences can be found in Zweimueller (1996, 2000) and Foellmi (1999). Zweimueller (1996) is the first model with hierarchic preferences and a continuous range of goods where the consumption of a single good $c(j)$ is continuous variable. In particular, he assumed $v(\cdot)$ to be quadratic such that product demand is linear.

tion allows us to focus on the effects of different endowments alone. In addition, the assumption, that the poor like to consume more bread, e.g., would lead to tautological statements concerning the consumption structure and inequality.

The presence of a hierarchic weight $\xi(j)$ does not imply that the utility function $u(\{c(j)\})$ is non-homothetic. Whether $u(\{c(j)\})$ is homothetic or not depends on the form of the sub-utility function $v(\cdot)$ alone. Non-homotheticity implies that the expenditure shares of the different goods j differ or, equivalently, that the income elasticities of the different goods may differ from one. This will be the case whenever the elasticity of substitution $-\frac{v'(c)}{v''(c)c}$ varies with c. Put in other terms, preferences of the form (2.1) are homothetic if and only if $\frac{v'(c)}{v''(c)c}$ is constant.[2]

It will turn out below that the income elasticity for good j is proportional to $-\frac{v'(c)}{v''(c)c}$. To match the stylized fact that the income elasticity for a certain good declines with consumption / income we therefore assume that $-\frac{v'(c)}{v''(c)c}$ decreases in c. Hence, the elasticity of substitution between two goods should be falling. This assumption means that there is a "relative" satiation in a single good. Having already consumed so much of a good, an individual is increasingly less willing to consume more of that good in exchange for a reduction in consumption of another good.[3] In addition we assume that the marginal utility of consuming good j in quantity zero, $\xi(j)v'(0)$ is finite for all $j > 0$.[4] This implies that consumers may not want to consume all goods - although they have the same preferences - because the *non-negativity constraints may become binding.* If marginal utility at quantity zero were infinitely large, it would always be optimal to consume a (small) positive amount even when prices are very high and/or the budget is very low. Needless to say, non-negativity constraints are incompatible with homothetic preferences. Every good must be consumed at all income levels or it is never consumed. To see this formally, consider the utility function in the standard monopolistic competition model which uses homothetic preferences (Dixit and Stiglitz (1977)). In this model, the partial utility function is given by $v(c(i)) = \frac{1}{\alpha}c(i)^{\alpha}$, $\alpha < 1$, which implies a constant $\frac{v'(c)}{v''(c)c}$ and $v'(0) = \infty$. Thus in the

---

[2] These are the CES (constant elasticity of substitution) preferences used e.g. in Dixit and Stiglitz (1977).

[3] Trivially, this assumption is satisfied at points where there is full satifiation: $v'(c) = 0$. However, it is not necessary that the utility function exhibits a bliss point. To see this, consider the utility function $v'(c) = (c+q)^{-\sigma}$ where $q, \sigma > 0$. It is easy to check that $-\frac{v'(c)}{v''(c)c}$ is monotonically falling in c.

[4] Note that the latter assumption implies that $\partial\left(-\frac{v'(c)}{v''(c)c}\right)/\partial c < 0$ at $c = 0$. Hence, the former and the latter assumption are compatible. In particular, if $\frac{v'(c)}{v''(c)c}$ is constant (homothetic case), marginal utility at zero $v'(0)$ necessarily equals infinity.

standard monopolistic competition model all available goods are consumed in positive amounts.

The generalized version of Engel's law - as emphasized for example by Kindleberger (1989) cited in the introductory chapter - implies that *additional* income is spent primarily on low-priority goods (high income elasticity). This essential feature is caught by the formulation that the utility of consumption of different goods differs in the factor $\xi(j)$. As the hierarchy function $\xi(j)$ is decreasing in j the marginal utility of a high priority good (low j) falls quickly. Optimal consumer behavior implies that additional income is spent primarily on the low-priority goods with slowly falling marginal utilities.[5]

2.1.1 *Individual Demand*

To derive the individual demand curve we solve the consumer's static maximization problem. The total expenditures of a consumer are denoted by E_i, which are exogenous in the static problem. The consumer's objective function (2.1) will be maximized subject to the budget constraint $\int_0^\infty p(j)c(j)dj = E_i$ and the nonnegativity constraints $c(j) \geq 0$ for all j. The optimality conditions then read

$$\begin{aligned} \xi(j)\ v'(c_i(j)) &= \lambda_i p(j) \text{ if } c_i(j) > 0 \\ \xi(j)\ v'(c_i(j)) &\leq \lambda_i p(j) \text{ if } c_i(j) = 0. \end{aligned} \tag{2.2}$$

Equation (2.2) gives us the individual demand function: Consumer i's optimal consumption of good j, $c_i(j)$, depends on its price $p(j)$ and the Lagrangian multiplier λ_i, the marginal utility of income of consumer i. It is immediately transparent that $c_i(j)$ and income E_i cannot be proportional. Very poor consumers with low E_i and high λ_i will choose not to consume good j. The nonnegativity constraint may become binding since marginal utility at zero consumption is finite. It is instructive to look at how $c_i(j)$ varies with j, i.e. what shape the individual consumption profile takes. Throughout the chapter we will assume that $\xi(j)/p(j)$ is decreasing. If the goods are ordered in such fashion, the model formalizes the notion of a "hierarchy of wants": loosely speaking, units of goods with low i indices yields higher utility, and consumers give priority to them when choosing the optimal consumption patterns. In that case the optimal quantity $c_i(j)$ decreases

[5] Of course, the same consumption pattern could be generated by imposing a specific structure on prices. If the prices of the goods $p(j)$ would increase in j, consumption of low-j-goods would be higher and their income elasticity lower as required when $\partial \frac{v'(c)}{v''(c)c} / \partial c > 0$. However, there is no clear evidence that such a cost pattern can be found on the production side.

in j and the consumption range increases in income. Hence, consumer i will consume all goods $j < N_i$. where the critical good N_i is determined by the following condition

$$\xi(N_i)\ v'(0) = \lambda_i p(N_i). \tag{2.3}$$

The consumption of the last good $c_i(N_i)$ equals zero, as long as $\xi(j)/p(j)$ is continuous at $j = N_i$ (otherwise the consumption of good N_i is strictly positive). Importantly, condition (2.3) implies that consumption "follows the hierarchy". If an individual gets richer, he will not only consume more of the previous goods but he will consume also more goods. A richer consumer exhibits a lower marginal utility of income λ_i, hence equation (2.3) is fulfilled by a larger N_i. Panel a. of the figure below shows the i's demand curve for a high j and a low j good, respectively. Panel b. shows the demand curve for the same good j of a rich and a poor consumer, respectively. Both pictures look very similar. This arises from the multiplicative formulation of the hierarchy factor $\xi(j)$.

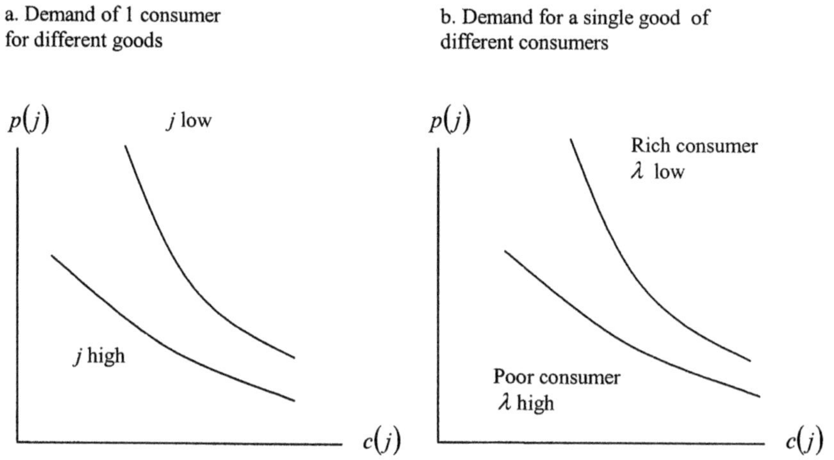

Fig. 2.1. Demand Patterns

To complete our discussion of the individual demand curve, calculate the price and income elasticity of demand. By differentiation of (2.2) we get the (direct) price elasticity

$$\begin{aligned} \varepsilon(c_i(j)) &\equiv \frac{dc_i(j)}{dp(j)}\frac{p(j)}{c_i(j)} = \frac{\lambda_i p(j)}{\xi(j)\ v''(c_i(j))c_i(j)} \\ &= \frac{v'(c_i(j))}{v''(c_i(j))c_i(j)}. \end{aligned} \tag{2.4}$$

We derive the income elasticity by differentiating (2.2) and the budget constraint. Income E and its marginal utility are negatively related

$$dE_i = \frac{d\lambda_i}{\lambda_i} \int_0^{N_i} p(j) \frac{v'(c_i(j))}{v''(c_i(j))} dj. \tag{2.5}$$

The income elasticity then reads

$$\begin{aligned} \frac{dc_i(j)}{dE_i} \frac{E_i}{c_i(j)} &= \frac{v'(c_i(j))}{v''(c_i(j))c_i(j)} \frac{\int_0^{N_i} \xi(j)\ v'(c_i(j))c_i(j)dj}{\int_0^{N_i} \xi(j)\ v'(c_i(j))c_i(j) \frac{v'(c_i(j))}{v''(c_i(j))c_i(j)} dj} \\ &= \varepsilon(c_i(j)) \left(\int_0^{N_i} e_{ij} \varepsilon(c_i(j)) dj \right)^{-1}. \end{aligned} \tag{2.6}$$

where e_{ij} denotes the expenditure share for good j which is given by $\frac{p(j)c_i(j)}{\int_0^{N_i} p(j)c_i(j)dj}$. The income elasticity for consumer i is proportional to $\frac{v'(c)}{v''(c)c} = \varepsilon(c)$. In particular, the income elasticity equals the direct price elasticity divided by an expenditure weighted average of the direct price elasticities.[6] Hence, the low i ("elementary") goods where consumption is higher exhibit a lower income elasticity than the high i ("luxury") goods. This is exactly the pattern required by Engel's law. In addition, the formula (2.6) suggests that richer individuals exhibit a lower income elasticity for a given good j than poorer individuals do. However, this relationship need not be strictly monotone without further assumption on the price structure and/or preferences. In the special cases below, we are able to present a clear answer to that question. Finally, we note that there is a correlation between income and price elasticity of a certain good: Goods with a low income elasticity also exhibit a low price elasticity in absolute value. This is due to the multiplicative manner that the hierarchy function $\xi(j)$ enters the utility function (see equation (2.1) and Figure 2.1).

2.1.2 Aggregate Demand

We turn to our question of primary interest, how income distribution affects aggregate demand. We continue to assume that all consumers have equal preferences and are different only with respect to their expenditure levels (with respect to E). By assumption of equal preferences consumers are systematically different with respect to their marginal utility of expenditures (richer consumers have a lower marginal utility of income) and the distribution of the marginal expenditure

[6] If $\frac{v'(c)}{v''(c)c}$ were constant, such that preferences are homothetic, the formula indeed shows that the income elasticity would equal unity for all goods j.

utilities derives from the distribution of the individuals' budgets. Assume that individual incomes E_i are distributed according to the distribution function $G(E_i)$. In principle, we get the aggregate demand function by summing up the individual demands $c_i(j)$ from (2.2) and using the density $g(E_i)$ as weight. However, with general functional form $v(\cdot)$, no explicit solution for $c_i(j)$ is available. Nonetheless, we can derive the slope of aggregate demand and the price elasticity of aggregate demand. Denote aggregate demand by $C(j) = \int_{E^*}^{\infty} c_i(j)dG(E_i)$, where E^* is the minimum income level such that good j is consumed. The marginal utility of income λ^* of the marginal consumer is given by: $\xi(j)\ v'(0) = \lambda^* p(j)$. Since $dE/d\lambda < 0$, the minimum income E^* depends negatively on $\xi(j)/p(j)$. Hence, for low priority goods (with low $\xi(j)/p(j)$), the share of consumers buying this good will be small. The slope of aggregate demand can be written as follows

$$\begin{aligned} \frac{dC(j)}{dp(j)} &= \frac{1}{\xi(j)} \int_{E^*}^{\infty} \frac{\lambda_i}{v''(c_i(j))} dG(E_i) \\ &= \frac{1}{p(j)} \int_{E^*}^{\infty} \frac{v'(c_i(j))}{v''(c_i(j))} dG(E_i) \end{aligned}$$

It is instructive to look at which parameters determine the slope of aggregate demand $dC(j)/dp(j)$. The integral tells us that it is given by the average of the slopes of individual demands because the individual demand curves are aggregated horizontally. First, the slope depends on the hierarchy parameter $\xi(j)$. For high priority goods, $dC(j)/dp(j)$ is very low or the demand curve is very steep. Second, it depends on the average of the λ_i's, the marginal utilities of income, of the consumers.[7] If good j is only consumed by a rich subset of the consumers who exhibit a low marginal utility of income, $dC(j)/dp(j)$ will be low (inelastic). Chapter 4 and 5 below present a specific example where this pattern can be discussed. To calculate the price elasticity of demand we use (2.2) to replace λ_i.

$$\begin{aligned} \frac{dC(j)}{dp(j)} \frac{p(j)}{C(j)} &= \int_{E^*}^{\infty} \frac{v'(c_i(j))}{v''(c_i(j))} \frac{1}{C(j)} dG(E_i) \\ &= \int_{E^*}^{\infty} \varepsilon(c_i(j)) \frac{c_i(j)}{C(j)} dG(E_i). \end{aligned}$$

We get the well known result that the price elasticity equals a quantity weighted average of individual price elasticities. Ceteris paribus, aggregate demand is more elastic if more consumers choose to consume good j, i.e. if E^* is lower, and if the total quantity is lower. The former is due to the higher price elasticity of

[7]The behavior of v'' is less clear since v''' may be either positive or negative. The second derivative v'' is constant if the partial utility function v is quadratic and demand is linear.

demand of poorer consumers. The latter comes from the fact that the individual demand becomes more inelastic when consumption rises, hence this holds also for aggregate demand.

Income distribution and aggregate demand structure with competitive markets

Continue to assume that $\partial\left(\xi(j)/p(j)\right)/\partial j < 0$. Markets are competitive, hence the prices $p(j)$ are determined by technology which is exogenously given (since we are considering a static problem). This assumption is necessary because prices will depend on distribution if markets are not competitive as we will see below. To study how the distribution affects demand we compare the derivatives of demand with respect to income across rich and poor consumers. From the income elasticity formula we can determine $\partial c(j)/\partial E$.

$$\frac{\partial c_i(j)}{\partial E_i} = \frac{v'(c_i(j))}{v''(c_i(j))}\left(\int_0^{N_i} p(j)\frac{v'(c_i(j))}{v''(c_i(j))}dj\right)^{-1}$$

The first general result is easily stated: More inequality increases the variety of goods consumed in the economy. The result directly follows from (2.3). An increase in inequality in the Lorenz-sense implies that the income of the richest consumer cannot fall (holding the average income constant, of course). If the richest' incomes rise, their marginal utility λ_i will be lower, hence their consumption range N_i is larger. The positive relationship between inequality and variety is exactly due to our assumption that marginal utility is finite: $v'(0) < \infty$.

However, with this general function form for $v(\cdot)$, there is no clear statement whether $\partial c(j)/\partial E$ is higher for goods where $c(j)$ is lower. This depends on the sign of $\partial\frac{v'(c)}{v''(c)}/\partial c$ which may be positive or negative. In addition, when we compare two individuals, we cannot even say whether the marginal propensity to consume is lower for the rich person. For an experienced reader who is acquainted with intertemporal models and inequality this should be no surprise. As mentioned above, an additively separable intertemporal utility function has, in principle, the same form as (2.1). The role of the hierarchy parameter $\xi(j)$ is taken by the discount rate. There, the individual chose consumption levels at different points in time, here, the agent chooses the consumption level of different goods. It can be shown (see Bertola, Foellmi and Zweimueller, 2005, chapter 3) that inequality will have no effects on aggregate savings if and only if $v(\cdot)$ takes a HARA form, because this is the only additive separable utility function that exhibits *linear* income expansion paths - as long as consumption is positive. Instead, if we allow $v(\cdot)$ to take a general form, the income expansion path could be convex or concave or both. Applying this to our problem here, everything may happen when inequality changes. So far I know there is no clear empirical evidence how the marginal propensity to consume of a single good changes with income holding the number of commodities bought constant. Since no general conclusion can be drawn from general functional forms, it seems useful to work with a HARA subutility function where $\partial c(j)/\partial E$ is constant when the consumption range N does not differ. The study of the HARA form will provide us a general intuition what sign the comparative statics will take. Needless to say, that the analytical complexity of our problem will be significantly reduced.

An important special case: The HARA class

Assume that the partial utility is given by the HARA form (we omit the individual index i in what follows)

$$u(\{c(j)\}) = \int_0^\infty \frac{1}{\beta}\frac{\sigma}{1-\sigma}\xi(j)\left(\frac{\beta c(j)}{\sigma} - \bar{c}\right)^{1-\sigma} dj \tag{2.7}$$

where $\beta > 0$, $\bar{c} < 0$, and $\sigma \in \Re$. The restrictions on the preference parameters guarantee that $-\frac{v'(c)}{v''(c)c}$ decreases in c. Again, the goods are arranged in such a way that the first N are consumed in positive amounts which must hold in equilibrium if $\partial\left(\xi(j)/p(j)\right)/\partial j < 0$.[8]

The first order conditions for an interior solution of individual consumption reads, by analogy to (2.2)

$$\xi(j)\left(\frac{\beta c(j)}{\sigma} - \bar{c}\right)^{-\sigma} - p(j)\lambda = 0, \forall i,$$

we obtain

$$c(j) = \frac{\bar{c}\sigma}{\beta} + \frac{\sigma}{\beta}\left(p(j)\lambda/\xi(j)\right)^{-1/\sigma}. \tag{2.8}$$

This characterizes the solution if the maximization problem is convex. The individual chooses to consume the first N goods since $\partial\left(\xi(j)/p(j)\right)/\partial j < 0$. Then, the budget constraint reads

$$\int_0^N p(j)c(j)dj = E.$$

[8] To prevent divergence of the integral we need $\lim_{x\to\infty} - \int_N^x \frac{1}{\beta}\frac{\sigma}{1-\sigma}\xi(j)\left(-\bar{c}\right)^{1-\sigma} dj \equiv \Xi$. The limes exists if $\lim_{x\to\infty}\int_N^x \xi(j)dj$ converges, i.e. $\xi(j)$ goes to zero at a rate fast enough ("steep hierarchy"). If we want to study a "flat hierarchy" where the latter integral does not converge, we must normalize $v(c(j))$ such that $v(0) = 0$. In that case $\int_N^x \xi(j)v(0)dj = 0\ \forall x$ and the normalized partial utility function is given by $\tilde{v}(c(j)) = \left(\frac{\beta c(j)}{\sigma} - \bar{c}\right)^{1-\sigma} - (-\bar{c})^{1-\sigma}$ (note that $\bar{c} < 0$). See also the discussion about finite utility in the next subsection.

Inserting the consumption levels (2.8) in the budget constraint, we have

$$\int_0^N p(j)\left(\frac{\bar{c}\sigma}{\beta}+\frac{\sigma}{\beta}\left(p(j)\lambda/\xi(j)\right)^{-1/\sigma}\right)dj=E,$$

hence

$$\lambda^{-1/\sigma}=\frac{\int_0^N p(j)\frac{\bar{c}\sigma}{\beta}dj-E}{\int_0^N p(j)\left(\xi(j)/p(j)\right)^{1/\sigma}dj}.$$

Thus, the (interior) consumption level of good i is given by

$$c(j)=\frac{\bar{c}\sigma}{\beta}+\frac{\left(\xi(j)/p(j)\right)^{1/\sigma}}{\int_0^N p(j)\left(\xi(j)/p(j)\right)^{1/\sigma}dj}\left(E-\frac{\bar{c}\sigma}{\beta}\int_0^N p(j)dj\right) \tag{2.9}$$

for a consumer who is faced by prices $\{p(j)\}$ and spends an amount E on a set of measure N of the goods.

At this point, we note that if $0>\sigma>-1$ (which implies $v''>0$) the allocation problem has a corner solution: the consumer should allocate his expenditure to the goods with the highest $\xi(j)/p(j)$ ratio and consumption of these goods equals $\frac{\bar{c}\sigma}{\beta}>0$. As $\xi(j)/p(j)$ decreases, the consumer chooses $c(j)=1$ for goods $j\in[0,N]$ and $c(j)=0$ for goods $j\in(N,\infty)$ in the optimum. Obviously, this solution can also be derived by considering a consumer with utility $V(\{c(j)\})=-\int_0^\infty \xi(j)c(j)dj$ where $c(j)\in\{0,1\}$ and $\frac{\bar{c}\sigma}{\beta}$ is normalized to one. This special case (*"0-1-preferences"*) is very convenient since it is extremely simple and it will be used in the applications (chapter 5) below.

¿From (2.9) the marginal propensity of agent i to consume good j can be derived.

$$\frac{\partial c_i(j)}{\partial E_i}=\begin{cases}\left(\frac{\xi(j)}{p(j)}\right)^{\frac{1}{\sigma}}\left(\int_0^{N_i}p(j)\left(\frac{\xi(j)}{p(j)}\right)^{\frac{1}{\sigma}}dj\right)^{-1} & j\in[0,N_i],\\ 0 & j\notin[0,N_i].\end{cases}$$

The HARA assumption provides us the required clear result. The marginal propensity to consume $\partial c_i(j)/\partial E_i$ is lower for richer agents because their N_i is higher. Hence, the Engel curve is strictly concave for $c_i(j)>0$ (see also Figure 3.2). This implication may seem restrictive because some empirical evidence suggests that Engel curve take a logistic shape. This would mean that for low levels of $c_i(j)$ the Engel curve is convex and for higher values it is concave. However, if we consider a range of goods and draw the corresponding Engel curve for this range, the curve takes indeed a logistic shape. This will be done in the section dealing with structural change in chapter 3 (Figure 3.3). The reason is that at low income levels only a subset of the given range will be consumed.

It is interesting to note how the derivative varies across goods taking expenditures E as constant, i.e. whether additional income is put . Note that $\partial c_i(j)/\partial E$ falls in j if $\sigma > 0$ which is somewhat unintuitive but follows from the fact that $\partial \frac{v'(c)}{v''(c)}/\partial c < 0$ if $\sigma > 0$. However, the increase is less than proportional for low j - goods since their income elasticity is below one. Put differently, although the consumption of "elementary" goods (low j) increases more strongly than that of "luxury" goods in absolute terms, the consumption of luxuries will always increase more strongly in relative terms even when $\sigma > 0$. For $\sigma \to -\infty$ where $v(\cdot)$ takes the CARA form, the propensity to consume is constant: $\partial c_i(j)/\partial E = 1/\int_0^{N_i} p(j)dj$. For HARA preferences with exhibit a bliss point which is the case if $\sigma < 0$, $\partial c_i(j)/\partial E$ increases in j. This is perhaps the most intuitive.

The income elasticity reads for goods where $c_i(j) > 0$:

$$\frac{dc_i(j)}{dE_i}\frac{E_i}{c_i(j)} = E_i\left(\frac{\bar{c}\sigma}{\beta}\left[\left(\frac{p(j)}{\xi(j)}\right)^{\frac{1}{\sigma}}\int_0^{N_i} p(j)\left(\frac{\xi(j)}{p(j)}\right)^{\frac{1}{\sigma}} dj - \int_0^{N_i} p(j)dj\right] + E_i\right)^{-1} \tag{2.10}$$

The income elasticity monotonically increases along the hierarchy, i.e. it is higher for goods of lower priority where $\xi(j)/p(j)$ is low (note that $\bar{c} < 0$). The value of the income elasticity allows us to give an intuitive condition of an "elementary" good. We define the goods with income elasticity below one as elementary. Therefore, good j is an elementary good if

$$\left(\frac{\xi(j)}{p(j)}\right)^{\frac{1}{\sigma}} > \int_0^{N_i} \frac{p(j)}{\int_0^{N_i} p(j)dj}\left(\frac{\xi(j)}{p(j)}\right)^{\frac{1}{\sigma}} dj \text{ for } \sigma > 0 \tag{2.11}$$

For $\sigma < 0$, the sign reverses. The formula tells us that good j is an elementary good if its utility / price ratio $\xi(j)/p(j)$ is higher than the weighted average of utility price ratios of all goods the agent consumes. From this condition it becomes also clear that the notion "elementary" versus "luxury" is a *relative one*. A given good j may be an elementary good for a rich consumer whereas it is viewed as a luxury from the viewpoint of a poor agent. In terms of the of the formula, the weighted average of utility / price ratios is lower for a rich individual because he consumes a large range of goods and $\xi(j)/p(j)$ decreases in j. Hence, the critical good j^*, where condition (2.11) holds with equality, is higher. The same pattern arises, if we looked at an economy with long run growth, where the range of goods

N expands over time: a given good j would be an luxury good at low stages of development and then become an elementary good at a mature stage.[9]

2.2 Hierarchy and CRRA

It is a commonly shared view that economic growth results in new and better products both for consumers and producers. In particular, many endogenous growth models (Grossman/Helpman, Romer) explain growth by expanding product variety. In a sharp contrast, however, final consumption is modeled as a composite commodity which is produced with an ever increasing variety of inputs but which itself does not change over time. In the optimum, consumers have the annoying duty to increase their consumption of an always identical good at a constant rate. If we now allow composity to vary, we confront the problem how to aggregate the different goods and if that is fulfilled how to get steady-states. However, and this is the purpose of the following section, there is a solution. We show that the (indirect) utility function is CRRA in expenditure levels if the hierarchic weight follows a power function and if the goods prices only depend on their relative position in the hierarchy.[10] In particular, the supply side assumptions are satisfied if all goods are produced with the same marginal costs (symmetry) and goods markets are competitive. In such a case the utility function would exhibit the CRRA form not only over time but also across agents.[11]

The deciding assumption is that the hierarchic weight takes a power function $\xi(j) = j^{-\gamma}$ where $\gamma > 0$. From (2.1) the preferences are given by

$$U(\{c_i(j)\}) = \int_0^\infty j^{-\gamma} v(c_i(j)) dj \tag{2.12}$$

where $c_i(j)$ denotes the level of consumption level of good j by a household of type i with expenditures $E_i \int_0^\infty p(j)c_i(j)dj$.

---

[9]As already mentioned in the introduction, the relative notion of elementary vs. luxury goods is illustrated by many examples: cars, vacuum cleaners, washing machines, tv etc. were luxuries when they were developed and they were bought only by a small part of the population. Nowadays, these products are widespread among households. See chapter 3 below.

[10]Note, however, that the utility value across (rich and poor) agents does not exhibit a CRRA form because they do not consume the same goods in the same proportions. Hence, they face different price indices.

[11]The following exposition is based on the derivations in Foellmi (2003).

Maximizing (2.12) with respect to the individual's budget constraint we get the first order conditions

$$\begin{aligned} j^{-\gamma}v'(c_i(j)) &= \lambda_i p(j) \text{ if } c_i(j) > 0 \\ j^{-\gamma}v'(c_i(j)) &\leq \lambda_i p(j) \text{ if } c_i(j) = 0 \end{aligned} \tag{2.13}$$

Inserting the optimal quantities back into the utility function (2.12) gives us the indirect utility function. Since utility is defined over an infinite sum of needs, we have to state conditions when the integral converges. In the appendix it is shown that for $\gamma < 1$ we can find a normalization of the integral such that convergence is always ensured. For $\gamma \geq 1$ the integral will only converge (after normalization) for partial utility functions $v(\cdot)$ which are bounded from above.

The following central proposition states how the value of utility changes when the range of goods available $N(t)$ changes over time. If hierarchy follows a power function and the goods' prices only depend on their relative position, expenditures $E_i(t)$ and the range of consumed goods $N_i(t)$ are proportional. This proportionality implies that utility is CRRA in expenditures.

Proposition 1 *From viewpoint of an individual, the indirect utility function is CRRA in expenditures over time if the relative price structure remains constant over time. If these conditions hold, the* inter*temporal rate of substitution does not differ across agents.*

Proof. See Appendix. ■

It is important to note that the utility function across agents at a given point in time does *not* exhibit a CRRA form. The reason is that poor and rich agents do not consume the same goods, hence they face a different price index. But this is not a problem for the steady state behavior. We need only that the indirect utility is CRRA from the viewpoint of a single agent, as stated in the Proposition, because this implies that all agents will save the same constant fraction of income in steady state.

How severe is the assumption that the relative price structure remains constant over time? Actually, this price pattern is the equilibrium outcome in a broad range of models. In particular, we will see in the chapters below that a possible economic situation which will give rise to such an price structure is the following: All goods are produced with the same marginal costs (i.e. the supply structure is symmetric) and the share of monopolists is constant over time (this will be the case e.g. if the economy is in steady state and the patent duration is constant).[12] Thus, a constant relative price structure can be found in many models with imperfect competition.

Heterogeneous Agents and Competitive Markets

An important special case where the relative price structure will remain constant is a situation where all goods are produced with the same marginal costs and markets are competitive. Obviously, in this case all prices are equal and constant over time. In addition, utility is CRRA not only over time but also across agents because the individual price indices are the same for all agents although they consume different goods.

Assume all products are produced with the same marginal costs and markets are competitive. The price of all products j equals unity. From (2.13) we conclude that $j^{-\gamma}v'(c_i(j)) = \lambda_i$ which implies that $c_i(j)$ is decreasing in j. Furthermore, the restriction $v'(0) < \infty$ means that there is a good, call it N_i, for which we have $c_i(N_i) = 0$. The first order condition for good N_i is

$$N_i^{-\gamma}v'(0) = \lambda_i. \tag{2.14}$$

Inserting this into the first order condition yields

$$v'(c_i(j)) = \frac{j^{\gamma}}{N_i^{\gamma}}v'(0) \tag{2.15}$$

Hence, $c_i(j)$ is a monotonically decreasing function of $\left(\frac{j}{N_i}\right)^{\gamma}$. Put in other terms, the consumption profile is decreasing in j and thus follows the hierarchy. The case where all prices are equal illustrates the key difference between homothetic and hierarchic non-homothetic preferences. With homothetic preferences, the consumption profile expands *vertically* as income rises. Compared to a poor consumer, a rich agent with the double amount of income will consume the double amount of every good. Instead, with hierarchic preferences (where $\xi(j) = j^{-\gamma}$ and prices are equal) the range of consumed goods N_i and the expenditures E_i are proportional. Hence, the consumption profile expands *horizontally*. In relative terms it looks the same for rich and poor but the rich agent consumes more goods.

For this symmetric price structure, we can derive a simple expression for the income elasticity of demand. Differentiate (2.15) with respect to N_i we get $\frac{dc_i(j)}{dN_i} =$

[12]Of course, these assumptions are sufficient but not necessary. For example, it would still be consistent with the proposition if the marginal costs on the supply side differed because of an exogenous learning-by-doing process where marginal costs fall at a constant rate over time. We will come back to this issue in the following chapter 3.

$-\frac{\gamma}{N_i}\frac{v'(c_i(j))}{v''(c_i(j))}$. As expenditures and the range of consumed goods are proportional we note that $dE_i/E_i = dN_i/N_i$. Hence, we get the consumer's i income elasticity of demand for product j

$$\frac{dc_i(j)}{dE_i}\frac{E_i}{c_i(j)} = -\gamma\frac{v'(c_i(j))}{v''(c_i(j))c_i(j)}$$

Because we assumed that $-\frac{v'(c)}{cv''(c)}$ falls in c (declining rate of substitution), the income elasticity of a product is lower when consumed quantity is lower. We already calculated the income elasticity for the general hierarchic function and a general price structure (see equation (2.6)). For this special case we see the pattern suggested by Engel's law much more easily: Since the consumption profile is decreasing along the hierarchy: $c_i'(j) < 0$, consumption of low-i-goods ("necessities") is higher, hence, they have a lower income elasticity whereas high-i-goods ("luxuries") face a high elasticity. In contrast to the general case, we are able to give a clear statement how income elasticities vary across different consumers: Poor consumers exhibit a higher income elasticity on all products they consume than rich consumers.

2.3 Non-Homothetic Utility in the Previous Theoretical Literature

First of all, there are a plenty of functional forms for utility functions and Engel curves proposed in empirical work. Of course, the use of flexible functional forms minimizes the risk of empirical misspecifications which could occur if we imposed too restrictive functional forms on the data. However, these functional forms are seldom tractable for theoretical (macroeconomic) models. In fact, the small existing literature that uses non-homothetic preferences is forced to adopt quite restrictive utility functions - which are still much more general than their homothetic counterpart, of course.

The well-known paper by Murphy, Shleifer and Vishny (1989) discusses how the degree of industrialization depends on income distribution. They use the following utility function over differentiated products j (rewritten in our notation, note that the utility function in their paper contains some typographic errors): $U = -\int_0^1(1-c(j))\frac{1}{j}dj + \int_1^\infty c(j)\frac{1}{j}dj$ where $c(j) \in \{0,1\}$. Obviously, this utility function is a special case of the utility function $U = \int_0^\infty j^{-\gamma}v(c(j))dj$ discussed above where $\gamma = 1$. In addition, the subutility function $v(\cdot)$ takes the simple form of 0-1-preferences and $v(\cdot)$ is normalized such that the utility integral converges (see section 2.4.1 in the Appendix). The growth model of Zweimueller (2000) uses a similar utility function. Matsuyama (2000) explains trade flows between (rich) north and (poor) south. The structure of demand differs between the two regions because the agents have non-homothetic preferences. His utility function is given by $U = \int_0^\infty \xi(j)dj$, hence he also uses 0-1-preferences but the hierarchic weight takes a general form.[13]

Stokey (1988, 1991) analyzes a growth and a trade model, respectively, where the sectoral structure changes as a result of non-homothetic preferences. She adopts a Lancaster-approach where preferences are defined over characteristics j. Preferences over the characteristics $q(j)$ are given by $U = \int_0^\infty u\left(q(j)\right) dj$. The subutility function $u\left(\cdot\right)$ satisfies exactly the same properties as our subutility function $v(\cdot)$ defined above. In particular, she assumes that $u'(0)$ must be bounded. Apart from the Lancaster approach, the only difference to our specification is the lack of a hierarchy. The impact of inequality on the degree of product market imperfections when preferences take this "symmetric" form is analyzed by Foellmi and Zweimueller (2003, 2004) and Saint-Paul (2005). We will come back to this type of preferences in chapter 5 of this book.

Other models of growth and structural change (Kongsamut, Rebelo, and Xie (2001), Echevarria (1997)) adopt a discrete specification of the differentiated goods.[14] Both models assume that there are three goods or sectors. Kongsamut et al. (2001) choose a Stone-Geary utility: $U(c_1, c_2, c_3) = \left(c_1 - \bar{c}_1\right)^{\beta} c_2^{\gamma} \left(c_3 + \bar{c}_3\right)^{\theta}$ where all parameters are positive constants such that the income elasticity of sector 1 ('agriculture') is below unity whereas for sector 3 ('services') the opposite holds. Thus, they do not use a hierarchy function but they directly manipulate the function $v(\cdot)$ to generate different income elasticities of the goods and sectors. This approach has the important disadvantage, however, that a further knife-edge assumption linking preferences and technology is needed to generate steady states. This Stone-Geary-type specification with different subsistence levels of the different goods is perhaps the most popular in the literature. However, it is only applicable when only a small number of goods is under consideration. If many

[13] A predecessor to Matsuyama's model is the trade model by Flam and Helpman (1987). They assume that the consumer has nonhomothetic preferences over two goods.

[14] Other models that use non-homothetic preferences in two- or three-goods models include de Janvry and Sadoulet (1983), Flam and Helpman (1987), Baland and Ray (1991), and Chou and Talmain (1996).

goods or even a continuous range of goods are considered, the model becomes intractable.[15]

An important special case of hierarchic preferences are the *lexicographic preferences.* Preferences are lexicographic if a consumer strictly prefers to consume good k than a whole bundle of goods j where all $j > k$. Lexicographic preferences are an extreme version of the 0-1-hierarchic preferences: A given need must be absolutely satiated before the consumer moves to next in his hierarchy. Obviously, in such a case the consumer will always consume along the hierarchy no matter what their prices are. A possible formulation of lexicographic utility is given in Matsuyama (2002).[16] He studies a development process where a series of industries takes off one after another. The utility of differentiated products is given by $U = \sum_{k=1}^{J} \prod_{j=1}^{k} x_j$ where $x_j \in \{0, 1\}$. As required, the marginal utility of good k is zero if one of the goods $j \leq k-1$ has not been consumed. Another possibility to model lexicographic preferences with many goods would be to specify directly the expenditure function (see Falkinger (1990)).

[15] For that reason, the Stone-Geary-type is very popular in models with two goods (see e.g. Matsuyama (1992)). The Stone-Geary is also common in (two-goods-)models where the individuals decide how much to consume and to bequest. Examples include Galor and Moav (2002) and Mani (2001).

[16] Eswaran and Kotwal (1993) and Laitner (2000) use lexicographic preferences in a two goods model (agricultural and manufacturing good).

2.4 Appendix

2.4.1 Convergence of the Utility Integral

To get a well defined problem, we assume that there are no free goods, i.e. $\exists \varepsilon > 0$ s.t. $p(j) \geq \varepsilon \; \forall j$, and that expenditures are positive, $E_i > 0$. We distinguish whether $v(c)$ is bounded from above or not. The individual index i is omitted in what follows. Before proceeding, we state and prove a Lemma.

Lemma 0 *Assume* $p(j) = \zeta < \infty$ *for* $0 \leq j < a$.
a. $\frac{dc(j)}{dj} \equiv c'(j) = \frac{\gamma v'(c(j))}{j v''(c(j))}$
b. If $\gamma < 1$, $\lim_{j->0} \frac{j^{1-\gamma}}{1-\gamma} v(c(j)) = 0$.
c. If there exists a finite saturation point s, *s.t.* $s = \arg\max v(c(j))$ *and* $v(s) =: \Xi$ *or if* $v(c(j))$ *is bounded from above, then* $\lim_{j->0} \frac{j^{1-\gamma}}{1-\gamma} \left(v(c(j)) - \Xi\right) = 0$ *for all* $\gamma \geq 0$.

Proof. a. Follows directly by applying the implicit function theorem to equation (2.13).
b. $\lim_{j->0} \frac{j^{1-\gamma}}{1-\gamma} v(c(j)) = \lim_{j->0} \frac{1}{(1-\gamma)^2} \frac{v'(c(j))}{j^{\gamma-2}} c'(j)$
$= -\lim_{j->0} \left(\frac{1}{(1-\gamma)^2} \frac{v'(c(j))}{j^{\gamma-1}} \frac{\gamma v'(c(j))}{v''(c(j))} \right) = -\lim_{j->0} \left(j^{-\gamma} v'(c(j)) j c(j) \frac{\gamma v'(c(j))}{v''(c(j)) c(j)} \right)$
$= -\lim_{c->c(0)} \frac{\gamma v'(c)}{v''(c)c} \lambda p(0) \lim_{j->0} j c(j) = 0$.
The term $-\lim_{c->c(0)} \frac{\gamma v'(c)}{v''(c)c}$ is finite because $-\frac{v'(c)}{v''(c)c}$ was assumed to be decreasing in c and. Finally, $\lim_{j->0} jc(j) = 0$ This limit being zero means that $c(j)$ goes to infinity at a lower rate than j. This is exactly what we need to have a well defined problem - otherwise we want to consume only good 0 and the budget constraint is already exhausted at $j = 0$.
c. The proof is analogous to b. ■

The following proposition states that for all utility functions $v(c(j))$ which are bounded, there can be found a normalization of the hierarchic utility function such that the optimal solution is associated with a finite value of utility. In particular, this proposition can be applied for all preferences which exhibit a bliss point, i.e. there exists a finite saturation point $s \; \forall j$, s.t. $s = \arg\max v(c(j))$. Trivially, saturation preferences are bounded, because it holds $v(c(j)) \leq v(s) < \infty$.

Proposition 2 *Assume that* $v(c(j)) \leq \Xi$, *i.e. it is bounded from above. The normalized utility function*

$$\tilde{U}(\{c(j)\}) = \int_0^1 j^{-\gamma} \left(v(c(j)) - \Xi\right) dj + \int_1^\infty j^{-\gamma} \left(v(c(j)) - v(0)\right) dj$$

is finite for all $\gamma \geq 0$ if $p(j)$ for $0 \leq j < a$ is finite.

Proof. Note that there are no free goods: $p(j) \geq \varepsilon \ \forall j$. The first order conditions (2.13) and $v'(0) < \infty$ directly imply that all goods $j \geq N_i$ are not consumed. Good N_i is given by $N_i^{-\gamma} v'(0) = \lambda_i \varepsilon$ and $j^{-\gamma} v'(0) < \lambda_i \varepsilon$, if $j > N_i$. Further, $c(j)$ and $v(c(j))$ are finite. This implies that the second integral converges.

To check convergence of the first integral, it suffices to check whether it converges for $0 \leq j < a$. As the integral is negative and indirect utility is non-increasing in prices we get a lower bound for the utility value if we evaluate it at a constant price $\zeta =: \max_{0 \leq j < a} p(j)$. we integrate by parts and get

$\int_0^a j^{-\gamma} v(c(j)) dj = \frac{j^{1-\gamma}}{1-\gamma} \left(v(c(j)) - \Xi\right)\Big|_0^a - \int_0^a \frac{j^{1-\gamma}}{1-\gamma} v'(c(j)) c'(j) dj$
$= \frac{1}{1-\gamma} \left(v(c(a)) - \Xi\right) - 0 - \int_0^a \frac{j}{1-\gamma} \lambda p(j) \frac{\gamma v'(c(j))}{j v''(c(j))} dj$
$= \frac{1}{1-\gamma} \left(v(c(a)) - \Xi\right) - \int_0^a \frac{\gamma}{1-\gamma} \lambda p(j) c(j) \frac{v'(c(j))}{v''(c(j)) c(j)} dj$, which is finite because the Lemma can be applied and the budget constraint must hold. ■

The normalization of the first integral prevents divergence at $j = 0$. If $\gamma \geq 1$, the integral $\int_0^1 j^{-\gamma} dj$ diverges. Hence, the utility function must be normalized such that the partial utility value at equals zero. Individual optimization implies that good 0, which has an infinite weight in the hierarchy, is consumed at full saturation if the preferences exhibit a bliss point: $c(0) = s$. The reason is that the first order condition (2.13) is only fulfilled if $c(0) = s$ as long as $\lambda_j p(0) > 0$. For preferences $v(\cdot)$ which are bounded but exhibit no bliss point, the consumer will choose $c(0) = \infty$ because $\lim_{c \to \infty} v'(c) = 0$ when $v(c)$ is bounded. In both cases $v(c(0)) = \Xi$ holds, thus the normalization yields the required result. On the other hand, the normalization of the second integral prevents divergence for $j \to \infty$. As goods $j > N_i$ are not consumed, the integrand equals zero for all these goods. Of course, we only need one of the two normalizations if we restrict the values the hierarchy parameter γ can take. If $\gamma > 1$ ("steep" hierarchy), the second integral will not diverge because $\int_1^\infty j^{-\gamma} dj$ converges for $\gamma > 1$. (for every good j there exists a finite saturation point $s \ \forall j$, s.t. $s = \arg\max v(c(j))$.) Therefore, with steep hierarchy we can simply work with the utility function $U = \int_0^\infty j^{-\gamma} \left(v(c(j)) - \Xi\right) dj$. On the other hand, if we consider only values of $\gamma < 1$ ("flat" hierarchy), the first integral will not diverge, as $v(c(j)) \leq \Xi < \infty$ and $\int_0^1 j^{-\gamma} dj$ converges for $\gamma < 1$. In this case, the normalized utility function $\int_0^\infty j^{-\gamma} \left(v(c(j)) - v(0)\right) dj$ already guarantees a finite utility value of the consumer's optimal decision. Finally, the assumption that prices of goods for small j are bounded is sufficient but not necessary. For $\gamma \geq 1$, the utility integral would diverge at $j = 0$, if the price $p(j)$ would go to infinity at a too fast rate when j approaches zero. Intuitively, the consumers would like to consume good 0 at its saturation point but they cannot reach the saturation point any more because its price is infinite. This problem, however, does not arise if we consider the case of flat hierarchy ($\gamma < 1$), as we will do below.

If we consider preferences $v(\cdot)$ which are unbounded if $c(j) \to \infty$ (as for example the logarithmic Stone-Geary-preferences where $v(c(j)) = \ln(c(j) + q)$ and $q > 0$) the normalization of the first integral can no longer be applied, of course. Hence, we *must* restrict the hierarchy parameter γ to values below unity, if we use a model where $\lim_{c \to \infty} v(c)$ diverges. This is simply due to the mathematical fact that the integral $\int_0^1 j^{-\gamma} dj$ diverges for $\gamma \geq 1$. The following proposition shows that the normalized utility function takes a finite value for all functions $v(\cdot)$ if $\gamma < 1$. In contrast to the proposition above, we do not need any assumptions about prices.

Proposition 3 *The normalized utility function*

$$\tilde{U}(\{c(j)\}) = \int_0^\infty j^{-\gamma} \left(v(c(j)) - v(0) \right) dj$$

is finite for all $\gamma < 1$.

Proof. The normalized utility function takes a positive value. As indirect utility is non-increasing in prices, if suffices to show that indirect utility is bounded from above if $p(j) = \varepsilon \ \forall j$. The first order conditions (2.13) and $v'(0) < \infty$ then directly imply that there exists a good N_i such that $N_i^{-\gamma} v'(0) = \lambda_i \varepsilon$ and $j^{-\gamma} v'(0) < \lambda_i \varepsilon$, if $j > N_i$. Integrating by parts we find $\int_0^\infty j^{-\gamma} v(c_i(j)) dj = \int_0^{N_i} j^{-\gamma} v(c_i(j)) dj + \int_{N_i}^\infty j^{-\gamma} v(0) dj = \int_0^{N_i} j^{-\gamma} v(c_i(j)) dj = \frac{j^{1-\gamma}}{1-\gamma} v(c_i(j)) \Big|_0^{N_i} - \int_0^{N_i} \frac{j^{1-\gamma}}{1-\gamma} v'(c_i(j)) c_i'(j) dj = 0 - \int_0^{N_i} \frac{j^{1-\gamma}}{1-\gamma} v'(c_i(j)) c_i'(j) dj$ which is finite according to the Lemma. The Lemma can be applied because $p(j) = \varepsilon$. ■

2.4.2 Proof of Proposition 1

The price of good j only depends on its relative position $p(j) = \tilde{p}\left(\frac{j}{N(t)}\right)$. We further assume that (i) $\tilde{p}(\cdot)$ is continuously differentiable (the proof can be extended to the case where $\tilde{p}(\cdot)$ is not continuous at a finite number of points) and that (ii) the goods prices do not fall more quickly than the hierarchy $\tilde{p}'\left(\frac{j}{N(t)}\right) \geq -\gamma \left(\frac{j}{N(t)}\right)^{-\gamma-1}$ (this corresponds to our usual assumption about the hierarchic ordering of the goods). From (2.13) we know that $j^{-\gamma} v'(c_i(j)) = \lambda_i p(j)$. Our assumption concerning the price structure $\tilde{p}(\cdot)$ implies that $c_i(j)$ is nonincreasing in j. Furthermore, the restriction $v'(0) < \infty$ means that there is a good, call it N_i, for which we have $c_i(N_i) = 0$. The first order condition for good N_i is

$$N_i^{-\gamma} v'(0) = \lambda_i$$

Combining the last two expressions yields

$$\begin{aligned} v'(c_i(j)) &= \frac{j^\gamma}{N_i^\gamma} v'(0) \tilde{p} \left(\frac{j}{N} \right) \\ p(j) &= \tilde{p} \left(\frac{j}{N(t)} \right) \end{aligned}$$

This relation implicitly determines the consumption profile of consumer i.

Now we want to calculate the value of the utility function once consumers have made an optimal choice of all consumption levels (the indirect utility function). To do this let us draw the consumption profile ($c_i(j)$ in dependency of j). Then consider a marginal increase in expenditures. This leads to an outward shift of the consumption profile because the resulting decrease in λ leads to an increase in $c_i(j)$ and N_i.

In the optimum, marginal utilities have to be equal across goods

$$v'(c_i(j)) = \frac{j^\gamma}{N_i^\gamma} v'(0) \tilde{p} \left(\frac{j}{N} \right)$$

Implicitly differentiate this equation with respect to $c_i(j)$, j and N_i. To simplify notation we suppress the argument of $\tilde{p}(\cdot)$. This gives

$$\begin{aligned} v''(c_i(j)) dc_i(j) &= \left(\gamma \frac{j^\gamma}{N_i^\gamma} v'(0) \tilde{p} \frac{1}{j} + \frac{j^\gamma}{N_i^\gamma} v'(0) \tilde{p}' \cdot \frac{1}{N} \right) dj \\ &\quad + \left(\gamma \frac{j^\gamma}{N_i^\gamma} v'(0) \tilde{p} \frac{1}{N_i} \frac{\partial N_i}{\partial N} + \frac{j^\gamma}{N_i^\gamma} v'(0) \tilde{p}' \cdot \left(-\frac{j}{N^2} \right) \right) dN \end{aligned}$$

$$\frac{dc_i(j)}{dj} \equiv c_i'(j) = \left(\gamma \frac{j^\gamma}{N_i^\gamma} v'(0) \tilde{p} \frac{1}{j} + \frac{j^\gamma}{N_i^\gamma} v'(0) \tilde{p}' \cdot \frac{1}{N} \right) / v''(c_i(j))$$

and

$$\begin{aligned} \frac{dc_i(j)}{dN} &= \left(-\gamma \frac{j^\gamma}{N_i^\gamma} v'(0) \tilde{p} \frac{1}{N_i} \frac{\partial N_i}{\partial N} + \frac{j^\gamma}{N_i^\gamma} v'(0) \tilde{p}' \cdot \left(-\frac{j}{N^2} \right) \right) / v''(c_i(j)) \\ &= -\frac{j}{N} \left(\gamma \frac{j^\gamma}{N_i^\gamma} v'(0) \tilde{p} \frac{1}{j} \frac{N}{N_i} \frac{\partial N_i}{\partial N} + \frac{j^\gamma}{N_i^\gamma} v'(0) \tilde{p}' \cdot \frac{1}{N} \right) / v''(c_i(j)). \end{aligned}$$

Assume now that N_i is proportional to N. In that case $\frac{N}{N_i} \frac{\partial N_i}{\partial N}$ equals unity. Note that we can write $\frac{dc_i(j)}{dN}$in terms of $c_i'(j)$ by using the latter two equations

$$\frac{dc_i(j)}{dN} = \frac{-jc_i'(j)}{N} \text{ or } dc_i(j) = -jc_i'(j) \frac{dN}{N}$$

For the price formula $p(j) = \tilde{p} \left(\frac{j}{N(t)} \right)$ we proceed analogously.

$$dp(j) = \tilde{p}' \cdot \frac{1}{N} dj + \tilde{p}' \cdot \left(-\frac{j}{N^2} \right) dN$$

$$\frac{dp(j)}{dN} = \frac{-jp'(j)}{N}$$

Totally differentiating the budget constraint with respect to E_i, N_i, and $c_i(j)$ yields

$$dE_i = \int_0^{N_i} (p(j)dc_i(j) + dp(j)c_i(j))\, dj + dN_i c_i(N_i)$$

where $c_i(N_i) = 0$. We now substitute $\frac{dc_i(j)}{dN}$ into the differentiated budget constraint to get

$$\begin{aligned}\frac{dE_i}{dN} &= \int_0^{N_i} \left(p(j)\frac{-jc_i'(j)}{N} + \frac{-jp'(j)}{N}c_i(j) \right) dj \\ &= -\int_0^{N_i} \frac{j}{N} \frac{\partial\left[p(j)c_i(j)\right]}{\partial j} dj\end{aligned}$$

Integrating by parts yields

$$\begin{aligned}\frac{dE_i}{dN} &= \frac{1}{N}\left(-jp(j)c_i(j)\right)_0^{N_i} + \frac{1}{N}\int_0^{N_i} p(j)c_i(j)dj \\ &= \frac{1}{N}E_i.\end{aligned}$$

Here we have used $lim_{j\to 0}\left[jp(j)c_i(j)\right] = 0$. This limit being zero means that the hierarchy may not be too steep so that $p(j)c_i(j)$ goes to infinity at a lower rate than j. However, this is exactly what we need to have a well defined problem - otherwise we want to consume only good 0).

We assumed that N_i is proportional to N. If this assumption holds therefore, we have shown that E_i is proportional to N and proportional to N_i. Aggregating across individuals, aggregate expenditures E must be proportional to N. This in turn implies that the relative expenditures E_i/E of all agents remain constant. This confirms our initial claim that N_i is proportional to N.

The last step is to show that the indirect utility function is CRRA in expenditures E_i where the intertemporal elasticity of substitution equals $1/\gamma$ constant for all agents. We have

$$\frac{dU_i}{dE_i} = \lambda_i = N_i^{-\gamma}v'(0) = (kE_i)^{-\gamma}\, v'(0)$$

where $k = N_i/E_i > 0$ is the proportionality factor. From the above equation it follows that U_i is proportional to $\frac{E_i^{1-\gamma}}{1-\gamma}$ (up to an additive constant).

3

Structural Change and Balanced Growth

3.1 Introduction

Fundamental changes in the structure of production and employment occur in the process of development. The emergence of new and the decline of old industries has led to a dramatic reallocation of labor between sectors of production in historical perspective.[1] Despite these large structural changes, the long-term growth process turns out remarkably stable in the aggregate. As mentioned by Kaldor (1961) in his famous stylized facts, a situation where growth rate, interest rate, capital output ratio, and labor share are constant over time is a reasonable approximation of the long-run growth experience of a modern economy.

In this chapter we present a model that accounts both for structural change and for the Kaldor facts. On the one hand, industries with a growing share in aggregate production co-exist with declining industries, and each such industry is going (or has already gone) through a cycle of take-off, maturity, and stagnation. Hence

[1] The following figures referring to a familiar trichotomy of sectors - agriculture, manufacturing, and services - demonstrate the impressive size of these structural changes (Maddison, 1987): In 1870 the employment share in agriculture amounted to 50 % in the U.S., to 67.5 % in Japan, and to 49.2 % in France. In 1984, the corresponding numbers decreased to 3.3 % in the U.S., 8.9 % in Japan, and 7.6 % in France. During the same period the employment share in the service sector increased from 25.6 % to 68.7 % in the U.S., from 18.7 % to 56.3 % in Japan, and from 23 % to 60.4 % in France.

there is continuous structural change. On the other hand, our model features a situation where all macroeconomic aggregates grow at the same constant rate, and where the interest rate and the labor share are constant over time. Thus, our model meets Kaldor's criteria. In contrast, standard theories of economic growth have been predominantly concerned with models that exhibit a 'balanced' growth path and have almost entirely ignored the issue of structural change.[2]

Generally speaking, changes in the structure of production and employment result either from differences in productivity growth or from differences in the growth of product demand across sectors. To focus on the demand side we abstract from technological differences across sectors. Thus the driving force behind structural changes are differences in the income elasticities of demand across sectors. We already discussed in the introductory chapter the importance and almost universal validity of Engel's law. This underlines that such systematic differences exist. Engel (1857) himself saw the implications of this law for development and structural change very clearly: a declining relative demand for food would inevitably decrease the share of output and employment in the agricultural sector, and would provide the resources for the emergence of new industries. Many writers since Engel have emphasized that Engel's law holds not only for food, but is a more general law of consumption. Kindleberger (1989, p. 9) notes that "*new products expand rapidly, (...) and then must slow down in rate of growth. This is Engel's law in extension.*" Pasinetti (1981) has emphasized that the typical Engel-curve has a logistic shape: expenditures for certain goods grow only slowly initially, then take off, and finally stagnate as demand approaches the saturation point.[3]

Our formulation of preferences introduced in chapter 2 captures a generalized version of Engel's law. We show that the resulting non-linear Engel-curves are consistent with a growth path that otherwise satisfies the stylized facts mentioned by Kaldor. The basic idea is that households expand their *consumption along a hierarchy of needs.* When the basic needs are saturated, consumers move on to more advanced needs. As incomes grow, more and more goods and services enter the consumption bundle, and more and more wants can be satisfied.

The supply side of our model has a simple structure. We study a situation where growth is endogenous and driven by industrial R&D. There are interindus-

---

[2]A noteable exception is Pasinetti (1981) who presents a systematic analysis of economic growth and structural change in the post-Keynesian tradition.

[3]In a recent contribution Matsuyama (2002), has studied a model of income distribution and mass consumption in which industries take off, one after the other, generating patterns of demand consistent with the generalized version of Engel's law.

try spillovers of knowledge, so innovative activities in one sector add to the economy-wide stock of knowledge and increase productivity in all other sectors. The assumption of economy-wide spillover effects rules out sector-specific technical progress, the second possible source of structural change. The main reason why we disregard uneven technical change is to keep the model tractable and to concentrate on the role of demand. The second reason is that, in contrast to demand side explanations, there are less clear supply side arguments how the expenditure and labor shares of sectors change over time.[4]

The equilibrium outcome of our model has the following features. First, the dynamic equilibrium is characterized by a situation of continuous structural change. At each date, there co-exist goods that have a high income elasticity (luxuries) with goods that have a low income elasticity (necessities). And over time each good starts off as a luxury with a high income elasticity and ends up as a necessity with a low income elasticity. In this sense, each sector goes through the same cycle of take-off, maturity, and stagnation. Hence the equilibrium is characterized by non-linear Engel-curves due to the non-homotheticity of hierarchic preferences.

Second, the dynamic equilibrium meets Kaldor's criteria. Prima facie reconciling structural change and non-linear Engel-curves with the Kaldor facts seems to be a difficult task. What is the crucial assumption that makes this possible? Necessary conditions for a steady growth path are a constant interest rate on the supply side and a constant elasticity of intertemporal substitution on the preference side. With many goods and a constant interest rate, steady growth is possible if the optimal growth rate of total consumption expenditures is constant over time. The demand and expenditure levels of the various products, however, *need not change in proportion with total expenditures.* It is exactly this pattern that our model generates. With our model of hierarchic preferences, it turns out that the constancy of the optimal growth rate of consumption expenditures depends critically on a function that characterizes the 'steepness' of the hierarchy of

[4]The literature discusses two important arguments. On the one hand, the transition towards a service economy implies the emergence of new industries with little scope for technical progress (Baumol, 1967, Baumol et al., 1985). On the other hand, the *new* expanding markets consist to large extent of high-tech products and sophisticated services where the potential for technological improvements is high. (In fact, the very recent U.S. experience suggests that technical progress is actually concentrated in these new sectors). Furthermore, while the empirical evidence shows that the service sector has grown more slowly (Maddison, 1987), is not clear to which extent this is due to measurement error. The particular problem is mismeasurement in the quality improvements of services (see Shapiro and Wilcox, 1996, and Hornstein and Krusell, 1996).

needs, that is the willingness of consumers to move from goods that satisfy needs of higher priority towards goods that satisfy needs of lower priority.

Third, in our model there is an interesting two-way causality between technological progress and the incentives for innovators. On the one hand, the aggregate growth rate is endogenously determined by industrial R&D due to our assumptions regarding productivity improvements. On the other hand, the incentives for innovators depend crucially on the economy-wide growth rate, because all sectors have a positive (albeit non-unitary) income elasticity of demand. This dynamic complementarity between aggregate and sectoral dynamics may give rise to multiple equilibria. Optimistic (pessimistic) expectations of a high (low) growth rate provide an incentive for a high (low) level of innovative activities that makes expectations come true.

Fourth, as mentioned in chapter 1, the growth process is maintained through demand only - the growth path follows the hierarchy of needs. R&D for new product will only take place as long as the individuals exhibit a sufficient willingness to pay for new products. Although the utility (in absolute value) of new products becomes lower over time, the growth process does not come to an end. We show that the marginal utility of income falls at the same rate as the utility of the latest product, hence, the willingness to pay for new products remains constant and steady growth is sustained.

Fifth, the dynamic equilibrium may be characterized by a situation where consumers cannot afford all products that are available on the market. In particular, this means that the non-negativity constraints for the most luxurious (= brand-new) products are binding. For this reason innovators have a 'waiting time' until consumers are rich enough to purchase a new product. Firms may nevertheless incur the R&D costs to get a patent and to prevent potential competitors conquering the market.

Finally, hierarchic preferences imply that incumbent firms have increasing market power as the price elasticities of demand decrease during the product cycle. Rising incomes lead to a higher willingness to pay and hence to higher mark-ups. The growing mark-ups imply strong static price distortions and the socially optimal patent policy is characterized by a finite patent length.

As mentioned above the previous literature has largely failed to analyze the simultaneity of structural change and steady growth. To our knowledge, the only paper that explicitly addresses this question is the one by Kongsamut, Rebelo, and Xie (2001). They show in the context of a three-goods economy that a 'generalized' balanced growth path is only possible if technology and taste parameters satisfy a certain knife-edge condition. No such link is necessary in our model. In the present set-up new goods are continuously introduced, each of which starts off as a luxury with a high income elasticity and ends up as a necessity with a low income elasticity. Moreover, in Kongsamut et al. (2001) productivity growth is exogenous whereas in our model innovations play a central role, and interesting interactions between aggregate and sectoral dynamics arise.[5]

There are several other papers that are related to the present analysis. As explained in the section above, in Matsuyama (2002) the structure of preferences is similar in spirit to our framework as the various goods are ranked according to priority. In equilibrium, consumer goods industries take off one after another, and new goods are initially luxuries and finally become necessities. Stokey (1988) also analyzes a growth model in which changes in the sectoral structure occur as a result of non homothetic preferences (for her utility specification see section above). Consumers value new goods because they have more characteristics, while old goods with less characteristics disappear. Neither of these papers focuses on the consistency of the changing sectoral structure with the Kaldor facts. Moreover, those papers assume a learning-by-doing mechanism, while in the present model growth is driven by innovations. Thus, the dynamic demand externalities in our model do not show up there. A further related paper is Laitner (2001) who analyzes changes in the measured savings rate that occur during the process of growth and structural change. Contrary to our model, productivity growth is exogenous and the process of structural change is modeled in a two-sector framework.[6]

The chapter is organized as follows. Section 2 presents the general set-up of the model, solves the static problems of consumers and firms, and discusses the resulting structure of demand and prices in the static equilibrium. In Section 3 we present our assumptions on technology, the labor market, and the determinants of aggregate savings. Section 4 discusses the equilibrium growth path and describes the patterns of structural changes that occur along this path. Section 5 contains a discussion of multiple equilibria and Section 6 applies the model to optimal patent policy. Section 7 summarizes the results and discusses possible extensions.[7]

---

[5]Also Echevarria (1997) studies the patterns of structural change in three-sector growth model. However, the focus of her paper is not to reproduce the Kaldor facts.

[6]Other papers where non-homothetic preferences have an impact on macroeconomic outcomes study the role of income inequality and/or unemployment. See, for instance, Murphy, Shleifer and Vishny (1989), Eswaran and Kotwal (1993), Baland and Ray (1991), for static models, and Falkinger (1990, 1994), Chou and Talmain (1996), Zweimüller (1996, 2000), Bertola and Zweimüller (2000), and Zagler (2000) for dynamic models. Flam and Helpman (1987), Stockey (1991) and Matsuyama (2000) study international trade in the context of non-homothetic preferences.

[7]The chapter follows Foellmi and Zweimueller (2001) and Foellmi and Zweimueller (2002a).

3.2 Static Equilibrium

3.2.1 Preferences and Demand

Consider a representative agent economy with infinitely many potentially producible goods ranked by an index j. We study the structure of consumption that is generated by preferences of the form

$$u(\{c(j)\}) = \int_0^\infty \xi(j)\ v(c(j))\ dj$$

To keep the analysis tractable we make two assumptions concerning the functional forms of the weighting function $\xi(j)$ and the baseline utility $v(c(j))$. First we assume that the weighting function is a power function $\xi(j) = j^{-\gamma}$ with $\gamma \in (0,1)$. It will turn out below that it is exactly this assumption which will allow us to study an equilibrium growth path that meets the Kaldor facts. Second, we assume that the baseline utility is quadratic, $v(c(j)) = \frac{1}{2}[s^2 - (s - c(j))^2]$. This allows us to find explicit solutions both for the optimal quantities consumed by the households and for the profit-maximizing prices charged by firms. At the same time this specification features the possibility that non-negativity constraints may become binding, as marginal utility at quantity zero is finite, $\xi(j)v'(0) = j^{-\gamma}\frac{1}{2}s^2 < \infty$ for all goods $j > 0$.

With these assumptions, we can now specify the objective function of the consumer's static maximization problem. Assume that only goods with high priority $j \in [0, N]$ are available on the market, whereas all $j > N$ have not yet been invented. In that case the consumers' objective function is[8]

$$u(\{c(j)\}) = \int_0^\infty j^{-\gamma}\ \frac{1}{2}[s^2 - (s - c(j))^2]\ dj. \tag{3.1}$$

which will be maximized subject to the budget constraint $\int_0^N p(j)c(j)dj = E$ and the non-negativity constraints $c(j) \geq 0$ for all j. The optimality conditions require

[8] $v(c(i)) = \frac{1}{2}[s^2 - (s - c(i))^2]$ has been normalized such that $v(0) = 0$. This normalization is necessary to prevent divergence of the utility integral because the consumer's preferences are defined over an *infinite* number of goods and $\gamma < 1$ (see Chapter 2.4.1). Since only goods in the interval $i \in [0, N]$ can be consumed in positive amounts the consumer's objective can be written as $u(\{c\}) = \int_0^N i^{-\gamma}\frac{1}{2}[s^2 - (s - c(i))^2]di + \int_N^\infty i^{-\gamma}\frac{1}{2}[s^2 - s^2]di$. To prevent divergence of the first integral we must have $\gamma < 1$. By the normalization of $v(.)$ the second integral is zero and does not diverge. We can then restrict our attention to the utility function $u(\{c\}) = \int_0^N i^{-\gamma}\frac{1}{2}[s^2 - (s - c(i))^2]di$.

that the above constraints and the first order conditions

$$\begin{aligned} c(j)\left[j^{-\gamma}(s-c(j))-\lambda p(j)\right] &= 0 \quad \forall j \\ j^{-\gamma}(s-c(j))-\lambda p(j) &\leq 0 \quad \forall j. \end{aligned} \tag{3.2}$$

be satisfied, where λ denotes the Lagrangian multiplier.

3.2.2 Optimal Price Setting

We assume there are constant marginal cost in production, equal for all goods, and we normalize these marginal costs to unity. Goods $j \in [0, aN]$ are supplied on competitive markets and goods $j \in (aN, N]$ are supplied by monopolistic firms. This means that high priority (low-j) goods are supplied by competitive producers and low priority (high-j) goods are supplied by monopolists.[9]

The prices for goods in the interval $j \in [0, aN]$ are equal to marginal costs which are unity. Determining the prices for the goods $j \in (aN, N]$ is less trivial but straightforward. The market demand function is given by the representative household's optimality conditions (3.2). The price that the monopolist charges maximizes the objective function $\pi(p(j)) = [p(j)-1]\left[\max\left(0,\ s - j^{\gamma} p(j)\lambda\right)\right]$. The solution is given by

$$p(j) = \max\left[1,\ \frac{s + j^{\gamma}\lambda}{2j^{\gamma}\lambda}\right] \quad \text{for } j \in (aN, N]. \tag{3.3}$$

3.2.3 Demand and Price Structure

We can now characterize the composition of demand and the structure of prices in the static equilibrium, given the representative agent's budget E and the measure of available goods N. This will be done separately for the two scenarios that can occur in equilibrium. In the first case, the consumer cannot afford all supplied goods because the non-negativity constraints for low-priority goods become binding. In the second case, the consumer is rich enough to purchase all goods that are supplied on the market. We discuss these two cases in turn. (The conditions under which the two respective regimes occur are studied in Section 4 below.)

---

[9] While this particular structure is an assumption at this stage, we will see below that it will be the equilibrium outcome of the model. Over time new goods are continuously introduced and the chronological sequence of innovations follows the hierarchy of wants. When innovators are protected by patent with finite duration, the 'new 'goods are protected and charged the monopoly price, whereas the patents for 'old' goods have expired and supplied on competitive markets.

When the consumer does not purchase all available goods, the measure of products consumed in positive amounts falls short of the measure of available goods N. If good j is consumed in positive amounts and supplied at the monopoly price, we know from (3.2) and (3.3) that the consumed quantity equals $c(j) = \frac{1}{2}(s - j^{\gamma}\lambda)$. The equilibrium demand is decreasing in j which means that the optimal quantity of low-priority goods is smaller. It also means that there is a good, call it n, such that for goods $j > n$ the optimal level of demand is zero and all goods $j < n$ are consumed in positive amounts. It turns out convenient to express the endogenous variables $c(j)$ and $p(j)$ in terms of the endogenous variable n rather than λ. ¿From $c(n) = \frac{1}{2}(s - n^{\gamma}\lambda) = 0$ it is straightforward to calculate $\lambda = \frac{s}{n^{\gamma}}$. Substituting this into equations (3.2) and (3.3) we get the equilibrium composition of demand, and the equilibrium structure of prices

$$c(j) = \begin{cases} s\left[1 - \left(\frac{j}{n}\right)^{\gamma}\right], & j \in [0, aN] \\ \frac{s}{2}\left[1 - \left(\frac{j}{n}\right)^{\gamma}\right], & j \in (aN, n] \\ 0, & j \in (n, N] \end{cases} \tag{3.4}$$

and

$$p(j) = \begin{cases} 1, & j \in [0, aN] \\ \frac{1}{2}\left[1 + \left(\frac{n}{j}\right)^{\gamma}\right], & j \in (aN, n] \\ 1, & j \in (n, N]. \end{cases} \tag{3.5}$$

According to equations (3.4) and (3.5), what matters for prices and quantities is the *relative position* in the hierarchy of needs, j/n. We also see that the 'steeper' the hierarchy (the higher is γ) the more important is the relative position. The above expressions for $p(j)$ and $c(j)$ are determined for a given measure of consumed goods n. However, n itself is an endogenous variable. To get the optimal value of n we substitute equations (3.4) and (3.5) into the budget constraint to get

$$E = \int_0^n p(j)c(j)dj = sn\left[\frac{aN}{n} - \frac{1}{4}\left(\frac{3(\frac{aN}{n})^{1+\gamma} + 1}{1+\gamma} - \frac{1 - (\frac{aN}{n})^{1-\gamma}}{1-\gamma}\right)\right]. \tag{3.6}$$

This equation implicitly defines the number of consumed goods n as a function of expenditures E, available goods N, and other parameters of the model.[10] In

[10] It is straightforward to verify that the right-hand-side of (3.6) is monotonically increasing in n. When no intersection occurs for $n \leq N$, the equilibrium is characterized by $n = N$. In that case equation (3.6') below is relevant. Note that when, respectively, $n = N$ and $p = 1$, the right-hand-sides of the equations (3.6) and (3.6') become identical.

particular, we note that E and N are exogenous from the point of view of the consumer. Moreover, we see from the above equation that n is homogenous of degree one in E and N: when E and N increase by some factor, the equilibrium value of n increases by the same factor.

Now consider the alternative scenario that the consumer chooses to consume all available goods in positive amounts. Obviously, this is the case if $c(N) = \frac{1}{2}(s - N^{\gamma}\lambda) > 0$. Also here it is convenient to replace λ. However, we cannot express λ in terms of the optimal bundle of consumed goods n which is trivially determined by the number of available goods N. Instead we express λ in terms of the price of the good that has least priority in consumption, that is by the endogenous variable $p(N) \equiv p$. From (3.3) it is straightforward to express the marginal utility of income as $\lambda = \frac{s}{N^{\gamma}(2p-1)}$. The same expression (3.3) can be used to express the monopoly prices for the goods $j \in (aN, N]$ in terms of p as $p(j) = \frac{1}{2}[1 + \left(\frac{N}{j}\right)^{\gamma}(2p-1)]$. The structure of prices and the equilibrium composition of demand can now be expressed as

$$c(j) = \begin{cases} s[1 - \left(\frac{j}{N}\right)^{\gamma} \frac{1}{2p-1}] & j \in [0, aN] \\ \frac{s}{2}[1 - \left(\frac{j}{N}\right)^{\gamma} \frac{1}{2p-1}], & j \in (aN, N] \end{cases} \tag{3.4'}$$

and

$$p(j) = \begin{cases} 1, & j \in [0, aN] \\ \frac{1}{2}[1 + \left(\frac{N}{j}\right)^{\gamma}(2p-1)], & j \in (aN, N]. \end{cases} \tag{3.5'}$$

Note that, in equilibrium, a higher p means higher prices for all goods and this goes hand in hand with higher equilibrium consumption for all goods. The reason for this apparently strange result is that the equilibrium depends crucially on the consumer's budget E relative to the measure of supplied goods N. If E is large relative to N, there is high demand for each good which means that monopolists can charge high prices.

The variables $c(j)$ and $p(j)$ are determined by the endogenous variable p, the profit-maximizing price chosen by the monopolist who supplies the good N. Just like before, the equilibrium depends on the consumer's budget E, the measure of available goods N, and other parameters of the model. To see the relationship between p, E, and N, we insert equations (3.4') and (3.5') into the consumer's budget constraint

$$E = \int_0^N p(j)c(j)dj = sN\left[a - \frac{1}{4}\left(\frac{3a^{1+\gamma}+1}{(1+\gamma)(2p-1)} - (2p-1)\frac{1-a^{1-\gamma}}{1-\gamma}\right)\right] \tag{3.6'}$$

This expression implicitly defines p as a function of E, N, and other parameters of the model. We observe that p is homogenous of degree zero in E and N: when E and N grow pari passu, p remains unchanged.

3.3 Dynamics of the Economy

3.3.1 R&D and the Resource Constraint

To keep things simple we develop our arguments assuming that labor is the only production factor. (In Section 5 below we will discuss the more general case when not only labor but also physical capital is used in production.) Production requires a fixed ('innovation' or 'research') input of $\tilde{F}(t)$ units of labor, and a variable labor input of $\tilde{b}(t)$ per unit of output (t denotes a continuous time index). Denoting by $w(t)$ the wage rate, we have innovation costs $w(t)\tilde{F}(t)$ and marginal costs of production $w(t)\tilde{b}(t)$. We assume $\tilde{b}(t) = \frac{b}{A(t)}$ and $\tilde{F}(t) = \frac{F}{A(t)}$, where $A(t)$ is the aggregate knowledge stock, and $F, b > 0$ are exogenous parameters. These assumptions imply that productivity growth, an increase in $A(t)$, is uniform across sectors and also across activities. Assuming uniform productivity growth across *products* makes sure that all heterogeneity comes from the demand side which is the focus of our analysis. Assuming uniform productivity growth across (production and research) *activities* is important for the existence of a constant growth path. Along this path wages grow with productivity so that marginal production costs $w(t)b(t)$ and innovation costs $w(t)F(t)$ are constant over time. In what follows we take marginal cost as the numeraire, hence $w(t)b(t) = 1$ for all t.

In accordance with much of the endogenous growth literature we assume that the aggregate knowledge stock is proxied by the amount of previous innovations activities. These consist of the measure of goods that are actually available on the market, so we have $A(t) = N(t)$ and $\tilde{b}(t) = \frac{b}{N(t)}$ and $\tilde{F}(t) = \frac{F}{N(t)}$.[11]

---

[11]Note that our assumption on knowledge spillovers differs from the standard 'love-for-variety' model (Grossman and Helpman, 1992). In that model productivity grows only in research but not in production. In the hierarchical model instead there has to be technical progress otherwise innovations comes to a halt because consumers are not willing to reduce consumption on high-priority goods if new goods come along. Hence without technical progress in production, sooner or later the whole labor force will be employed to satisfy the demand of consumers on the already existing goods. Our assumption can be justified using the argument of Young (1993): If the invention of a new good i leads as a by-product to the discovery of a new intermediate input and if the final goods are produced by combining these inputs using a constant returns

The labor force is normalized to 1 and, in equilibrium, there is full employment. At date t, $\dot{N}(t)$ new goods are introduced and the necessary employment level to perform the innovation input is $\dot{N}(t)\frac{F}{N(t)}$. The necessary employment level to produce the demanded consumers goods is $\frac{b}{N(t)}\int_0^{n(t)} c(j,t)dj$. Thus with full employment of the labor resources we have

$$1 = \frac{\dot{N}(t)}{N(t)}F + \frac{b}{N(t)}\int_0^{n(t)} c(j,t)dj. \tag{3.7}$$

Innovations occur because firms are granted patents and earn profits as long as their market is protected from competitors. The value of an innovation that occurs at date t, $\Pi(t)$, equals the present value of the profit flow that accrues to the innovating firm. This flow starts at the date when consumers begin to purchase this product and ends when patents have expired. We denote the flow profit at date τ of the date-t innovator (the firm which produces good $N(t)$) by $\pi(N(t),\tau) = [p(N(t),\tau) - 1]\ c(N(t),\tau)$.

When consumers purchase all available varieties $n = N$ the date-t innovator earns positive profits right from the start, that is throughout the interval $[t, t+\Delta]$ where the exogenous policy parameter Δ denotes the duration of the patent. When consumers cannot afford all available varieties $n < N$, the innovator has initially no demand. Consumers purchase only the goods with high priority, that is all goods in the interval $[0, n(t))$ and no goods in the interval $[n(t), N(t)]$. In that case, innovators have a waiting time until consumers are willing to purchase their product. Denoting this waiting time by δ, the profit flow $\pi(N(t),\tau)$ is zero at dates $\tau \in [t, t+\delta]$, positive at all dates $\tau \in (t+\delta, t+\Delta]$, and zero for $\tau > t+\Delta$. To see how δ is determined note that, when consumers start to buy good $N(t)$ at date $t+\delta$, $N(t)$ is the good with least priority in the consumption bundle. Hence δ is given by $n(t+\delta) = N(t)$. In the dynamic equilibrium $n(t)$ grows at the constant rate g and we have $n(t+\delta) = n(t)e^{\delta g} = N(t)$.

Innovation costs are constant over time and given by wF. Assuming free access to the research sector, there is entry as long as innovation costs fall short of the value of an innovation. Hence in equilibrium, when all profit opportunities are exploited, we must have $wF \geq \Pi(t)$, with strict equality whenever innovations take place. The zero-profit condition can be stated as

$$wF = \int_{t+\delta}^{t+\Delta} [p(N(t),\tau) - 1]\ c(N(t),\tau)\ e^{-r(\tau-t)}d\tau. \tag{3.8}$$

---

to scale CES technology, the productivity of the output sector rises linearly in the number of these inputs.

3.3.2 Intertemporal Consumption Choice

The representative consumer maximizes utility over an infinite horizon. Assuming intertemporal separability of lifetime utility we can apply two-stage budgeting. This means we can treat the dynamic problem (optimal allocation of lifetime expenditures across time) separately from the static problem (optimal allocation of a given amount of expenditures across goods at a given date). In Section 2 above we have studied the solution to the static problem. Now we turn to the consumer's dynamic problem. For the solution of this problem the following Lemma is helpful.

Lemma 1 *In the static equilibrium the maximized instantaneous utility at date t, $\hat{u}(t)$, can be written as* $\hat{u}(t) = \frac{E(t)^{1-\gamma}}{1-\gamma} K\left(\frac{n(t)}{N(t)}, p(t), a(t); s, \gamma\right)$.

Proof *see Appendix.*

Note that the function $K(\cdot)$ in the Lemma depends on the fraction of consumed relative to available goods $n(t)/N(t)$, the innovators entry price $p(t)$, and the fraction of competitive sectors $a(t)$. These variables can, in principle, change over time which makes the analysis potentially complicated. We are interested in a growth path that satisfies the Kaldor facts, that is on a situation where expenditures and productivity ($E(t)$ and $N(t)$) grow at the same constant rate. In that case we know from equation (3.6) and (3.6') that, in the respective regimes, $n(t)/N(t)$ and $p(t)$ are constant over time. In addition, when $N(t)$ grows at the constant rate g, the fraction of competitive markets $a(t)$ equals $e^{-g\Delta}$ which is independent of t.[12]

Two-stage budgeting implies that, along the equilibrium growth path, the consumers' static and dynamic decisions can be conveniently separated. The static choices determine the equilibrium value of the function $K(.)$, taking $E(t)$ as constant, and the dynamic choice problem is to decide on the time path of $E(t)$, taking the equilibrium value of $K(.) = \bar{K}$ as constant. The solution to the latter problem is equivalent to maximizing

$$U(t) = \bar{K} \int_t^{\infty} \left(\frac{E(\tau)^{1-\gamma}}{1-\gamma}\right)^{1-\sigma} \frac{e^{-\rho(\tau - t)}}{1-\sigma} d\tau$$

[12]To see the relationship between a, g, and Δ, note that, at date $t+\Delta$ all patents granted at t and before are expired, and all patents granted after t are not yet expired. With $N(t)$ markets at date t, there are $N(t+\Delta) = e^{g\Delta}N(t)$ markets at date $t+\Delta$. Hence, at date $t+\Delta$, the measure of competitive markets equals $N(t)$. Obviously, a fraction $a = e^{-g\Delta}$ is competitive and a fraction $1-a = 1-e^{-g\Delta}$ is monopolistic.

subject to the lifetime budget constraint

$$\int_t^\infty E(s)e^{-R(s)}ds \leq \int_t^\infty w(s)e^{-R(s)}ds + V(t)$$

where ρ is the rate of time preference, σ is a parameter that describes the willingness to shift 'utilities' across periods,[13] $R(s) = \int_t^s r(\tau)d\tau$ is the cumulative interest rate, and $V(t)$ denotes the assets that the consumer owns at date t.

The path of expenditures that maximizes the above objective function has to satisfy the Euler equation

$$\frac{\dot{E}(t)}{E(t)} = g = \frac{r(t) - \rho}{\sigma(1-\gamma)+\gamma}. \tag{3.9}$$

Clearly, when $E(t)$ grows at a constant rate, the interest rate $r(t)$ is also constant. In the symmetric case ($\gamma = 0$) we get the usual form $g = \frac{r-\rho}{\sigma}$. Note that the effect of γ on the growth rate of consumption is ambiguous (remember $\gamma < 1$). A higher γ raises g when $\sigma > 1$ and it decreases g if $\sigma < 1$. The intuition is subtle: With $\gamma > 0$, the expenditures $E(t)$ enter themselves as a concave function in the utility function. The growth rate of consumption depends on how fast marginal utility falls. In the symmetric case marginal utility declines at rate σ. The asymmetry has two effects. On the one hand, the *inter*temporal substitution effect causes marginal utility to fall only at the rate $\sigma(1-\gamma)$; on the other side the *intra*temporal substitution implies that marginal utility falls at rate γ. In total, marginal utility falls at rate $\sigma(1-\gamma)+\gamma$ which is less than σ if $\sigma > 1$ and bigger than σ if $\sigma < 1$.

3.4 Equilibrium Growth Path

We now describe the general equilibrium of the model. We start by defining the equilibrium growth path. Then we establish the conditions under which a unique path exists. A discussion of the consistency of this equilibrium with the Kaldor facts of economic growth and of the patterns of structural change along this path is devoted to the next Section.

---

[13]The reason why we take per-period utility to the power of σ is that this allows us to separate the intra- and intertemporal substitution. Alternatively, think of $u(\{c(i,\tau\})$ as a consumption aggregator and of $\frac{u(\{c(i,\tau\})^{1-\sigma}}{1-\sigma}$ as the instantaneous utility function.

3.4.1 Definition of Equilibrium Growth Path

The equilibrium growth path is characterized by the following conditions: (i) consumers allocate lifetime expenditures optimally across time and goods, (ii) firms set prices that maximize profits, (iii) research firms leave no profit opportunities unexploited, (iv) the labor force is fully employed and (v) aggregate consumption and investment expenditures and the value of aggregate production grow at the same rate.

When consumers do not purchase all available goods, $n < N$, conditions (i) and (ii) are satisfied when, for each date t, equations (3.9), (3.4) and (3.5) hold.[14] Equation (3.9) implies that consumer allocate expenditure optimally across time. If equations (3.4) and (3.5) are satisfied consumers allocate expenditures optimally across goods, given profit maximizing prices of firms; and firms set profit-maximizing prices given the optimal quantities of consumers. Condition (iii) is satisfied when the resource constraint (3.7) holds, and condition (iv) is satisfied when the zero-profit equation (3.8) holds. Condition (v) is satisfied because our specification of preferences boils down to a (maximized) felicity function that is CRRA in total consumption expenditures. The critical underlying assumption is that the weighting factor is a power function $\xi(j) = j^{-\gamma}$ - as we know from chapter 2 - and that technologies are symmetric across industries.

The model has a convenient recursive structure and we can reduce the above system of equations to two equations in two unknowns: the economy-wide growth rate g and the innovator's waiting time δ. To obtain the first equation substitute equation (3.4) into the resource constraint (5.2) and use the definition $g = \frac{\dot{N}(t)}{N(t)}$. Moreover we make use of the fact that in the dynamic equilibrium we have $n(t) = e^{-\delta g} N(t)$ and $aN(t) = N(t)e^{-\Delta g}$. The former relation says that the relation between consumed and available goods is constant and given by $e^{-\delta g}$. The latter relation says that the fraction of competitive markets among all markets is constant and given by $e^{-\Delta g}$. Thus the resource constraint (3.7) can be rewritten as

$$1 = gF + \frac{bs}{2} e^{-g\delta} \left[e^{-g(\Delta-\delta)} - \frac{e^{-g(1+\gamma)(\Delta-\delta)} + 1}{1+\gamma} + 1 \right]. \tag{3.10}$$

The second equation is obtained by substituting equations (3.9), (3.4) and (3.5) into the zero profit condition (3.8). Note that $c(N(t), \tau) = \frac{s}{2}\left[1 - \left(\frac{N(t)}{N(\tau)}\right)^{\gamma}\right] = \frac{s}{2}\left[1 - e^{-g\gamma(\tau-t)}\right]$ and $p(N(t), \tau) = \frac{1}{2}\left[1 + \left(\frac{N(\tau)}{N(t)}\right)^{\gamma}\right] = \frac{1}{2}\left[1 + e^{g\gamma(\tau-t)}\right]$. This

[14] The time index t enters equations (3.4) and (3.5) because n depends on t.

yields

$$wF = \frac{s}{4}\left(\frac{1-e^{-\phi(\Delta-\delta)}}{\phi} - 2\frac{1-e^{-(\phi+g\gamma)(\Delta-\delta)}}{\phi+g\gamma} + \frac{1-e^{-(\phi+2g\gamma)(\Delta-\delta)}}{\phi+2g\gamma}\right)\cdot e^{-\delta(\phi+g\gamma)} \tag{3.11}$$

where we used the definition $\phi = r - g\gamma$ and the fact that from (3.9) $r = \rho + g(\sigma(1-\gamma)+\gamma)$.

Similarly, when consumers purchase all available goods, $n = N$, conditions (i) and (ii) are satisfied when equations (3.9), (3.4') and (3.5') hold; and conditions (iii) and (iv) are also given by equations (3.7) and (3.8). This system of equations can be conveniently reduced to two equation with two unknowns: the growth rate g and the innovator's entry price p. The solution procedure is analogous to before except that now (3.4') and (3.5') are relevant. This yields

$$1 = gF + \frac{bs}{2}\left[e^{-g\Delta} - \frac{e^{-g\Delta(1+\gamma)}+1}{(1+\gamma)(2p-1)} + 1\right] \tag{3.10'}$$

for the resource constraint, and

$$wF = \frac{s}{4}\left(\frac{1-e^{-\phi\Delta}}{\phi}(2p-1) - 2\frac{1-e^{-(\phi+g\gamma)\Delta}}{\phi+g\gamma} + \frac{1-e^{-(\phi+2g\gamma)\Delta}}{\phi+2g\gamma}\frac{1}{2p-1}\right) \tag{3.11'}$$

for the zero-profit condition.

3.4.2 A Unique Equilibrium

To examine existence and uniqueness of the dynamic equilibrium we analyze the respective equilibrium conditions graphically. We denote the resource constraint by R and the zero profit condition by Π and draw R and Π in a (δ, g, p)-diagram. This allows us to discuss the above two scenarios simultaneously (Figure 3.1). In both parts of Figure 3.1 the vertical axis measures the growth rate g. In the left part of Figure 3.1 the horizontal axis measures the innovator's waiting time δ (from right to left, starting at $\delta = 0$), and in the right part of Figure 3.1 the horizontal axis measures the innovators' entry price p (starting at $p = 1$). Observe that $\delta = 0$ and $p = 1$ is the limiting case where the innovator has neither a waiting time nor enough demand to charge a price above marginal cost.

We now discuss the shape of the two curves in turn. To avoid confusion we denote the resource constraint in (g, δ)-space by $\tilde{R}$ and the one in (g, p)-space by R. Similarly, we have Π and $\tilde{\Pi}$ for the zero-profit condition. The R-curve in (g, δ) space is defined by the equation $1 = \tilde{R}(g, \delta)$ and $\tilde{R}(g, \delta)$ is given by the right-hand-side of equation (3.10). The Π-curve is defined by the equation $wF = \tilde{\Pi}(g, \delta)$

where $\tilde{\Pi}(g, \delta)$ is given by the right-hand-side of equation (3.11). Similarly, the R- and the Π-curve in (g, p) space are defined by $1 = R(g, p)$ and $wF = \Pi(g, p)$ where $R(g, p)$ and $\Pi(g, p)$ by given by the right-hand-side of equations (3.10') and (3.11').

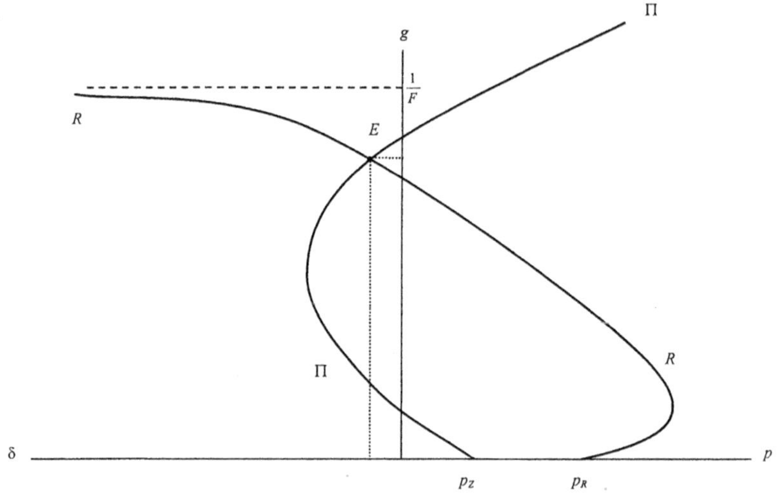

Fig. 3.1. The Equilibrium of the Growth Rate g and Waiting Time δ

The shape of the Π*-curve*

Consider first the (g, δ) space. When the consumer does not buy all available goods, $n < N$, innovators have a waiting time $\delta > 0$ until they can sell their product. The slope of the $\tilde{\Pi}$-curve is given by $dg/d\delta = -\tilde{\Pi}_\delta/\tilde{\Pi}_g$. A higher δ decreases profits so $\tilde{\Pi}_\delta < 0$ (where $\tilde{\Pi}_x$ denotes the partial derivative of $\tilde{\Pi}$ with respect to x). This simply results from discounting: the longer one has to wait for a given profit flow, the lower is the present value of this flow. This effect is enhanced by the fact that, due to a fixed patent duration Δ, the period during which the innovator earns positive profits does not only start later but also becomes shorter (recall that we measure δ from left to right).

The impact of the growth rate g on the value of an innovation Π, i.e. the of $\tilde{\Pi}_g$ is ambiguous. In a world with homothetic preferences where all goods enter the utility function in a symmetric way, a higher growth rate always lowers the value of an innovation. This is because in equilibrium, a higher growth rate is always associated with a higher interest rate that discounts future revenues more strongly (see the discussion in Romer, 1990). With hierarchic preferences instead, we have a second effect: a higher growth rate raises demand for the most recent innovator's product and leads to faster growth of the innovator's market. This leads to higher future prices and higher future profits which raises the value of an innovation. The size of the latter effect depends crucially on the value of γ, the steepness of the hierarchy: Lemma 2 below shows that the first effect always dominates if γ is low. Instead, if the hierarchy parameter γ is large, the demand effect of higher growth dominates the interest rate effect at low level of g (see Figure 3.1). It is important to note that a steep hierarchy is a necessary condition for the regime $n < N$ to be possible at all. When innovators have no initial demand, there are innovation incentives only if, after the waiting period δ, demand grows very quickly.

When consumers purchase all available products, $n = N$, innovators have no waiting time $\delta = 0$ and charge an entry price larger than marginal cost $p \geq 1$. The slope of the Π-curve is given by $dg/dp = -\Pi_p/\Pi_g$. How does the value of an innovation depend on p? We know from (3.5') that a higher entry price p for the most recent innovator's product means higher prices for all other goods in equilibrium. Moreover, from equation (3.4') a higher p is also associated with larger equilibrium consumption of each variety. Hence each monopolist has larger profits, so we have $\Pi_p > 0$.

The impact of the growth rate g on the value of an innovation is just like before. The demand effect increases, whereas the interest effect decreases the value of an innovation. The demand effect can dominate at low growth rates when the hierarchy is steep enough, whereas the interest effect dominates at high growth rates.

Lemma 2 *a. At* $pz = 1 + \left((1 + \frac{bs}{F}\frac{1-e^{-\Delta\rho}}{\rho})^{\frac{1}{2}} - 1\right)^{-1}$ *the Π-curve crosses the p-axis.*

b. The value of an innovation falls monotonically in the growth rate if $\gamma \leq \frac{\sigma(pz-1)}{1+\sigma(pz-1)}$ (flat hierarchy). *In this case, the zero profit constraint is a monotonically increasing curve in the (g, p)-space.*

c. For g sufficiently high, $\Pi_g < 0$ *and* $\tilde{\Pi}_g < 0$.

Proof *see Appendix.*

The shape of the R-curve

The slope of the resource constraint R can be derived in an analogous way as before by calculating, respectively, $dg/d\delta = -\tilde{R}_\delta/\tilde{R}_g$ and $dg/dp = -R_p/R_g$ for the two regimes. A higher waiting time δ reduces labor demand. The reason is that a higher δ decreases the demand for each product. (To see this use $n = e^{-\delta g}N$ in equation (3.4)). This means that $\tilde{R}_\delta < 0$. Similarly, a higher entry price p is associated with higher consumption levels for all goods (see equation (3.4')), and thus with a larger demand for labor in the whole economy. For this reason $R_p > 0$.

A higher growth rate g has an ambiguous effect on the demand for labor resources. On the one hand, there is the direct effect from a larger demand for workers in the research sector. On the other hand, there is an indirect effect which is due to the increase in the size of the monopolistic sector. (Recall from Section 3 above that, with a given patent duration Δ, a fraction $e^{-g\Delta}$ of all goods is supplied by competitive producers and a fraction $1 - e^{-g\Delta}$ by monopolistic firms). The larger the monopolistic sector, the higher the overall price level, and the lower consumption demand. Hence an increase in g leads to a lower demand for production workers. The following Lemma shows that the latter effect may dominate at low g, whereas the former effect always dominates at high g. We therefore have $R_g > 0$ if g is high and vice versa. We summarize this discussion in the following

Lemma 3 *a. The R-curve crosses the p-axis at* $p_R = \frac{1}{2}\left[1 + \frac{1}{1+\gamma}\frac{bs}{bs-1}\right]$ *if* $1 < bs \leq \frac{1+\gamma}{\gamma}$.

b. If $bs \leq 1$, *the resource constraint is monotonically falling in the* (g,p)*- and* (δ, g)*-space and reaches asymptotically the growth rate* $\hat{g}$ *implicitly defined by* $1 = \hat{g}F + \frac{bs}{2}\left(1 + e^{-\hat{g}\Delta}\right)$.

c. If $bs > \frac{1+\gamma}{\gamma}$, *even at* $g = 0$ *not all products can be produced, the share of products consumed* $x = \frac{n}{N}$ *is then given by the equation* $1 = \frac{bs}{2}\left[1 - x^{-\gamma}\frac{1}{1+\gamma} + x\frac{\gamma}{1+\gamma}\right]$.

d. For g *sufficiently high,* $R_g > 0$ *and* $\tilde{R}_g > 0$.

Proof *see Appendix.*

Remark *If* $bs \leq 1$, *the* $R-$*curve never hits the* $p-$*axis. All consumers could consume all varieties at the saturation level and there are still resources available for research.*

Having discussed the shape of the two curves we can consider the general equilibrium of the model. In this equilibrium both the resource constraint and the zero profit condition have to be satisfied which is the case at the point of intersection E in Figure 3.1.[15] A sufficient condition for uniqueness is $\gamma \leq \frac{\sigma(p_Z - 1)}{1+\sigma(p_Z - 1)}$ (flat hierarchy) and $bs \leq 1$, since then the two equilibrium curves are monotonically increasing or falling, respectively.

[15] Figure 1 suggests that the equilibrium exists if the Π-curve hits the p-axis to the left of R-curve. For most parameter values, simulations show that the equilibrium is unique.

Proposition 4 *a. If the exogenous parameters satisfy* $p_Z < p_R$ *or if* $bs \leq 1$*, there exists a general equilibrium with positive growth rate. b. A sufficient condition for a unique general equilibrium is* $bs \leq 1$ *and* $\gamma \leq \frac{\sigma(p_Z-1)}{1+\sigma(p_Z-1)}$.

Proof *Part b. see Appendix.*

3.5 Structural Change and the Kaldor Facts

In this Section we discuss of how the famous stylized facts mentioned by Kaldor (1961) can be reconciled with a continuous change in the structure of production and employment. We proceed in three steps. First, as the Kaldor facts of economic growth are partly concerned with physical capital, we have show that the equilibrium established in the last Section - when enriched with physical capital - meets Kaldor's criteria. Second, we describe the patterns of structural change that occur along the long-run growth path, in particular the rise and fall of the employment shares in the various sectors that occurs during the process of economic development. Finally, we study the critical role of the two taste parameters that characterize the hierarchy of needs, the saturation level s and the steepness of the hierarchy γ.

3.5.1 The Kaldor Facts

In a celebrated paper, Kaldor (1961) mentions that a reasonable growth model should capture the following criteria: (i) a constant growth rate of output and labor productivity; (ii) a constant increase in capital per worker; (iii) a constant long-term interest rate; (iv) a constant capital-output ratio; (v) a constant share of profits in output; and (vi) differences in growth rate of labor productivity across countries.

The long-run growth equilibrium established above assumes that labor is the only production factor. In order to discuss Kaldor's stylized facts in a meaningful way, we have to bring physical capital into the picture. Assume that each consumer good is produced with the same constant-returns-to-scale technology $F[k(j,t), A(t)l(j,t)]$ and that also capital goods are produced with that technology. $k(j,t)$ and $l(j,t)$ denote, respectively, the amounts of physical capital and labor employed in sector j at date t.[16] $A(t)$ is the stock of (labor-augmenting)

[16]Since technology is linear homogenous, the distribution of capital on the several firms in sector i plays no role.

technical knowledge and it is again assumed that $A(t) = N(t)$. Given the linear homogeneity of the production function we can write $f(\kappa(j,t)) = F[\frac{k(j,t)}{A(t)l(j,t)}, 1]$ with $\kappa(j,t)$ as the capital-labor ratio in efficiency units of labor and $f(\kappa(j,t))$ as the production function in intensive form.

When financial markets are perfect, savings yield the same returns, irrespective of whether they are invested in physical capital or in research. With a competitive market for capital goods, the rental price of capital equals $r(t) + \delta$, where δ is the rate of depreciation of physical capital. The rental price is the same in each sector. Each firm has to pay a wage rate w and a rental price of physical capital $r + \delta$. Cost minimization implies that each firm chooses the same capital-labor ratio. This implies that marginal production costs are the same in all sectors. In a steady state, where the interest rate is constant, the capital labor ratio is constant over time. For firms that operate under competitive conditions we must have $f'(\kappa(j,t)) = r$. Because *all* firms choose the same capital labor ration we have, for all j and t, $\kappa(j,t) = \kappa$. When κ is constant, the wage rate per efficiency unit of labor is also constant. Obviously, the wage rate per worker grows at the same rate as productivity.

The final step is to show that the capital output ratio is constant. To see this, suppose that employment in investment sector is constant. First, since κ is constant, output of investment goods j grows at the same rate as productivity. Physical capital evolves according to $\dot{K} = j - \delta K$, thus the capital stock grows also at the same rate as productivity. Second, output in the research sector is given by $w(t)gF$ which also grows at the same rate as productivity. Third, the value of output in the consumption sector also grows at the same rate. This is because, with marginal costs constant over time, the price setting behavior is the same as before. Hence the profit share in the consumption goods sector is constant and the Euler equation (3.9) still holds. In the steady state, the optimal growth rate of consumption expenditures equals the growth rate of productivity. Hence when wages grow at this rate, employment in the consumption goods sector is constant. This confirms our initial guess that employment in the investment sector is constant. Output equals $Y(t) = E(t) + j(t) + w(t)gF$ and therefore grows at the same rate as productivity. Hence the capital-output ratio is constant. We summarize this discussion in the following Proposition.

Proposition 5 *When production takes place with labor and physical capital the long-run equilibrium of the model satisfies the Kaldor facts.*

3.5.2 Structural Change

The equilibrium growth path exhibits *continuous structural change:* At a given date, many different goods exist and each good has a different income elasticity. Declining sectors with a low income elasticity and a falling share of production and employment co-exist with expanding sectors that have a high income elasticity and expanding share of production and employment. Hence there is uneven development and continuous reallocation of labor across sectors of production. In this Section we describe the pattern of structural change in more detail. We will concentrate on the regime $n < N$ and briefly discuss the regime $n = N$ at the end of the section.

To make the changes in the structure of consumption and employment explicit consider the life cycle of product j. How does demand and employment of an innovator increase over time? To answer this question take equation (3.4) and note that along the long-run growth path we have $n(t) = e^{-\delta g}N(t)$. Given the initial value of N, the growth rate g, and the innovator's waiting time δ, we know the equilibrium value of $n(t)$. From equation (3.4) the consumption level $c(j,t)$ and the corresponding level of employment $l(j,t) = b\frac{c(j,t)}{N(t)}$ can be calculated.

Figure 3.2 shows the Engel-curves for good $j = N(t)$. We draw $c(j,t)$ against total output in the production sector $E(t)$. As $E(t)$, $N(t)$, and $n(t)$ grow at the same rate the shape of the Engel-curve can be derived from (3.4). Demand is initially zero and the non-negativity constraints are still binding. This means at low income levels consumers cannot afford the product. Once a critical income level has been reached consumers start to buy. Increases in income initially lead to a strong expansion of the market, followed by decreasing growth rates and finally stagnating demand in the long term once consumption approaches the saturation level s. We note further that Engel-curves show a discontinuity at the point of time when patents expire. At this date the market opens up for competition, the price falls to marginal cost, and the demand level jumps up.

The following proposition summarizes the patterns of structural change by referring to the income elasticities of demand and employment. The 'gross' income elasticities take account of both the direct income effect on demand and of the indirect effects due to changes in the own price and the prices of all other (monopolistically supplied) products as incomes grow.

Proposition 6 *a. The 'gross' income elasticity of demand for good j is* $\gamma\frac{s-c(j,t)}{c(j,t)}$.

b. The 'gross' income elasticity for employment is $\gamma\frac{s-c(j,t)}{c(j,t)} - 1$.

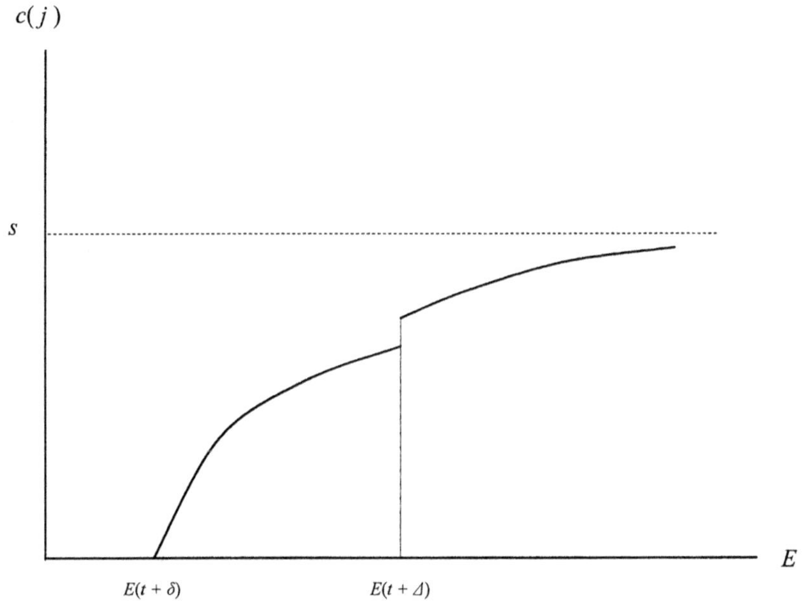

Fig. 3.2. The Engel-Curve for Good $j = N(t)$

This proposition holds for both regimes. As $E(t)$, $N(t)$ and $n(t)$ grow at the same rate, we can calculate the income elasticity as $\frac{dc(j,t)}{dn(t)}\frac{n(t)}{c(j,t)}$ or $\frac{dc(j,t)}{dN(t)}\frac{N(t)}{c(j,t)}$. For both regimes, the expressions in the proposition can be derived, respectively, from equations (3.4) and (3.4'). Part b) of the proposition obtains because the employment required to produce $c(j,t)$ is $l(j,t) = b\frac{c(j,t)}{N(t)}$, hence $\frac{dl(j,t)}{dN(t)}\frac{N(t)}{l(j,t)} = \frac{dc(j,t)}{dN(t)}\frac{N(t)}{c(j,t)} - 1$.

The above proposition shows that, for a given product, the demand elasticity is initially high and then decreases monotonically towards zero as consumption approaches the saturation level s.[17] *Despite that the model generates constant growth rates of macroeconomic aggregates, goods with high and low income elasticities coexist and continuous structural change takes place.*

We make two further interesting observations. The first refers to the definition of luxury versus necessary goods. In order to determine whether a good is a necessity or a luxury one frequently refers to the income elasticity of a product. Luxury goods are goods with a high income elasticity (higher than unity), whereas

[17] Also with respect to demand elasticities note the discontinuity at the date when patents expire. At this date the demand level jumps up and thus there is a sudden decrease in the income elasticity.

necessities are goods with a low income elasticity. The above proposition shows that, whether or not a good is a luxury or a necessity, depends on the level of development. Income elasticities change as the economy gets richer, and a good that has been a luxury good in the initial period of the product cycle becomes a necessity after incomes have sufficiently grown.

The second interesting observation refers to typical patterns of industry demand. Many writers have suggested that a stylized path of industry demand imply an Engel curve that has a logistic shape (for an explicit treatment see, for instance, Pasinetti, 1981). Initially demand is low and it also expands slowly. In this initial stage industry growth rates increase, reach a maximum and then start to decrease again. For Figure 3.2 above we see that, for a single product such a pattern emerges with the exception that the slowly growing initial stage is not present. However, when we consider a *range of products* (an 'industry'), increasing income effects in the early stage of the product cycle are generated because demand increases both at the intensive and at the extensive margin. As incomes grow consumers purchase more of the same products as well as new products. After a critical income level has been reached all products have positive demand, income effects decrease, and once incomes have sufficiently grown demand approaches the saturation level.

Panel a) of Figure 3.3 simulates industry demand and shows that industry Engel-curves have logistic shape. When the industry is small, the Engel-curve is convex because some sectors of the industry are not producing. The Engel-curve becomes concave at the point where the 'last' sector of the industry (here $i = kn$) starts production. In panel b) of Figure 3.3 we show the corresponding development of industry employment. Whether or not employment increases or decreases, depends on whether demand grows faster or slower than productivity. Hence the employment level reflects the outcome of a race between the growth of demand and productivity as the economy gets richer. Initially the growth of demand is larger than the growth of productivity and employment increases over time. However, after incomes have sufficiently grown, the growth of market demand lags behind the growth of productivity. Hence the industry labor share decreases. We also note that the discontinuities in product and labor demand due to expired patents smooth out as we consider a whole range of products rather than a single variety. We summarize our discussion in the following

Proposition 7 *The Engel curve for a range of products has a logistic shape, and the corresponding Engel curve of employment is bell-shaped.*

Industry Range: $[n, kn]$

Parameter Values:
$n = s = 1, k = 3, \gamma = 0.7, \delta = 0, \Delta = \infty$

Expenditures E, when good $i = n$ starts production, are normalized to 1

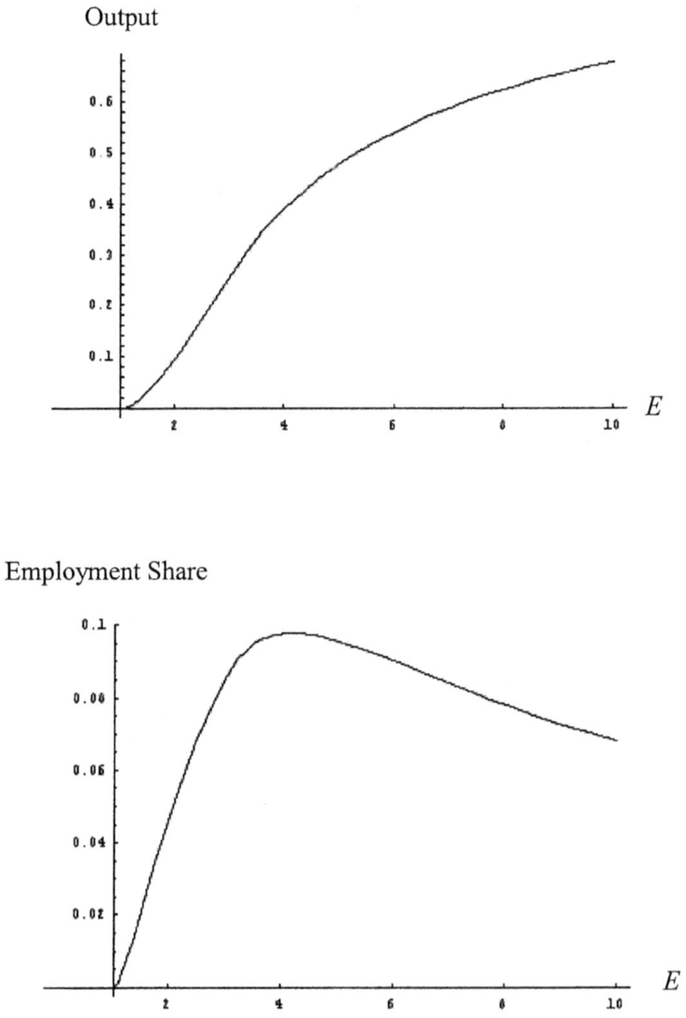

Fig. 3.3. Output and Employment Share of an Industry

3.5.3 The Impact of Hierarchic Preferences

The assumptions which are crucial for the results of this model refer to the preference side. We have already mentioned the importance of the hierarchy function $\xi(j) = j^{-\gamma}$ to generate constant growth rates for macroeconomic aggregates. We now consider the two parameters that characterize the hierarchy of needs, the steepness γ and the saturation level s.

The impact on growth

An *increase in the hierarchy parameter* γ has two competing effects on growth (Figure 3.4). On the one side, a higher γ raises both prices and demanded quantities. The resulting higher profits tend to increase the incentive to innovate and raise growth. The zero-profit curve Π shifts to the left. On the other side, with a steeper hierarchy more labor is used in production because a higher γ increases the demand for each good. This raises the demand for production labor and leaves less resources for innovation and growth. The resource constraint R shifts to the left. In general, either effect can dominate so we can conclude that the steepness of the hierarchy γ has no systematic effect on growth.

However, a rise in γ clearly implies that the innovator's waiting time δ increases (regime $n < N$) or that the innovators' entry price p falls (regime $n = N$). This should come to no surprise, as with a steeper hierarchy γ, the low-j goods get more weight in the utility function. Thus the utility drawn from consuming many different goods - the love for variety - becomes less pronounced.

The effects of *a higher saturation level* s are similar to those of a higher γ. As s rises, the demand for each good increases (see equations (3.4) and (3.4')). This raises the profitability of an innovation and the Π-curve shifts to the left. But obviously the demand change leads also to an increase in the demand for production labor and leaves less resources for research. As a result, the resource constraint R also shifts to the left. Just like an increase in γ, a larger s has no systematic effect on the growth rate g but leads to an increase in the innovator's waiting time δ (when $n < N$) or to lower prices p (when $n = N$).

The analysis above suggests that we can interpret s and γ as parameters for 'variety-aversion'. This becomes clear when we look at the utility function (3.1). For a given s, the steepness of the hierarchy says how much weight a certain product gets in the objective function and if γ is larger, the most basic goods get disproportionately high importance. For a given γ, the parameter s is a scaling factor, which determines how many units of good j are to be consumed to achieve a certain utility level. As marginal utility is falling, a large s is equivalent to a slowly falling marginal utility. A consumer does not want to consume a lot of a given product does not want to consume many different goods, in this sense a low s reinforces a given variety-aversion as measured by γ.

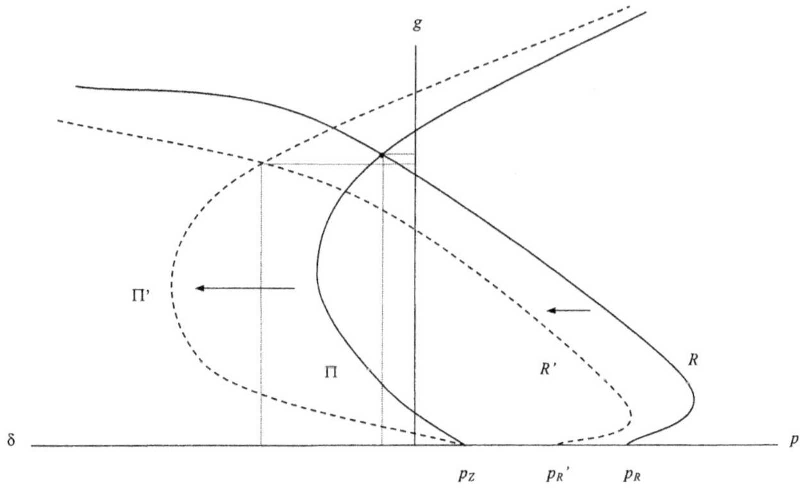

Fig. 3.4. A Rise in γ

The impact on patterns of structural change

The preference parameters determine the extent of structural change both directly and indirectly via the growth rate. Below, we will focus on the direct effect and ask how do the hierarchy parameter γ and the saturation level s affect the patterns of structural change, *given the equilibrium values of g and δ (or p).* Of course, the growth rate itself is crucial for structural change. If growth is higher, expenditures rise faster, hence we see from Figure 4 that the velocity of structural change is increased. Without growth no structural change takes place at all.

If the hierarchy is steep, γ is high, the gross income elasticity implies that demand increases strongly and approaches the saturation level quickly. In this sense, we have a lot of structural change. Intuitively, a steeper hierarchy implies a shift of demand away from the most recent (and least priority) goods to necessities. To see this more clearly, consider the other extreme, when no hierarchy exists and $\gamma = 0$. Here structural change is reduced to a minimum: with symmetry across products, the demand for an innovator jumps to its steady-state level at the period when the product is introduced and stays at this level forever. (The 'gross' income elasticity of demand is equal to zero). The whole increase in income takes place at the extensive margin: an increase in consumption means purchasing new goods whereas the consumption level of the old goods is not affected. Reallocation of labor takes the form of a proportional reduction of labor in the existing firms which are employed in the new firms. When $\gamma > 0$ the consumption level of all sectors is affected and the reallocation of labor affects sectors differently. Sectors with a 'gross' income elasticity larger than unity attract workers from sectors with an elasticity lower than unity. Additional income is to a smaller extent directed towards new goods.

The saturation level s only scales up demand but has otherwise no effect on the patterns of structural change. Inserting (3.4) into $\gamma\frac{s-c(j,t)}{c(j,t)}$, we directly see that s does not affect the gross elasticity of demand.

3.6 Calibration

The model was designed to explain structural change and the constant long run growth rate at the same time. Hence, it is at least instructive to examine the model's *quantitative* predictions although we should interpret the results only as an illustrative example. Among others, these include "realistic predictions" of the growth rate g, the corresponding saving rate, and the speed of structural change.[18] As some of these statistics are easy to obtain in reality, namely the growth and the saving rate, we should be able to draw some conclusions from the obtained data, regarding certain variables of the model, which are difficult or impossible to observe. Such variables include the steepness of the hierarchy γ, the fixed labor input F or the saturation level s.

Empirical findings give us a frame to work with and benchmarks to which we can compare and evaluate the results deriving from our model. We know that the growth rate g should be below 4%, as it is observed in most developed countries. For the saving rate, the picture is not so clear. As there is no capital in the standard setting of our model, the saving rate corresponds to the share of R&D expenditures to GDP. Formally, the saving rate is defined in our model as $\frac{s}{c+s}$, we get

$$\frac{s}{c+s} = \frac{g\frac{F}{bs}}{B+g\frac{F}{bs}}$$

where

$$B = e^{-g(\Delta-\delta)} - \frac{1}{4}\left(\frac{3e^{-g(\Delta-\delta)(1+\gamma)}+1}{(1+\gamma)(2p-1)} - (2p-1)\frac{1-e^{-g(\Delta-\delta)(1-\gamma)}}{1-\gamma}\right).$$

[18]Some parts of these calibrations are due to the excellent research assistance of David Kocher, who wrote a student thesis in 2001 ("Semesterarbeit") under supervision of mine.

The share of the labor force employed in R&D is around 0.5 percent in industrialized countries (see e.g. Jones (1995)).[19] R&D expenditures totally amount to around 5% of GDP. Because these ratios are not constant in the data (this is the problem of the "Scale effect"), there must be a *caveat* about the model's quantitative predictions concerning growth and R&D. However, our main points of interest concern growth and structural change.

Values of the Variables Used in the Calibration

For the rate of time preference, ρ, we may refer to King and Rebelo (1996). They estimated a value of 0.016 for ρ. We will therefore keep ρ as close as possible to that value, but definitely not lower than 0.01, nor larger than 0.04. The inverse of the intertemporal rate of substitution $\sigma(1-\gamma)+\gamma$ should lie somewhere within the range of 2 and 6 which seems to be the consensus of the present literature. The classical reference is Friend and Blume (1975). They come to the conclusion, that there is sufficient evidence to assume that $\sigma(1-\gamma)+\gamma$ has to be at least 2 or larger.

The work from David and Olsen (1992) gives us some insight on the optimal patent length, Δ. They came to the conclusion that optimal patent duration had to be somewhere within the range of 14 to 26 years. But they also mentioned in their paper, that under certain circumstances, a somewhat longer patent duration may also be acceptable, as there are differences in the way, patents are being handled in different countries. There are patents granted from the date of innovation as well as those granted from the date of the first production of the good. For our model, these differences do not have very strong implications, as patent duration is regarded within our model merely as a metaphor for the time, before an innovation is being imitated. We therefore keep the range for patent duration for our model a bit larger, from 10 to 35 years.

The parameter F and s are included in the variables c and d: $\frac{F}{bs}=d$ and $\frac{L}{bs}=\frac{1}{bs}=c$.

Calibration: Structural Change

We already did a small calibration exercise in Figure 3.3 above. There, the output and the employment share of industry $[n,3n]$ was plotted in dependence of (real) expenditures. At date t where $j=3n$ is the newest product consumed, the indus-

[19]However, the employment share of researchers has grown over time although the aggregate growth rate did not increase. Hence, the scale effect in the growth mechanism used in the present model lacks empirical foundation. One could eliminate this scale effect by using a semiendogenous growth model à la Jones (1995).

try covers two thirds of all available products. Hence, the industry is relatively large. The peak of the employment share is a sign for the speed of structural change. This peak is achieved at an income level four times larger than at the start of the industry. If the growth rate equals 3 percent, e.g., this takes approximately 47 years which seems quite reasonable. However, the employment share of this industry never exceeds 10 percent. Hence, a hierarchy parameter γ of 0.7, as it is chosen in the figure, is already relatively steep. If γ would be smaller, the employment share would be larger. With symmetry ($\gamma = 0$) this industry would employ in the maximum 2/3 of the workers employed in manufacturing.

Calibration: Equilibrium Growth Rate

We consider parameter values such that the $n = N$ regime (no waiting time) is the equilibrium outcome. We are investigating the effects of γ on the two curves and their equilibria, by assigning two different values (0.2 and 0.3) to the variable γ. The default parameter values for this calibration are $\sigma = 6$, $\Delta = 25$, $\rho = 0.01$, $c = 2.2$, $d = 0.6$. The result of this exercise is depicted in Figure 3.5. In this diagram, the p-axis is vertical and the g-axis is horizontal. An increase in the steepness of the hierarchy leads to a downward shift of both curves. For these parameter values, an increase in γ leads to a smaller growth rate. Hence, this exercise shows that γ has an ambiguous effect on the growth rate. Note that, if $\gamma > 0.3436$, the curves do not cross at all with these parameters, and the resulting equilibria for steeper hierarchies are stagnation equilibria, with $g = 0$.

In Figure 3.6, we keep γ fixed at 0.3 and manipulate σ. The R-curve is of course unaffected from a change of σ (the resource allocation does not directly depend on the interest rate), while the Π-curve shifts to the right, as σ increases. (The value of an innovation depends negatively on g for the chosen parameter values). A higher σ raises the interest rate which decreases the present value of profits ceteris paribus. Within the limits of σ (5 to 6), there are only unique equilibria. As σ increases, the growth rate decreases.

Figure 3.7 then shows the effects of different patent duration Δ, while we keep $\gamma = 0.3$ and $\sigma = 6$ constant. A change in duration has only a weak effect on the Π-curve, shifting it downwards for increasing patent durations. The effect is diminishing in size though, for increasing growth rates. The effect on the R-curve is just the opposite, as it shifts the R-curve upwards for increasing patent durations. We get either stagnatory equilibria (for $\Delta < 22.2$) or unique equilibria (for $\Delta \geq 22.2$). For durations above 22.2, the growth rate increases as the duration increases, as required.

$\delta = 0$ $\rho = 0.01$ $c = 2.2$ $d = 0.6$ $\sigma = 6$ $\Delta = 25$

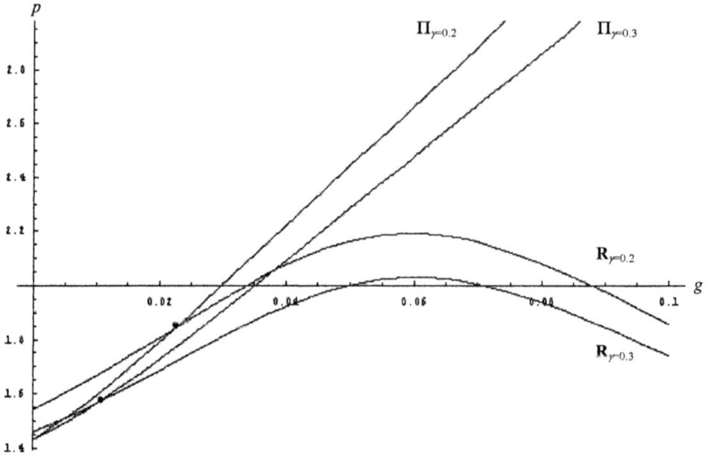

Fig. 3.5. Changes in the Hierarchy Parameter γ; $\gamma = 0.2$; $\gamma = 0.3$

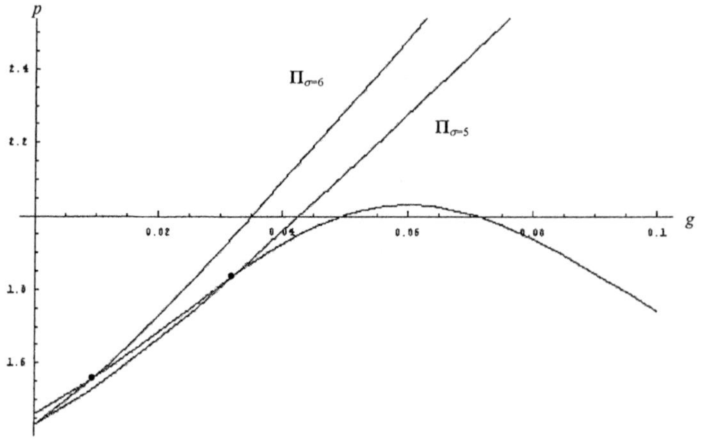

Fig. 3.6. Different Intertemporal Rates of Substitution σ; $\sigma = 5$; $\sigma = 6$

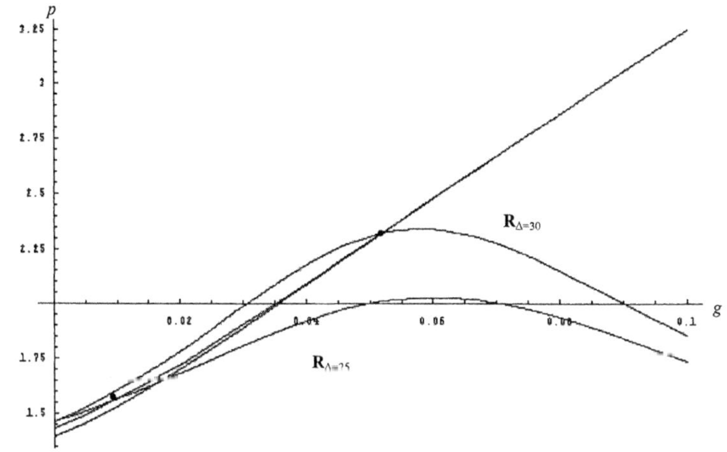

Fig. 3.7. Changes in Patent Duration: $\Delta = 25$; $\Delta = 30$

Implications for macroeconomic variables

The default parameter values used in the calibration $\sigma = 6$, $\Delta = 25$, $\rho = 0.01$, $c = 2.2$, $d = 0.6$ lead to a growth rate $g = 1.00\%$ and a corresponding price $p = 1.56$. This leads to a R&D rate of 3.5%, which is not unrealistic.

3.7 Other Types of Equilibria

If the parameter values satisfy $p_Z \geq p_R$ a *stagnation* equilibrium or *multiple* equilibria may arise (see Lemmas 2 and 3 for the definitions of p_Z and p_R). In that case, the Π-curve cuts the p-axis to the right of the R-curve.

Stagnation

In a stagnation equilibrium the value of an innovation is (equal or) *smaller* than the costs of an innovation, which implies that no research will be undertaken. Not surprisingly, this outcome is likely if research costs F are high. Also in the stagnatory state, the full employment condition has to be satisfied, hence the equilibrium point lies *on* the R-curve and is located where the R-curve intersects the horizontal axis (at $g = 0$). If $n = N$, the R-curve hits the horizontal axis in the right part of Figure 3.1. This occurs at $p_R > 1$. When this inequality is violated the regime $n = N$ is not feasible and we are in the regime $n < N$. As the economy does not grow, the waiting time δ is not a meaningful endogenous variable because δ will necessarily be infinite. As stated in Lemma 3c, the resource constraint has to be solved for $x = n/N$, the share of available products that is actually consumed. In such an equilibrium there are firms that know how to produce the goods $j \in (n, N]$, but no production ever takes place since demand given the (constant) income level is too small.

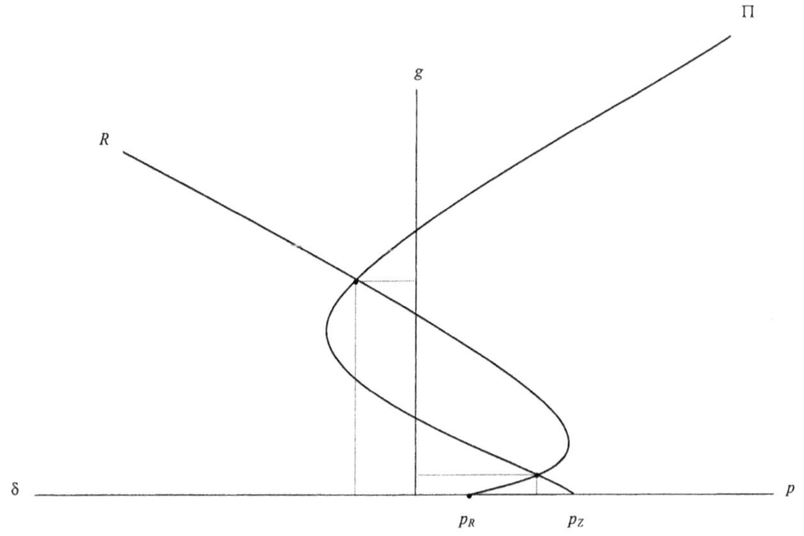

Fig. 3.8. Multiple Equilibria

Multiple equilibria

If $p_Z \geq p_R$ and if the two curves cross the model exhibits multiple equilibria. We then have three equilibria: the stagnation point and the two points of intersection of the Π- and the R-curve. There are two potential sources of multiplicity: the first is due to *finite patent length*; the second is due to *a hierarchic structure of preferences*. To identify the critical assumptions we compare the behavior of an economy where consumers have symmetric preferences ($\gamma = 0$) to the case when preferences are hierarchic ($\gamma > 0$).

With symmetric preferences ($\gamma = 0$) each good faces the same demand, hence all monopolistic prices are equal to $p > 1$. A situation where $p = 1$ and $\delta > 0$ cannot arise in an equilibrium with positive growth since a new good is *immediately* purchased in the same amounts as all other goods supplied by the monopolists. The zero profit condition and the resource constraint, respectively, read

$$\frac{F}{bs} = \frac{1 - e^{-\phi\Delta}}{\phi} \frac{(p-1)^2}{2p-1}, \quad \text{and} \quad 1 = gF + bs\left(1 + e^{-g\Delta}\right) \frac{p-1}{2p-1}.$$

The slope of the zero profit condition is positive because a demand externality does not arise: higher economy-wide growth has no impact on the market demand for previous innovators. Instead demand jumps from zero to a positive level and stays there until the patent has expired.[20] Hence there is always a positive association between the entry price p and the growth rate g.

The resource constraint, however, still has an ambiguous slope. A higher growth g not only raises the demand for labor in research but it also decreases the demand for production labor. The larger fraction of monopolistic markets implies high prices on more markets leading to lower aggregate consumption demand. High growth can be sustained due to lower equilibrium employment in production and vice versa. When patent length is *infinite*, this complementarity vanishes. In that case changes in the growth rate do not affect market structure because all markets are monopolized. This point has been made by Laussel and Nyssen (1999) who showed that multiple equilibria can arise in a standard endogenous growth model when patent length is finite.

With hierarchic preferences ($\gamma > 0$) the situation is different. Multiple equilibria can arise even when there are infinitely lived patents because the Π-curve is not necessarily monotonic. With a steep hierarchy (high γ) the Π-curve is backward bending at low levels of g (see Lemma 2b). The reason is a demand externality: when preferences have a hierarchic structure the demand of a previous innovator depends on the economy-wide growth rate. If innovators expect high growth they expect that the demand for their products expands more quickly so that future prices, quantities, and profits are larger. So higher economy-wide growth stimulates the incentive to innovate. If innovators expect low growth, profit expectations and the resulting incentives to innovate are correspondingly low. Hence low growth rates are sustained by pessimistic expectations and vice versa. Obviously, this *demand externality* is at work independently of the particular length of a patent; in particular it holds even when protection is forever.

It is worth noting that the intercept of the resource constraint with the horizontal axis, p_R, shifts to the left with an increase in γ. According to Proposition 1, this implies that multiple equilibria become more likely. We summarize this discussion in the following Proposition 8.

Proposition 8 *A hierarchic structure of preferences ($\gamma > 0$) may lead to multiple equilibria even when patent length is infinite.*

---

[20]Thereafter demand makes a further jump due to the fall in prices that occurs as soon as the competitive producers take over the market; needless to say, this demand increase is irrelevant for the innovation incentives.

3.8 Is the Optimal Patent Duration Infinite?

Patent policy always faces a trade-off. On the one hand, patents create mark-ups and these mark-ups distort relative prices. On the other hand, patents stimulate R&D by allowing the successful firms to earn profits which may imply a dynamic efficiency gain. In a symmetric world this trade-off is trivial as there are no relative price distortions when patent length is infinite (see also the discussion in O'Donoghue and Zweimueller, 2004). As long as innovators are not displaced by future innovators (as in models of expanding product variety) it is optimal to set the patent length to infinity. With hierarchic preferences instead such price distortions exist as the mark-ups of innovators increase over time.

In such a set-up it is interesting to study the question whether a higher utility level can be achieved by finite patents. Proposition 6 says that social welfare can always be increased by moving from infinite to finite patent duration.

Proposition 9 *Welfare is maximized at a finite patent length.*

Proof *see Appendix.*

The result in Proposition 6 does *not* depend on the rate of time preference. Intuitively, the static inefficiency of the price distortions is always too strong to make an infinite patent length socially optimal. To illustrate this result graphically, we have plotted the value of intertemporal utility for different hierarchy levels in dependency of the inverse patent duration $1/\Delta$, so that a value of zero for this variable corresponds to infinite patent length (Figure 3.9). We see that social welfare increases at $1/\Delta = 0$ but the dynamic efficiency loss as a result of lower R&D ultimately dominates the static efficiency gain from the reduction of price distortions of shorter patents.

Furthermore, it is interesting to note that the optimal patent length becomes shorter as the hierarchy gets steeper. Intuitively, a steeper hierarchy implies stronger price distortions and bigger static inefficiency. For the parameter values chosen in Figure 3.9, the optimal patent length is about 18 years when $\gamma = 0.7$.

Default Parameter values:

$\sigma = 2 \qquad \rho = 0.02 \qquad \frac{F}{bs} = 1.46 \qquad \frac{1}{bs} = 0.6$

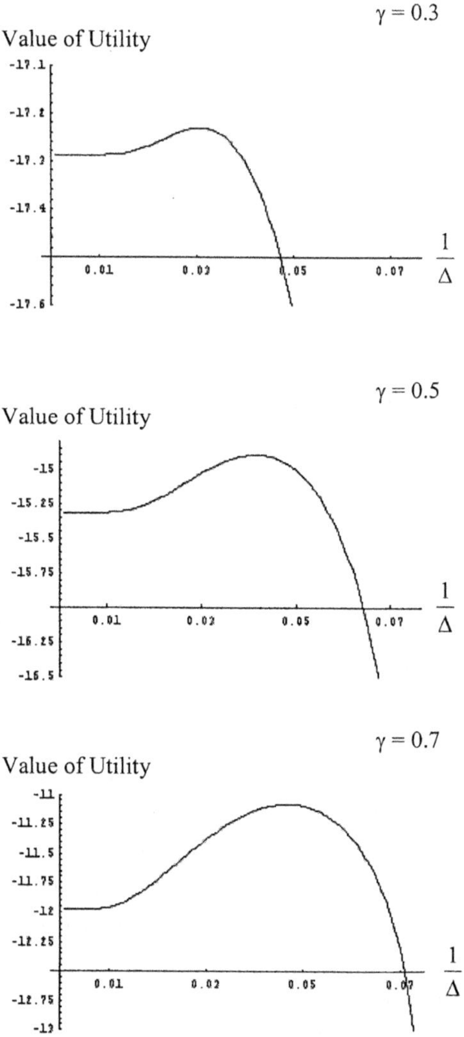

Fig. 3.9. The Impact of Different Patent Durations on Welfare

3.9 Discussion and Extensions

In this section we have presented a model that captures two of the most important features of the long-run growth process: the dramatic changes in the structure of production and employment; and the Kaldor facts of economic growth. Our model has focused on the demand-explanation of structural change according to which the dramatic reallocation of labor is driven by differences in income elasticities across sectors. The basic idea of our analysis is that household expand their consumption along a hierarchy of needs. If the 'hierarchy function' that characterizes the willingness of consumers to move from goods with high priority to goods with lower priority takes a particular form, the equilibrium process of growth and structural change is consistent with the Kaldor facts.

Innovations play a crucial role in our model. Innovations drive productivity growth and this leads to interesting interactions between sectoral and aggregate dynamics: Economy-wide growth prospects are of central importance for the emergence of new industries; and the industrial R&D that leads to these new industries is central for improvements in productivity. These complementarities open up the possibility for multiple equilibria. Hence our model is not only capable of yielding insights into the process of growth and structural change, but sheds also light on the question why some countries experience high long-term growth and many industries take off, while in other countries we see neither a change in the production structure nor increases in aggregate productivity.

The way we have discussed the interactions between structural change and economic growth depends on several assumptions and suggests interesting extensions. We want to mention four points. First, our discussion of the model was based on a particular endogenous growth mechanism. However, our main results do not depend on a specific mechanism that drives aggregate productivity. For instance, an exogenous growth mechanism would reproduce similar patterns of structural change as presented in this chapter,[21] as would a semi-endogenous growth model in the spirit of Jones (1995) that does not exhibit the scale effects that characterizes the present model. Instead, removing the scale effect by introducing a quality dimension (as in the models survey by Jones, 1999) would add a qualitatively new feature to our model. Structural change could also take place within industries as better goods would replace old goods and incumbent firms may either change

---

[21] Of course, exogenous growth would only allow for a one-way causality from aggregate to sectoral dynamics without any further feedback mechanism.

their own structure of production or may be displaced by new firms supplying better qualities at lower prices.

Second, our results are based on the assumption that the baseline utility function is quadratic. We have used this specific formulation because it illustrates the idea that consumers get saturated with goods of high priority and move on to goods with lower priority. However, we have shown in section 2 above that this specific formulation of the baseline utility is not crucial. The two important conditions are that the hierarchy function takes the particular form of a power function; and that the relative price structure remains the same over time. In this section, the former condition is met by the assumption that the hierarchy function $\xi(j) = j^{-\gamma}$. The latter condition is guaranteed in equilibrium because the supply conditions are symmetric across sectors. This assumption could be relaxed because the second condition only requires that the supply side should keep the same relative structure such that the equilibrium price structure remains constant, in relative terms.

3.10 Appendix

3.10.1 Proof of Lemma 1

Consider first the regime $n < N$. To get the maximized utility $\hat{u}$ for a given level of expenditures E and a given menu of goods N, we insert equilibrium quantities (3.4) into the utility function (3.1) After some manipulations this yields

$$\hat{u} = \frac{n^{1-\gamma}}{1-\gamma}\frac{s^2}{8}\left(3 + \left(a\frac{N}{n}\right)^{1-\gamma} + 2(1-\gamma)\frac{aN-n}{n} - (1-\gamma)\frac{1+3\left(a\frac{N}{n}\right)^{1+\gamma}}{(1+\gamma)}\right)$$

which we can write as $\hat{u} = \frac{n^{1-\gamma}}{1-\gamma}\psi(\frac{n}{N}, a; \gamma, s)$. We know from (3.6), that we can write $E = sn\phi(\frac{n}{N}, a; \gamma, s)$ which implies $n = \frac{E}{s\phi(\frac{n}{N}, a;\gamma,s)}$. Inserting this latter expression into the above utility function yields

$$\hat{u} = \frac{E^{1-\gamma}}{1-\gamma}K\left(\frac{n}{N}, p = 1, a; s, \gamma\right)$$

where $K\left(\frac{n}{N}, p = 1, a; s, \gamma\right) = \frac{\psi(\frac{n}{N},a;\gamma,s)}{\left[s\phi(\frac{n}{N},a;\gamma,s)\right]^{1-\gamma}}$.

We proceed in a similar way for regime $n = N$. This yields for maximized utility

$$\hat{u} = \frac{N^{1-\gamma}}{1-\gamma}\frac{s^2}{8}\left(3 + a^{1-\gamma} + \frac{2(1-\gamma)(a-1)}{2p-1} - \frac{(1-\gamma)(1+3a^{1+\gamma})}{(1+\gamma)(2p-1)^2}\right),$$

which can be written as $\hat{u} = \frac{N^{1-\gamma}}{1-\gamma}\Psi(p, a; \gamma, s)$. We know from equation (3.6') that we can write $E = sN\Phi(p, a; \gamma, s)$. Solving for N and substituting into the above utility expression yields

$$\hat{u} = \frac{E^{1-\gamma}}{1-\gamma}K\left(\frac{n}{N} = 1, p, a; s, \gamma\right),$$

where $K\left(\frac{n}{N} = 1, p, a; s, \gamma\right) = \frac{\Psi(p,a;\gamma,s)}{[s\Phi(p,a;\gamma,s)]^{1-\gamma}}$.

3.10.2 Proof of Lemma 2

We know from the zero-profit condition (3.11') that

$$\begin{aligned}
\Pi_g &\equiv \frac{\partial \Pi(t)}{\partial g} \\
&= \frac{s}{4}\int_t^{t+\Delta}\left[\begin{array}{c} -\sigma(1-\gamma)(2p-1) \\ -\frac{\sigma(1-\gamma)+2\gamma}{2p-1}e^{-2g\gamma(\tau-t)} \\ +2(\sigma(1-\gamma)+\gamma)e^{-g\gamma(\tau-t)} \end{array}\right](\tau - t)e^{-(r-g\gamma)(\tau-t)}d\tau \\
&\equiv \frac{s}{4}\int_t^{t+\Delta}\Theta(p,g)(\tau-t)e^{-[\rho+g\sigma(1-\gamma)](\tau-t)}d\tau
\end{aligned}$$

We will show the following: If $\left.\frac{\partial\Pi(t)}{\partial g}\right|_{g=0} \leq 0$ then $\frac{\partial\Pi(t)}{\partial g} < 0$ for all $g > 0$. Hence, $\left.\frac{\partial\Pi(t)}{\partial g}\right|_{g=0} \leq 0$ is sufficient for Π to have always a positive slope. $\left.\frac{\partial\Pi(t)}{\partial g}\right|_{g=0}$ can be calculated as

$$\frac{s}{4}\Theta(p,0)\int_t^{t+\Delta}(\tau-t)\,e^{-\rho(\tau-t)}d\tau \leq 0.$$

This is equivalent to

$$\begin{aligned}
\Theta(p,0) &= -\sigma(1-\gamma)\,(2p-1) - \frac{\sigma(1-\gamma)+2\gamma}{2p-1} + 2\,(\sigma(1-\gamma)+\gamma) \leq 0 \\
&\iff \gamma \leq \frac{\sigma(p-1)}{1+\sigma(p-1)} \iff p \geq \frac{\sigma(1-\gamma)+\gamma}{\sigma(1-\gamma)} \\
&\iff 2p-1 \geq \frac{\sigma(1-\gamma)+2\gamma}{\sigma(1-\gamma)}.
\end{aligned}$$

Note that p depends on g. If $\left.\frac{\partial\Pi(t)}{\partial g}\right|_{g=0} \leq 0$, the zero profit constraint has a positive slope, i.e. we must have $p'(g) \geq 0$. Together with the lower bounds of p above we can determine the sign of the partial derivatives of $\Theta(p,g)$

$$\begin{aligned}
\Theta_p &= -2\sigma(1-\gamma) + \frac{2}{(2p-1)^2}\,(\sigma(1-\gamma)+2\gamma)\,e^{-2g\gamma(\tau-t)} \\
&\leq -2\sigma(1-\gamma) + \frac{2\sigma^2(1-\gamma)^2}{(\sigma(1-\gamma)+2\gamma)^2}e^{-2g\gamma(\tau-t)} < 0 \\
\Theta_g &= -2\gamma\,(\tau-t)\left((\sigma(1-\gamma)+\gamma)\,e^{-g\gamma(\tau-t)} + \frac{\sigma(1-\gamma)+2\gamma}{2p-1}e^{-2g\gamma(\tau-t)}\right) \\
&\leq -2\gamma\,(\tau-t)\left((\sigma(1-\gamma)+\gamma)\,e^{-g\gamma(\tau-t)} + \sigma(1-\gamma)e^{-2g\gamma(\tau-t)}\right) < 0
\end{aligned}$$

Hence $\Theta(p(g),g) < \Theta(p(0),g) < \Theta(p(0),0) \leq 0$ which completes the proof.

b. Insert $g = 0$ into the zero profit condition (3.11') (since demand does not grow when $g = 0$, an equilibrium with positive waiting time δ is impossible)

$$\begin{aligned}
\frac{F}{b} &= \frac{s}{4}\frac{1-e^{-\rho\Delta}}{\rho}\left(2p_z - 1 + \frac{1}{2p_z-1} - 2\right) \\
4\frac{F}{bs}\frac{\rho}{1-e^{-\rho\Delta}} &= \left(\sqrt{2p_z-1} - \frac{1}{\sqrt{2p_z-1}}\right)^2 \\
2\sqrt{\frac{F}{bs}\frac{\rho}{1-e^{-\rho\Delta}}} &= \sqrt{2p_z-1} - \frac{1}{\sqrt{2p_z-1}}
\end{aligned}$$

Note that only the positive root is relevant since $2p_z - 1 > 1$. We denote $\sqrt{2p_z-1} = x$, the equation above can then be written as $x^2 - 2\sqrt{\frac{F}{bs}\frac{\rho}{1-e^{-\rho\Delta}}}x - 1 = 0$. This quadratic equation has the solution $x = \sqrt{2p_z - 1} = \sqrt{\frac{F}{bs}\frac{\rho}{1-e^{-\rho\Delta}}+\sqrt{\frac{F}{bs}\frac{\rho}{1-e^{-\rho\Delta}}+1}}$. Solving for p_z yields the claim of the Lemma.

c.

$$\lim_{g->\infty} \Pi_g = \int_t^{t+\Delta} \frac{s}{4}\Theta(p,g)\,(\tau - t)\, e^{-[\rho+g\sigma(1-\gamma)](\tau-t)} d\tau < 0$$

and

$$\lim_{g->\infty} \tilde{\Pi}_g = e^{-\delta r} \int_t^{t+\Delta-\delta} \frac{s}{4}\Theta(1,g)\,(\tau - t)\, e^{-r(\tau-t)} d\tau - \delta\sigma(1-\gamma)\Pi(t) < 0$$

since

$$\lim_{g->\infty} \Theta(p,g) = -\sigma(1-\gamma)\,(2p-1) < 0.$$

3.10.3 Proof of Lemma 3

a. Inserting $g = 0$ into the resource constraint (3.10') yields

$$1 = bs\left[1 - \frac{1}{(1+\gamma)\,(2p-1)}\right] =: f(p)$$

$1 \leq p < \infty$ implies $bs\frac{\gamma}{1+\gamma} \leq f(p) < bs$. Hence, the equation can only be fulfilled if $1 < bs \leq \frac{1+\gamma}{\gamma}$. Solving the equation yields $p_R = \frac{1}{2}\left[1 + \frac{1}{1+\gamma}\frac{bs}{bs-1}\right]$.

b. If p goes to infinity in equation (3.10'), the condition follows directly.

c. Replace δ by the new variable $x = \frac{n}{N} = e^{-\delta g}$. Equation (3.10) now reads:

$$1 = gF + \frac{bs}{2}\left[1 - \frac{e^{-g(1+\gamma)\Delta}}{1+\gamma}x^{-\gamma} + \frac{\gamma}{1+\gamma}x\right].$$

Inserting $g = 0$ yields the condition in the Lemma.

d. The derivatives with respect to g are, respectively, $\tilde{R}_g = F - \frac{bs}{2}(\Delta - \delta)e^{-g\delta}\left[e^{-g(\Delta-\delta)} - e^{-g(\Delta-\delta)(1+\gamma)}\right] - \delta\,(1 - gF)$ and $R_g = F - \frac{bs}{2}\Delta\left[e^{-g\Delta} - \frac{1}{2p-1}e^{-g\Delta(1+\gamma)}\right]$. Hence, $\lim_{g->\infty}\tilde{R}_g > \lim_{g->\infty} R_g = F > 0$ which proves the claim.

3.10.4 Proof of Proposition 4

With flat hierarchy, we showed that the Π-curve is monotonically increasing, and so an equilibrium is only possible with $p > 1$. It remains to show that the R-curve monotonically decreasing if $bs \leq 1$, which would guarantee uniqueness. Lemma 2b. says that R approaches $\hat{g}$, defined by $1 = \hat{g}F + \frac{bs}{2}\left(1 + e^{-\hat{g}\Delta}\right)$. The right hand side of the latter expression is a convex function in g and must therefore have a positive slope at $g = \hat{g}$. Thus, $F - \frac{bs}{2}\Delta e^{-\hat{g}\Delta} > 0$. But this implies $R_g = F - \frac{bs}{2}\Delta e^{-g\Delta} + \frac{bs}{2}\Delta\frac{1}{2p-1}e^{-g\Delta(1+\gamma)} > \frac{bs}{2}\Delta\frac{1}{2p-1}e^{-g\Delta(1+\gamma)} > 0$.

3.10.5 Proof of Proposition 9 (Patent Duration)

We will first consider the case where $p > 1$.

The longer patent protection the higher are profits. We see directly that $\frac{4}{s}\Pi_\Delta = e^{-\Delta[\phi+g\gamma]}\left((2p-1)\,e^{g\gamma\Delta} - 2 + \frac{1}{2p-1}e^{-g\gamma\Delta}\right) > 0$, thus, with a higher Δ, Π shifts to the right. A higher Δ is associated with a bigger share of the monopolistic sector, which reduces the total amount produced, therefore we see that $R_\Delta < 0$, R shifts to the left. Algebraically, the impact of Δ on the growth rate g and the price of the latest good p reads as follows.

$$\begin{pmatrix} \Pi_g & \Pi_p \\ R_g & R_p \end{pmatrix}\begin{pmatrix} dg \\ dp \end{pmatrix} = \begin{pmatrix} -\Pi_\Delta \\ -R_\Delta \end{pmatrix} d\Delta$$

Applying Cramer's Rule we get the desired expressions $dg/d\Delta$ and $dp/d\Delta$.

$$\frac{dg}{d\Delta} = \frac{\Pi_p R_\Delta - \Pi_\Delta R_p}{\Pi_g R_p - \Pi_p R_g}$$

$$\frac{dp}{d\Delta} = \frac{\Pi_g R_\Delta - \Pi_\Delta R_g}{\Pi_g R_p - \Pi_p R_g}$$

When the equilibrium is unique, the R-curve has a steeper slope - viewed from the g-axis - than the Π-curve at point of intersection. This implies that the denominator $\Pi_g R_p - \Pi_p R_g$ is negative. We then see directly that $\frac{dg}{d\Delta}$ is positive: Longer patents increase growth. The sign of $\frac{dp}{d\Delta}$ is ambiguous. Intuitively, as Δ increases a lower p satisfies the zero-profit condition, but a higher Δ increases the share of the monopolistic sector too. This implies that a higher p is allowed to fulfill the resource constraint.

We are now able to study the welfare effects of different patent durations Δ. We calculate the welfare of the representative agent. $N(t)$ is the inherited number of known designs, $n(t) = e^{-\delta g}N(t)$ is the number of goods consumed. Inserting the value of the instantaneous utility into the intertemporal utility function and evaluating yields

$$U(t) = \frac{K(e^{-(\Delta-\delta)g}, p; \gamma)^{1-\sigma}}{1-\sigma} \left(\frac{\left(N(t)e^{-\delta g}\right)^{1-\gamma}}{1-\gamma} \right)^{1-\sigma} \frac{1}{\rho - g(1-\gamma)(1-\sigma)}$$

Is the optimal Δ equal to infinity? Because $\Delta = \infty$ is associated with $a = 0$ when the growth rate is positive, we sign the partial derivative of the value of the intertemporal utility function with respect to a. Then we evaluate the derivative at $a = 0$. This allows us to answer how welfare changes with Δ, as $\frac{dU}{da} = \frac{dU}{d\Delta}\frac{d\Delta}{da}$.

With $p > 1$, δ is equal to zero. We get

$$\frac{dU}{d\Delta} = \Gamma \left(\frac{\partial K}{\partial \Delta} + \frac{\partial K}{\partial p}\frac{dp}{d\Delta} + \frac{\partial K}{\partial g}\frac{dg}{d\Delta} + \frac{(1-\gamma)K}{\rho - g(1-\gamma)(1-\sigma)}\frac{dg}{d\Delta} \right)$$

where Γ is given by $\Gamma = K^{-\sigma} \left(\frac{\left(N(t)e^{-\delta g}\right)^{1-\gamma}}{1-\gamma} \right)^{1-\sigma} \frac{1}{\rho - g(1-\gamma)(1-\sigma)}$. We note that Γ is well defined for every a.

The intuition of the derivative $\frac{dU}{d\Delta}$ is straightforward: $\frac{\partial K}{\partial \Delta} + \frac{\partial K}{\partial p}\frac{\partial p}{\partial \Delta}$ reflects the static efficiency losses due to an increasing Δ whereas $\frac{\partial K}{\partial g}\frac{\partial g}{\partial \Delta} + \frac{(1-\gamma)K}{\rho - g(1-\gamma)(1-\sigma)}\frac{\partial g}{\partial \Delta}$ measures the corresponding dynamic efficiency gains.

Recognize that the sign of $\frac{\partial U}{\partial a}$ is only determined by the coefficients of the a-terms with the lowest exponent: $a^{-\gamma}$. We have to rewrite the partial derivatives in terms of a. ($a = e^{-g\Delta}$ or $\Delta = -\frac{1}{g}\ln a$)

$$\begin{aligned}
\frac{4}{s}\Pi_g &= (2p-1)\,\sigma(1-\gamma)\frac{(-\frac{\phi}{g}\ln a + 1)a^{\frac{\phi}{g}} - 1}{\phi^2} \\
&\quad -2[\sigma(1-\gamma)+\gamma]\frac{(-\frac{\phi+g\gamma}{g}\ln a + 1)a^{\frac{\phi+g\gamma}{g}} - 1}{[\phi+g\gamma]^2} \\
&\quad +\frac{1}{2p-1}[\sigma(1-\gamma)+2\gamma]\frac{(-\frac{\phi+2g\gamma}{g}\ln a + 1)a^{\frac{\phi+2g\gamma}{g}} - 1}{[\phi+2g\gamma]^2} \\
\frac{4}{s}\Pi_p &= 2\frac{1-a^{\frac{\phi}{g}}}{\phi} - \frac{2}{(2p-1)^2}\frac{1-a^{\frac{\phi+2g\gamma}{g}}}{\phi+2g\gamma} \\
\frac{4}{s}\Pi_\Delta &= a^{\frac{\phi+g\gamma}{g}}\left((2p-1)\,a^{-\gamma} - 2 + \frac{1}{2p-1}a^{\gamma}\right) \\
R_g &= F - \frac{bs}{2}\Delta a\left[1 - \frac{1}{2p-1}a^{\gamma}\right] \\
R_p &= bs\frac{1+a^{1+\gamma}}{(1+\gamma)\,(2p-1)^2} \\
R_\Delta &= \frac{bs}{2}ga\left(\frac{1}{2p-1}a^{\gamma} - 1\right)
\end{aligned}$$

We calculate the partial derivatives $\frac{\partial g}{\partial \Delta}\frac{\partial \Delta}{\partial a}$ and $\frac{\partial p}{\partial \Delta}\frac{\partial \Delta}{\partial a}$ first. Remember that $a = e^{-g\Delta}$: by implicit differentiation we see that $\frac{\partial \Delta}{\partial a} = -\frac{1}{ga}$ (and $\frac{\partial g}{\partial a} = -\frac{1}{\Delta a} = -\frac{g}{a \ln a}$.). The denominator $\Pi_g R_p - \Pi_p R_g$ becomes a negative constant when a approaches zero. We denote this constant by H. It is given by $H = \Pi_g|_{a=0} \frac{bs}{(1+\gamma)(2p-1)^2} - \frac{sF}{4}\left(\frac{2}{\phi} - \frac{2}{(2p-1)^2}\frac{1}{\phi+2g\gamma}\right)$

If the intertemporal utility function takes a finite value, we have $\rho - g(1-\gamma)(1-\sigma) > 0$. This implies $r = \phi + g\gamma > g$. The lowest exponent of $\Pi_p R_\Delta$is 1 and the lowest exponent of $\Pi_\Delta R_p$ is $\frac{\phi}{g}$. If $\phi < g$, we get

$$\frac{\partial g}{\partial \Delta}\frac{\partial \Delta}{\partial a} \equiv \frac{dg}{da} = -\frac{1}{Hga}(\Pi_p R_\Delta - \Pi_\Delta R_p) \approx \frac{1}{Hg}\frac{bs}{(1+\gamma)(2p-1)} a^{\frac{\phi}{g}-1} < 0$$

as a goes to zero.

If $\phi \geq g$, the lowest exponent of $(\Pi_p R_\Delta - \Pi_\Delta R_p)$ equals 1. Hence, $\frac{dg}{da}$ approaches a negative constant as a goes to zero.

The lowest exponents of $\Pi_g R_\Delta$ and $\Pi_\Delta R_g$ are 1 and $\frac{\phi}{g}$, respectively. If $\phi < g$, we get for a near zero

$$\frac{\partial p}{\partial \Delta}\frac{\partial \Delta}{\partial a} \equiv \frac{dp}{da} = -\frac{1}{Hga}(\Pi_g R_\Delta - \Pi_\Delta R_g) \approx \frac{2p-1}{Hg}\frac{sF}{4} a^{\frac{\phi}{g}-1} < 0$$

If $\phi \geq g$, $\frac{dp}{da}$ approaches a negative constant as a goes to zero.

We are adding the pieces of the puzzle together. We rewrite the central derivative:

$$\frac{1}{\Gamma}\frac{dU}{da} = \frac{\partial K}{\partial a} + \frac{\partial K}{\partial p}\frac{dp}{da} + \frac{\partial K}{\partial g}\frac{dg}{da} + \frac{(1-\gamma)K}{\rho - g(1-\gamma)(1-\sigma)}\frac{dg}{da}$$

We need the following derivatives:

$K(a,p;\gamma) = \frac{s^2}{8}\left(3 + a^{1-\gamma} + 2(1-\gamma)\frac{a-1}{2p-1} - (1-\gamma)\frac{1+3a^{1+\gamma}}{(1+\gamma)(2p-1)^2}\right)$

$\frac{\partial K}{\partial a} = \frac{s^2}{8}(1-\gamma)\left(a^{-\gamma} + \frac{2}{2p-1} - \frac{3a^\gamma}{(2p-1)^2}\right)$

$\frac{\partial K}{\partial p} = \frac{s^2}{2}(1-\gamma)\left(\frac{1-a}{(2p-1)^2} + \frac{1+3a^{1+\gamma}}{(1+\gamma)(2p-1)^3}\right)$

$\frac{\partial K}{\partial g} = \frac{\partial K}{\partial a}\frac{\partial a}{\partial g} = -\frac{s^2}{8}\frac{1-\gamma}{g} a \ln a \left(a^{-\gamma} + \frac{2}{2p-1} - \frac{3a^\gamma}{(2p-1)^2}\right)$

If $\phi \geq g$, $\frac{dp}{da}$ and $\frac{dg}{da}$ approach constants, hence the derivative is dominated by the $\frac{\partial K}{\partial a}$-term which exhibits the lowest exponent $-\gamma$.

If $\phi < g$, the lowest exponent of $\frac{\partial K}{\partial p}\frac{dp}{da}$ is $\frac{\phi}{g} - 1$ (the exponent of $\frac{\partial K}{\partial g}\frac{dg}{da}$ is higher since $\lim_{a->0} a^{1-\gamma}\ln a = 0$). If the intertemporal utility function takes a finite value, we have $\rho - g(1-\gamma)(1-\sigma) > 0$. This implies $r = \phi + g\gamma > g$. From this follows $\frac{\phi}{g} + \gamma > 1$ or $\frac{\phi}{g} - 1 > -\gamma$. We conclude that the $\frac{\partial K}{\partial a}$-term will dominate again. The derivative of the utility function therefore approaches in both cases

$$\frac{1}{\Gamma}\frac{\partial U}{\partial a} \approx \frac{s^2}{8}(1-\gamma)a^{-\gamma} > 0$$

which is positive.

In the $\delta > 0$-case one gets a similar result with the same reasoning: $\frac{1}{\Gamma}\frac{\partial U}{\partial a} \approx \frac{s^2}{8}(1-\gamma)e^{\delta g(1-\gamma)}a^{-\gamma} > 0$.

4

Inequality and Research Incentives

4.1 Introduction

In this chapter we study the impact of inequality on the incentives to innovate. Recall that the structure of demand is affected by the distribution of income when consumers have hierarchic preferences. Poor people concentrate most of their expenditures on basic needs, whereas richer people direct their expenditures to more luxurious goods. The empirical relevance of a hierarchic structure of demand is documented by 'Engel's law', one of the most robust empirical findings in economics.

In the standard Schumpeterian growth models consumers have homothetic preferences. By this assumption, the level of demand for the various goods - including the innovator's product - does not depend on the income distribution. Instead, we study a situation where preferences are non-homothetic and income distribution has an impact, both on the *composition of consumer demand* and on the *structure of prices* that innovators charge for their product. This yields a rich set-up that allows us to study the inequality growth-nexus via a channel that has not attracted much attention in the recent literature.

When product demand is affected by the income distribution, inequality becomes a determinant of economic growth. The demand-channel has received little attention in the inequality-growth literature.[1] Instead, much of the recent literature has either focused on the role of capital market imperfections, (see Galor and Zeira (1993), Banerjee and Newman (1993), Aghion and Bolton (1997), and others) or on political mechanisms (Bertola (1993), Persson and Tabellini (1994), Alesina and Rodrik (1994), and others). In contrast, this chapter focuses on the role of inequality for the dynamics of an innovator's demand and does neither rely on imperfect capital markets nor on politico-economic arguments.

In this chapter, we introduce hierarchic preferences in the simplest possible way. In order to satisfy a certain want, consumers buy one unit of an indivisible good, i.e. the subutility function $v(\cdot)$ takes the form of 0-1-preferences. The hierarchy implies that poor consumers will only buy a small range of high priority goods, whereas richer people will consume a wider range including also goods of lower priority. Hence, the incentive to conduct R&D is affected by the distribution of income as inequality determines the level of demand and the optimal price of an innovator. Today, the good of an innovator may be purchased only by a small group of rich people and the willingness to pay for this product will initially be low. But as incomes grow the size of the market grows as also less wealthy people become willing to buy. One novel aspect of our approach is to study how income distribution affects the time path of demand for the innovator's good; the other novel aspect is that the prices and mark-ups of innovators are determined by the distribution. This means we can study a situation where both depend on the income distribution and both affect the reward to an innovation. We therefore have a set-up where inequality affects growth via its impact on product demand.

The following three points are the main findings of our analysis.

First, inequality alters the degree of competition in the economy. With poor and rich consumers, it may be profitable for the monopolist only to sell to the rich, whose demand is inelastic (relative to the poor), and thus to charge higher prices. However, this strategy implies that in the aggregate we have a distortion

[1] The empirical importance of the inequality-growth relationship is a matter of discussion in the empirical literature. A number of earlier studies have found a robust negative correlation between growth rates and income inequality in cross-country regressions (Persson and Tabellini (1994), Alesina and Rodrik (1994), Clarke (1995), and in particular Perotti (1996)). While more recent work by Deininger and Squire (1998) casts doubt on the robustness of the relationship between growth and the distribution of income, empirical regularities in the inequality-growth relationship remain. In this paper we do not aim to directly address findings from this empirical literature. Our aim is to study the interesting meachanisms and show under which conditions we get a positive and when we get a negative impact of inequality on growth.

in the price structure due to the fact that the poor are *excluded from consumption* due to too high prices.

Second, inequality has an a priori ambiguous impact on the incentive to innovate: On the one hand, with high inequality an innovator faces immediate demand with a high willingness to pay by the rich consumers; on the other hand, new markets are small for a long time since only the rich buy. However, we get the comparative-static result that the first effect dominates, if there is exclusion of the poor *and* if the increase in inequality is due to higher income of the rich group. Higher inequality increases the profit share of the economy; with profits being the reward for innovation, more resources are allocated in R&D which enhances growth. Instead, if higher inequality is due to an enlargement of the poor group although their relative wealth remains constant, higher inequality may reduce growth. The important message is that higher inequality *per se* is a too crude statement to decide how the demand structure is affected. The result suggests that higher inequality due to a smaller size of wealthy people is especially harmful for profits and thus for growth.

Third, if there is *no* exclusion of the poor, the inequality-growth relation changes its sign. The case of no exclusion can only arise, if for some goods in the economy no saturation point exists. The presence of those goods limits the scope for price setting by innovators, because the marginal willingness to pay for innovative products is bounded also for the very rich. Then, once a rather egalitarian distribution is considered, the innovator has no incentive to set prices that would exclude the poor. Thus, prices are determined by the willingness to pay of the poor. An even more egalitarian distribution allows the monopolist to set higher prices and earn higher profits as the poor are the 'critical' consumers that determine demand at the extensive margin.

The role of inequality and hierarchic preferences in the context of economic development has been studied in a few other papers. Our analysis is related to that of Murphy, Shleifer, and Vishny (1989). As in the present model, they show that the adoption of efficient methods of production requires large markets and excessive concentration of wealth may be an obstacle to economic development. However, Murphy, Shleifer, and Vishny (1989) focus on a static framework. As a consequence, changes in income distribution matter only if the demand of the marginal firm is affected. This is different from the present model where not only the level but also the time path of demand affects growth.[2] Models that study the impact of inequality and product demand on growth include Chou and Talmain (1996), Falkinger (1994), and Zweimueller (2000). These papers have in common that while income distribution affects demand there is no impact of the distribution on prices. Hence an important mechanism of the present model, namely that the poor may be excluded from the market as a result of the monopolists pricing decision, does not occur in these models.[3]

The chapter is organized as follows. Section 2 presents the model and Section 3 studies the static equilibrium in detail. Section 4 deals with the supply side of the economy, Section 5 discusses the innovation process. In Section 6 we introduce our assumption on inequality and Section 7 we can study the general equilibrium of the model. Section 8 discusses the impact of inequality on growth. Section 9 concludes.[4]

4.2 Static Equilibrium

4.2.1 Hierarchic Preferences and Consumption Choices

In an economy there exist many potentially producible, differentiated products indexed by a continuous index $j \in [0, \infty)$. Consumers have hierarchic preferences over the differentiated goods. Further, we assume that the choice to buy a certain differentiated product is a take-it or leave-it decision: either a good is consumed in which case one and only one unit is purchased, or is not consumed. This allows us to normalize the baseline utility (2.1) such that $v(0) = 0$ and $v(1) = 1$ ("0-1-preferences"). Again, the hierarchic weight follows a power-function, i.e. we assume $\xi(j) = j^{-\gamma}$ with $\gamma \in (0, 1]$. The preferences over the differentiated products can thus be represented by the following utility function

$$\tilde{u}(\{c(j)\}) = \int_0^\infty \xi(j) v(c(j)) dj = \int_0^\infty j^{-\gamma} c(j) dj$$

where we make use of the above normalization $v(c(j)) \equiv c(j)$. Evidently, $c(j)$ is a dummy variable indicating whether or not good j is consumed. Take the case when a consumer purchases the first n goods in the hierarchy. In this case the

---

[2]Other papers which study the impact of inequality on product demand are Eswaran and Kotwal (1993) and Baland and Ray (1991) both of which stick to a static framework. See also Bourguignon (1992).

[3]For models where inequality drives the incentive to improve the quality of products see Glass (1996, 2001), Li (1996), and Zweimueller and Brunner (1996, 2005).

[4]This chapter follows Foellmi and Zweimueller (2002b).

above utility is given by $\tilde{u}(\{c(j)\}) = \int_0^{\infty} j^{-\gamma} c(j) di = \int_0^{N} j^{-\gamma} di = \frac{N^{1-\gamma}}{1-\gamma}$ and, due to the restriction $\gamma \in [0,1)$, the integral $\int_0^N j^{-\gamma} di$ does not diverge. While the highest utility arises from consuming all goods in the interval $[0, N]$, it is also evident that the utility integral is finite for any arbitrary bundle of goods with measure N: any arbitrary interval of measure N (or sub-intervals that sum up to measure N) yields instantaneous utility larger than 0 but lower than $\frac{N^{1-\gamma}}{1-\gamma}$.

Apart from the sector of differentiated products, there exists also a second sector that produces a homogeneous good x that can be consumed in continuous amounts. A possible different interpretation of x to which we will frequently refer, is leisure. The total utility flow at any instant is given by the utility received from consuming differentiated products and the utility received from consuming the homogenous good. We assume that the two types of goods are linked by a Cobb-Douglas relationship with parameter ν, where $0 \leq \nu < 1$.[5] The instantaneous utility function takes the form

$$u(x, \{c(j)\}) = x^{\nu} \int_0^{\infty} j^{-\gamma} c(j) dj \tag{4.1}$$

Now consider the decision problem of household i. Households are heterogenous with respect to their available budget E_i but otherwise identical.[6] It is assumed that the first $\overline{N}$ products in the hierarchy are actually available on the market, whereas goods in the interval $(\overline{N}, \infty)$ have not yet been invented.[7] We denote by $p(j)$ the price of the differentiated product j and by p_x the price of one unit

[5] As it implies constant expenditure shares, the Cobb-Douglas is a fair formulation in the sense that higher inequality does not imply *per se* consumption of the traditional good to rise, as is done in other approaches.

[6] As we assume intertemporal additive separability of the utility function, we can apply two-stage budgeting: The consumers' decision can be split up into two parts: In the first stage, we look at the *intra*temporal decision problem by solving for the optimal structure of consumption at a point of time, given current prices of all goods $p(j)$ and p_x and the currently available budget E_i. In the second stage, we look at the *inter*temporal decision problem and calculate how to allocate the consumers' lifetime resources across time. While the time path of E_i is endogenous, we can take it as given when solving for the optimal structure of expenditures at a given point of time.

[7] We are making a shortcut here: more generally we could assume that a bundle of goods with measure N is available on the market but that this measure does not necessarily coincide with the interval $(0, N)$ in the hierarchy, i.e. there are ' andholes' in the sense that goods with higher priority are still not available whereas goods with low priority have already been invented.

We will abstract from this possibility here as we are primarily interested in the behavior of the economy along the balanced growth path. This means, we start here already with a situation which will prevail in the balanced growth equilibrium, namely when the introduction of new goods follows the prespecified hierarchy of needs and wants. In equilibrium, therefore, there will of the homogenous good x. Total expenditures of household i are given by $E_i = \int_0^{\overline{N}} c_i(j)p(j)dj + p_x x_i$ where $c_i(j)$ indicates whether household i consumes good j. Hence the static choice problem of consumer i can be written as

$$\max_{x,\{c(j)\}} x_i^{\nu} \int_0^{\overline{N}} j^{-\gamma} c_i(j)dj \qquad s.t. \qquad E_i \geq \int_0^{\overline{N}} c_i(j)\, p(j)dj - p_x x_i$$

Taking expenditures and prices as given, consumer i maximizes his utility by choosing which differentiated products to consume $\{c_i(j)\}_{j\in[0,\overline{N}]}$, and by choosing the optimal amount of the homogenous good x_i. To solve the above problem we can set up the Lagrangian as

$L = x_i^{\nu} \int_0^{\overline{N}} j^{-\gamma} c_i(j)dj + \lambda_i \left(E_i - \int_0^{\overline{N}} c_i(j)\, p(j)dj - p_x x_i\right)$

where λ_i is the Lagrangian multiplier, which in our context may be interpreted as consumer i's marginal utility of wealth. Maximization of the Lagrangian with respect to $\{c(j)\}$ and x yields following first order conditions

$$\begin{aligned} c_i(j) &= 1 \qquad p(j) \leq x_i^{\nu} j^{-\gamma}/\lambda_i \equiv q_i(j) \\ c_i(j) &= 0 \qquad p(j) > q_i(j) \\ v x_i^{\nu-1} \int_0^{\overline{N}} j^{-\gamma} c_i(j)dj &= \lambda_i p_x. \end{aligned} \tag{4.2}$$

The first two conditions say that consumer i will consume good j if its price $p(j)$ is lower than (or equal to) consumer i's willingness to pay $x_i^{\nu} j^{-\gamma}/\lambda_i$ which from now on we denote by $q_i(j)$.[8] The third condition is the familiar condition that says the homogenous good x is consumed up to the point where the marginal utility of consumption of x equals the utility-adjusted price $\lambda_i p_x$.

4.2.2 The Determination of Prices and the Structure of Consumption

Our next step is to discuss the determination of prices. It is assumed that the homogenous good is produced with constant marginal cost and supplied on a competitive market. Hence the price of the *homogenous* good p_x is constant, and exogenously given by the constant marginal cost. (As our aim is to study growth,

be no holes as the most recent innovator produces always the goods which has least priority among all goods that are actually available on the market.

[8]This condition comes from comparing the received utility from consuming good j, $x_i^{\nu} j^{-\gamma}$, with its price $p(j)$ times consumer i's marginal utility of wealth λ_i. Rearranging terms yields $p(j) \leq x_i^{\nu} j^{-\gamma}/\lambda_i$.

we will come back to the issue of how p_x changes over time below). Instead, each *differentiated* product is supplied by one single *monopolistic* supplier. Since we focus on heterogeneity of demand (because of the hierarchic preferences), we assume for simplicity that marginal costs are equal and constant for all monopolistic firms. Without loss of generality, we take the marginal cost of the differentiated product as numeraire.[9]

We now assume that there are only two types of households, rich R and poor P, where a fraction β is poor and $1-\beta$ are rich. Recall that each household either consumes one unit or does not consume good j. Hence the level of demand depends on how many consumers are willing to purchase good j at a given price $p(j)$. Consequently the market demand function is a step function (figure 4.1), where the steps are determined by $p(j) = q_R(j)$ and corresponding quantity $1-\beta$, the willingness to pay and group size of the rich, and by $p(j) = q_P(j)$ and maximum quantity 1, the poor' willingness to pay and the size of the whole population.[10] Consider now a monopolist which supplies good j, his price is then either at point A or at point B in figure 4.1, whichever yields the higher profits. The corresponding profit levels are, respectively, $[q_R(j) - 1]\,(1-\beta) \equiv \Pi_R(j)$ (selling only to the rich) and $[q_P(j) - 1] \equiv \Pi_{tot}(j)$ (selling to all consumers).

Note first that a situation where only the rich buy goods from monopolistic producers cannot be an equilibrium. If the poor would not buy any differentiated products at all, their willingness to pay would become infinitely large as their marginal utility of income would become zero. Hence it holds for some j, $\Pi_{tot}(j) \geq \Pi_R(j)$ or equivalently, $q_P(j) - q_R(j)(1-\beta) \geq \beta$, which implies that $q_P(j)/q_R(j) > 1-\beta$. Note that this ratio does not depend on j.

We can directly state the result.

Lemma 4 *a) 'Consumption along the hierarchy'. Prices are set such that for all goods $j \in [0, N_P]$, $p(j) = q_P(j)$, and for all $j \in (N_P, N_R]$ we have $p(j) = q_R(j)$, where $0 < N_P \leq N_R \leq \overline{N}$.*

b) 'Market exclusion of the poor'. If the willingnesses to pay of the rich and the poor are sufficiently different we get $N_P < N_R$. In such a situation the suppliers of low-priority goods set prices too high for the poor. In other words, the poor are

[9]When we discuss intertemporal issues below, we will see that the marginal production cost is also constant *over time*, as input prices grow pari passu with productivity

[10]Obviously, if there are more types of consumers, there are more such kinks, and in the case of continuous distribution we have a smooth demand function. In any case, under the take-it or leave-it assumption the shape of the demand function reflects the distribution of the consumers' budgets.

excluded from participation in the market for low-priority goods. If $\nu = 0$, *the poor will always be excluded from some goods in equilibrium.*

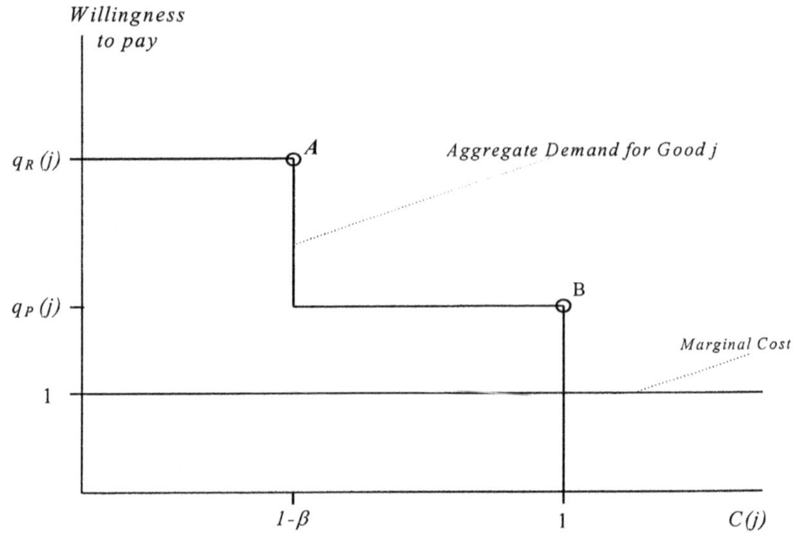

Fig. 4.1. Aggregate Demand for Good j and Decision Problem of the Monopolist

Proof. Part a. Recall that $q_i(j) = x_i^{\nu} j^{-\gamma}/\lambda_i$. Hence it is straightforward to calculate $\frac{\partial \Pi_R(j)}{\partial j} = -\frac{\gamma}{j} q_R(j)(1-\beta)$ and $\frac{\partial \Pi_{tot}(j)}{\partial j} = -\frac{\gamma}{j} q_P(j)$. Since $q_P(j)/q_R(j) > 1-\beta$, we see that $\frac{\partial \Pi_R(j)}{\partial j} > \frac{\partial \Pi_{tot}(j)}{\partial j}$, which means that the difference $\Pi_{tot}(j) - \Pi_R(j)$ decreases as we move along the hierarchy. Since poor consume a positive subset goods j, there must exist a good $N_P > 0$ such that for any $j \leq N_P$ we have $\Pi_{tot}(j) \geq \Pi_R(j)$.

Part b. Assume $\nu = 0$. If $N_P = N_R = \bar{N}$ were an equilibrium, then, rich and poor would consume exactly the same, since there is no expenditure for x-goods. This would imply that the rich have income left causing their marginal utility of income be zero and thus their marginal willingness to pay be infinity. Hence it would be profitable for a monopolist to deviate, since he could raise profits by selling only to the rich. ■

Lemma 4a implies that the poor consume all goods $j \in [0, N_P]$ and the rich consume all goods $j \in [0, N_R]$ where $0 < N_P \leq N_R \leq \overline{N}$. This means 'consumption follows the hierarchy' in the sense that consumer i purchases only the first N_i products in the hierarchy and no products $j > N_i$. This is an intuitive result: the goods with lower priority (high-j goods) are priced such that only the rich can afford them. Further, we observe that the equilibrium will be one of the following three scenarios. We could have a situation where (i) only the rich can buy all products that are available on the market, so that $N_P < N_R = \overline{N}$; (ii) both the poor and the rich will buy all products that are available on the market, so $N_P = N_R = \overline{N}$; and (iii) where neither the rich nor the poor can afford all $\overline{N}$ goods, so $N_P < N_R < \overline{N}$.[11] As we will show below, the first scenario will prevail if the willingnesses to pay are sufficiently different. For the second scenario exactly the opposite is true. The third scenario is possible if the inherited measure of producible goods is very large, even relative to willingness to pay of the richest consumer.

More generally, we observe that in our model of hierarchic preferences, the structure of prices is determined by the distribution of the willingnesses to pay of the various consumers, which themselves reflects the distribution of the households' budgets. This is a result that is absent from the standard monopolistic competition due to the assumption of homothetic preferences: total market demand there is independent of the income distribution and has therefore no effect of the structure of prices. (The same is true for previous attempts to combine a hierarchic structure of demand with market power, where a uniform mark-up is assumed for all products. Murphy, Shleifer, Vishny (1989), Zweimueller (2000)).

Finally, we observe that the distribution of the willingnesses to pay (which reflects the *personal* distribution of income) affects the choice of prices and therefore also the aggregate profits. So, in our model the *personal* distribution of income affects the *functional* distribution.

4.2.3 Solving the Static Consumers' Problem

We can now characterize the choice problem of the consumers in this economy. As mentioned above, consumers maximize utility over an infinite horizon and due to the additivity of the utility function we can solve the problem by two-stage budgeting. In their static choice consumers take expenditures at a given point of time as given and ask how to allocate these expenditures across the homogeneous good and the differentiated products along the hierarchy. The dynamic choice problem is then to ask for the optimal allocation of lifetime resources over time, taking the structure of consumption at a given point of time as given. We will first look at the static equilibrium before we discuss the dynamic solution of the consumers' problem. Furthermore, in presenting the static and the dynamic solutions we concentrate on the case when the rich but not the poor buy all products that are available on the market ($N_P < N_R = \overline{N}$) and describe the

[11]A case $N_P = N_R < \overline{N}$ cannot arise in equilibrium, as will be shown below.

corresponding equilibria in some detail. At the end of this section we will also briefly mention the two remaining scenarios namely, when neither the rich nor the poor can afford all $\overline{N}$ goods ($N_P < N_R < \overline{N}$); and when both the poor and the rich buy all available products ($N_P = N_R = \overline{N}$).

A static equilibrium is a structure of consumption of the differentiated products $\{c_i(j)\}_{j\in[0,\overline{N}]}$, a corresponding structure of prices of these products $\{p(j)\}_{j\in[0,\overline{N}]}$, the consumption levels of the homogeneous product x_i, and the marginal utilities of wealth λ_i, where $i = (R, P)$. When we present the solution we take as predetermined the measure of available products $\overline{N}$ (from the innovation process prior to the point of time we consider), the consumers' budgets E_i (from the first stage of our two-stage budgeting problem), the constant marginal production costs in the monopolistic sector (taken as numeraire) and in the competitive sector (equal to p_x). Exogenous are the utility parameters γ and ν and the population size of poor β.

To characterize the static equilibrium in the interesting case $N_P < N_R = \overline{N}$ it will be convenient to introduce two new variables, (i) the goods that the poor relative to the goods that the rich can afford, $n_P \equiv N_P/N_R$, which in the present regime equals $N_P/\bar{N}$ and (ii) the price of good $\overline{N}$, $\overline{p} \equiv p(\overline{N})$. It turns out that, once the equilibrium values of these two variables are known, the equilibrium structure of consumption $\{c_i(j)\}_{j\in[0,\overline{N}]}$ and the corresponding structure of prices $\{p(j)\}_{j\in[0,\overline{N}]}$ can be derived immediately. Hence when presenting the solution to the static equilibrium we can replace $\{c_i(j)\}_{j\in[0,\overline{N}]}$ and $\{p(j)\}_{j\in[0,\overline{N}]}$ by n_P and $\overline{p}$ and describe this solution in terms of the endogenous variables $n_P, \overline{p}, x_P, x_R, \lambda_P$ and λ_R.

The equilibrium structure of consumption $\{c_i(j)\}_{j\in[0,\overline{N}]}$ is determined by the equilibrium value of n_P alone, according to Lemma 4. To determine the equilibrium structure of prices $\{p(j)\}_{j\in[0,\overline{N}]}$ in terms of n_P and $\overline{p}$, consider first the lower priority goods $j \in (N_P, \overline{N}]$. These goods are priced at the willingness to pay of the rich $p(j) = q_R(j)$, and from (4.2) we know that $q_R(j) = q_R(\overline{N})\left(j/\overline{N}\right)^{-\gamma} = \overline{p}\left(j/\overline{N}\right)^{-\gamma}$. Now consider the goods with high priority $j \in [0, N_P]$. They are priced at the willingness to pay of the poor, together with (4.2) we thus know that $p(j) = q_P(j) = q_P(N_P)\,(j/N_P)$. It remains to determine $p(N_P)$ in terms of n_P and $\overline{p}$. Recall that, for the critical good N_P, the corresponding firm is indifferent between selling only to the rich at price $q_R(N_P) = \overline{p}n_P^{-\gamma}$ or by serving the whole market at price $p(N_P) = q_P(N_P)$. Hence we must have $q_P(N_P) - 1 = (\overline{p}n_P^{-\gamma} - 1)(1-\beta)$. Assuming the firm supplying good N_P charges the willingness to pay of the poor and serves the whole market, we get $p(N_P) = q_P(N_P) = \beta + \overline{p}n_P^{-\gamma}(1-\beta)$. Taken together we can express the equilibrium structure of prices as

$$p(j) = \begin{cases} \left[\beta n_P^\gamma + (1-\beta)\overline{p}\right]\left(\frac{j}{\overline{N}}\right)^{-\gamma} & j \in [0, N_P], \\ \overline{p}\left(\frac{j}{\overline{N}}\right)^{-\gamma} & j \in (N_P, \overline{N}]. \end{cases} \tag{4.3}$$

Having determined $\{c_i(j)\}_{j\in[0,\overline{N}]}$ and $\{p(j)\}_{j\in[0,\overline{N}]}$ in terms of n_P and $\overline{p}$ we are now ready to describe the solution to the static equilibrium of the model in terms of the six endogenous variables $n_P, \overline{p}, x_P, x_R, \lambda_P$ and λ_R. The six equations that determine this equilibrium are given by

$$\beta + (1-\beta)\overline{p}n_P^{-\gamma} = \frac{x_P^\nu \left(n_P\overline{N}\right)^{-\gamma}}{\lambda_P} \tag{S1}$$

$$\overline{p} = \frac{x_R^\nu \overline{N}^{-\gamma}}{\lambda_R} \tag{S2}$$

$$\nu x_P^{\nu-1}\frac{\left(n_P\overline{N}\right)^{1-\gamma}}{1-\gamma} = \lambda_P p_x \tag{S3}$$

$$\nu x_R^{\nu-1}\frac{\overline{N}^{1-\gamma}}{1-\gamma} = \lambda_R p_x \tag{S4}$$

$$\frac{E_P}{\overline{N}} = \left[\beta n_P^\gamma + (1-\beta)\overline{p}\right]\frac{n_P^{1-\gamma}}{1-\gamma} + \frac{p_x x_P}{\overline{N}} \tag{S5}$$

$$\frac{E_R}{\overline{N}} = \left[\beta n_P^\gamma + (1-\beta)\overline{p}\right]\frac{n_P^{1-\gamma}}{1-\gamma} + \overline{p}\frac{1-n_P^{1-\gamma}}{1-\gamma} + \frac{p_x x_R}{\overline{N}}. \tag{S6}$$

Equations (S1) and (S2) say that the price of good N_P equals to the willingness to pay of the poor for good N_P, and that the price for good $\overline{N}$ equals the willingness to pay of the rich for good $\overline{N}$. Equations (S3) and (S4) say that, for both types of consumers, the optimal level of x_i is determined such that the marginal utility of x_i equals its utility-adjusted price $\lambda_i p_x$. Finally, equations (S5) and (S6) state that the budget constraints have to be satisfied for both types of consumers.

4.2.4 Static Expenditures and Utilities

For further use, it is convenient to reduce this system to two equations in the two unknowns n_P and $\overline{p}$. These two interesting equations are the budget constraints when consumers have made optimal consumption choices, that is their 'expenditure functions'. Moreover, we can also express the maximized utility functions in terms of the endogenous variables in terms of n_P and $\overline{p}$, that is the 'indirect utility functions'.[12]

[12]We use the terms 'expenditure function' and 'indirect utility function' in the sense that expenditures (utility) evaluated after consumers have made optimal choices. We do not explicitely

Combining equations (S1) and (S3) of the above system we can write

$$p_x x_P = \frac{\nu \overline{N}}{1-\gamma}\left[\beta + (1-\beta)\overline{p} n_P^{-\gamma}\right] n_P \tag{4.4}$$

and

$$p_x x_R = \frac{\nu \overline{N}}{1-\gamma}\overline{p}, \tag{4.5}$$

and substitute these relations into equations (S5) and (S6) of the above system. This yields

$$\frac{E_P}{\overline{N}} = \left[\beta n_P^{\gamma} + (1-\beta)\overline{p}\right]\frac{n_P^{1-\gamma}}{1-\gamma} + \left[\beta + (1-\beta)\overline{p} n_P^{-\gamma}\right]\frac{\nu n_P}{1-\gamma} \tag{4.6}$$

and

$$\frac{E_R}{\overline{N}} = \left[\beta n_P^{\gamma} + (1-\beta)\overline{p}\right]\frac{n_P^{1-\gamma}}{1-\gamma} + \overline{p}\frac{1-n_P^{1-\gamma}}{1-\gamma} + \overline{p}\frac{\nu}{1-\gamma}, \tag{4.7}$$

we note that, for given values of n_P and $\overline{p}$, E_P and $\overline{N}$ as well as E_R and $\overline{N}$ are proportional. (This is a result of Cobb-Douglas preferences; the power-function for the hierarchy-index; and the constant marginal production cost of the differentiated products).

We proceed to calculate the maximized static utility function in terms of the endogenous variables n_P and $\overline{p}$. Substituting the relations (4.4) and (4.5) into the utility flow function (4.1). This yields for the rich

$$u_R(n_R = 1,\ n_P < 1,\ \overline{p} > 1) = \left(\overline{p}\frac{\nu}{1-\gamma}\frac{\overline{N}}{p_x}\right)^{\nu}\frac{\overline{N}^{1-\gamma}}{1-\gamma} \tag{4.8}$$

and for the poor

$$u_P(n_R = 1,\ n_P < 1,\ \overline{p} > 1) = \left(\left[\beta + (1-\beta)\overline{p} n_P^{-\gamma}\right]\frac{\nu}{1-\gamma}\frac{\overline{N}}{p_x}\right)^{\nu} n_P^{1+\nu-\gamma}\frac{\overline{N}^{1-\gamma}}{1-\gamma} \tag{4.9}$$

¿From (4.6) and (4.7) we know that, for given values of n_P and $\overline{p}$, the range of available goods $\overline{N}$ and the expenditure levels E_i are proportional for both types of consumers. And we will see below that also the price of the homogeneous goods p_x and $\overline{N}$ are proportional. It follows that the instantaneous utilities can be expressed as

specify the (minimized) expenditures in terms of utility and prices and the (maximized) utility in terms of prices and expenditures. It should be clear that using the relations derived in the text this can be easily done.

$$u_i(n_P,\ \overline{p}) = \mu_i(n_P, \overline{p}, \frac{\overline{N}}{p_x})\ \frac{E_i^{1-\gamma}}{1-\gamma}. \tag{4.10}$$

Equation (4.10) gives the important result that instantaneous utility is of the CRRA-type with hierarchy-parameter γ as the relevant parameter.[13]

4.3 Dynamics of the Economy

4.3.1 Intertemporal Allocation of Expenditures

We now ask the question how consumption expenditures are allocated over time. As we are interested in the balanced growth path of the economy, we will analyze a situation where $\overline{N}$ and E_i grow at the same rate. This means that, along a balanced growth path, (see equations (4.6) and (4.7)). To study the intertemporal problem we change notation slightly: as n_p and $\overline{p}$ are constant over time we drop the arguments $(n_P,\ \overline{p})$ in the utility function and replace it by the time index s. So $u_i(t)$ is the maximized instantaneous utility at date t.

Suppose time is continuous and consumers maximize lifetime utility $U(t)$ over an infinite horizon where lifetime utility is additively separable and the felicity function is given by equation (4.10). We assume that lifetime utility takes the CRRA-form

$$U_i(t) = \int_t^{\infty} e^{-\rho(s-t)} \frac{(u_i(s))^{1-\sigma}}{1-\sigma} ds \tag{4.11}$$

where the parameter $\rho > 0$ denotes the rate of time preference and the parameter $\sigma > 0$ describes the consumers' willingness to shift total consumption (as measures by $u_i(s)$) over time where $1/\sigma$ is the *inter*temporal elasticity of substitution. From (4.10) we know that also the instantaneous utility is of the CRRA-type (in expenditures) with parameter γ and we may interpret $1/\gamma$ as the *intra*temporal elasticity of substitution (among goods along the hierarchy).

The consumers' lifetime resources are given by the discounted value of a labor income flow $\{w(s)l_i\}_{s\in[t,\infty)}$, where l_i denotes the labor endowment of consumer

---

[13] An important observation can be made here though the utilities of the rich and the poor are CRRA in their expenditures over time, the ratio of utility between the poor and the rich at a given point of time does not exhibit a CRRA relationship, even if $v = 0$, i.e. $\frac{u(x_R(t),n_R(t))}{u(x_P(t),n_P(t))} \neq \left(\frac{E_R}{E_P}\right)^{1-\gamma}$ in general. The reason is that the expenditure share of a single good is not the same for the rich and the poor, they even do not consume the same goods. Since prices of the various goods are different, rich and poor face a different average price level.

i, and the value of assets individual i owns at date t, $V_i(t)$. The lifetime budget constraint is then given by

$$\int_t^\infty E_i(s)e^{-r(s-t)}ds \leq \int_t^\infty w(s)l_i e^{-r(s-t)}ds + V_i(t) \tag{4.12}$$

where r is the interest rate. Since expenditures are proportional to $N(t)$ in equilibrium, the growth rate of expenditures is constant, since we are in steady state. The Euler equation below, which is the solution to the intertemporal problem, then implies that the interest rate must be constant.

$$\frac{\dot{E}(s)}{E(s)} = g = \frac{r - \rho}{\sigma(1-\gamma)+\gamma}. \tag{4.13}$$

4.3.2 The Supply Side: Technology and Resource Constraint

As mentioned above, the aim of this chapter is to analyze the implications of hierarchic preferences for distribution and growth. This means the main focus comes of our analysis is on heterogeneity that comes from the demand side of the economy. The supply side plays a less central role and to keep things simple we assume symmetry of firms as far as production possibilities are concerned. This means that all monopolistic firms have access to the same production technology; and that it is equally costly to design the blueprint and set up the necessary production facilities for a new product, irrespective of the position of this good in the hierarchy.

In this section we describe the supply side of the economy, both the situation in the various sectors at a given point of time and the dynamics of productivity in that sector. Having done that, we can look at the resource constraint of the economy and can discuss the equilibrium allocation of resources across sectors. We will confine the analysis to the situation that prevails along a balanced growth path.

When describing the equilibrium allocation of resources across sectors in this Section, we still concentrate on the case where the rich, but not the poor, can afford all goods that are available on the market. That is we focus on the case $N_P < N_R = \overline{N}$. The equilibrium allocation of resources remaining two cases, $N_P < N_R < \overline{N}$ (when neither the rich nor the poor can afford all N goods), and $N_P = N_R = \overline{N}$ (all households purchase all N goods) are briefly discussed in Section 4.7. (The detailed derivations for these cases are presented in the Appendix).

Production technology and technical progress

To keep things as simple as possible we assume that labor is the only production factor and that the labor market is competitive. The market clearing wage at date t is denoted by $\widetilde{w}(t)$. Consider first the monopolistic sector that produces the differentiated goods along the hierarchy. We assume that the technology in this sector exhibits increasing returns to scale. Before a good can be produced a fixed cost has to be incurred. Having incurred this fixed cost the firm gets access to the blueprint of the new good in the hierarchy and gets a monopoly position on this new market.[14] (This is what we will call an 'innovation' henceforth). This fixed cost consist of a fixed labor input $\widetilde{F}(t)$ and the fixed cost is $\widetilde{w}(t)\widetilde{F}(t)$, equal for all goods. It is assumed that $\widetilde{F}(t)$ *decreases* over time as a result of technical progress. Just like in many recent endogenous growth models, we assume that technical progress is driven by innovations, that is we assume $\widetilde{F}(t)$ is inversely related to the aggregate knowledge stock of knowledge $A(t)$ that reflects the economy-wide productivity at date t. We assume that the knowledge stock of this economy equals the number of known designs, hence we have $A(t) = \overline{N}(t)$. We can thus write $\widetilde{F}(t) = \frac{F}{A(t)} = \frac{F}{\overline{N}(t)}$where $F > 0$ is an exogenous parameter. Once an innovation has taken place the corresponding output good can be produced with the linear technology

$$l(j,t) = \widetilde{b}(t)y(j,t) \tag{4.14}$$

where $l(j,t)$ is labor employed to produce good j at date t, $y(j,t)$ is the quantity produced and $b(t)$ is the unit labor requirement. Marginal cost at date t is $\widetilde{w}(t)b(t)$, equal for all goods, where $\widetilde{w}(t)$ is the wage rate that applies to the whole economy.

We assume that - as a result of technical progress - not only $\widetilde{F}(t)$ but also $b(t)$ decreases over time. Just like before we assume that technical progress in the production process is a result of innovations that produce new knowledge which leads also to higher productivity of the inputs in the monopolistic sector. Again we model this by assuming that $b(t) = \frac{1/w}{\overline{N}(t)}$, where $w > 0$ is an exogenously given parameter. Along the balanced growth path it must be that wages growth with productivity, so $\widetilde{w}(t)$ must be proportional to $\overline{N}(t)$. Moreover, we have normalized marginal production cost to unity so, for all t, we must have $\widetilde{w}(t)b(t) = 1$. But this can only be the case if wages grow according to $\widetilde{w}(t) = w\overline{N}(t)$.

---

[14] By assumption, we rule out that there is any duplication. So when a new good is 'invented' there is one and only one firm that incurs that fixed cost and captures the respective market.

We also note that our assumptions about technology and technical progress imply that the set-up cost of developing a new good is constant over time and equal to $\widetilde{w}(t)\widetilde{F}(t) = w\overline{N}(t)\frac{F}{\overline{N}(t)} = wF$.

Finally, the marginal cost of a traditional firm which produces good x has to be determined. We assume a linear technology $l_x = b_x x$ where l_x denotes the labor input for good x and b_x is the labor input coefficient which, by assumption, *does not change over time.* Since the wage at date t is given by $\widetilde{w}(t) = w\overline{N}(t)$, the marginal cost and hence the price of good x at date t is given by $p_x(t) = wb_x\overline{N}(t)$. But this also implies that $p_x(t)/\overline{N}(t)$ equals wb_x which is an exogenously given time-invariant constant.

Finally, we denote by g the growth rate of $\overline{N}(t)$. On a balanced growth path we have $g = \frac{\dot{E}(t)}{E(t)} = \frac{\dot{\overline{N}}(t)}{\overline{N}(t)} = \frac{\dot{N}_P(t)}{N_P(t)} = \frac{\dot{N}_R(t)}{N_R(t)}$, this implies that $\overline{N}(t) = \overline{N}(0)e^{gt}$.

The resource constraint

The economies' resources consist of the stock of knowledge $A(t)$ and homogeneous labor supplied by each household in the economy. The stock of knowledge is given by the measure of past innovations $\overline{N}(t)$ and the labor supply is normalized to unity. We now proceed by discussing how the labor force is allocated across the various sectors. We denote by L_N the number of workers employed in the sector producing the differentiated hierarchical products, by L_R the number of workers that employed in research to design the blueprints for new such products, and by L_x the number of workers employed in the sector producing the homogenous good. Obviously, in the full employment equilibrium we must have $1 = L_N + L_R + L_x$.

Consider first employment in the production of the differentiated products. Obviously, when $N_P < N_R = \overline{N}$, the resources necessary to produce the differentiated hierarchic products are given by

$$\begin{aligned} \int_0^{\overline{N}(t)} l(j,t)dj &= \beta \int_0^{N_P(t)} \frac{b}{\overline{N}(t)}di + (1-\beta)\int_0^{\overline{N}(t)} \frac{b}{\overline{N}(t)}di \\ &= b\left(\beta n_P + (1-\beta)\right) \end{aligned}$$

which means that along a balanced growth path employment in the production of final output of hierarchical products remains constant. Secondly, the level of employment in the research sector is given by the level of innovative activity at date t. Note that, at date t, $\dot{\overline{N}}$ new goods are introduced and each such innovation requires a unit labor input $\frac{F}{\overline{N}(t)}$. This means that

$$L_R = \dot{\overline{N}}(t)\frac{F}{\overline{N}(t)} = gF$$

workers are employed in the R&D sector at t. Finally, employment in the competitive sector producing the homogenous good is given by

$$\begin{aligned} L_x &= b_x \frac{\beta p_x(t) x_P(t) + (1-\beta) p_x(t) x_R(t)}{w b_x N(t)} = \frac{\beta p_x(t) x_P(t) + (1-\beta) p_x(t) x_R(t)}{w N(t)} \\ &= \frac{\nu}{1-\gamma} b \left(\beta^2 n_P + (1-\beta) \overline{p} n_P^{1-\gamma} + (1-\beta) \overline{p} \right) \end{aligned}$$

where we have used equations (4.4) and (4.5).

In sum, when the rich but not the poor can afford all available products in the economy, that is in the case $N_P < N_R = \overline{N}$, the resource constraint of the economy is given by the equation

$$1 = gF + b\left(\beta n_P + (1-\beta)\right) + \frac{\nu}{1-\gamma} b \left(\beta^2 n_P + (1-\beta) \overline{p} n_P^{1-\gamma} + (1-\beta) \overline{p} \right)$$

4.3.3 The Innovation Process

To study the impact of hierarchic preferences on distribution and growth we have to specify what determines the level of innovative activities in the economy. An incentive to devote additional resource to innovative activities exists as long as the return to an innovation is larger than the fixed cost to introduce a new good. Hence the equilibrium has to be characterized by a situation where the value of an innovation is less than or equal to the costs of an innovation. Above we have already seen that the innovations costs equal wF.

The value of an innovation depends on the resulting future profit flow. This in turn depends on (i) how the level of demand develops over time, and (ii) on how the prices that innovators can charge for their product change over time. Consider a firm, that at date t, incurs the set-up costs and is granted a patent of infinite length. First of all, it should be intuitively clear that this good is the one with least priority among all the goods actually available; and it is the good with the highest priority among those goods that have not yet been invented. This latter observation come from the fact that, as we have no uncertainty, new innovators will always target their innovation activities towards those goods for which the consumers have the highest willingness to pay. In other words, the R&D process leads to 'innovation along the hierarchy'.

Now consider how the flow profit of the innovator of good $\overline{N}(t)$ develops over time. In the case $N_P < N_R = \overline{N}$, on which we are focusing throughout this section, such a new firm has initially demand $1-\beta$ as only the rich can initially afford the new product. The price level is initially equal to $\overline{p}$ but changes over time as new innovations take place resulting in productivity increase and corresponding increases in income, which in turn lead to a higher willingness to pay for the existing good allowing previous innovators to charge higher prices. Denote by $\overline{N}(s')$ the good produced by the most recent innovator at date $s' > t$. Obviously the price this firm can charge is given by $\overline{p}$. The firm producing good $\overline{N}(t)$ can charge a higher price as good $\overline{N}(t)$ has a higher priority than good $\overline{N}(s')$, that is we have $\overline{N}(t) < \overline{N}(s')$. From equation (4.3) we know that, as long as only the rich purchase the product, the corresponding price equals $p(\overline{N}(t)) = \overline{p}\,[\overline{N}(t)/\overline{N}(s')]^{-\gamma}$.

After sufficient time has passed there will be enough growth in incomes that also the poor are willing to purchase good $\overline{N}(t)$. At that date, demand jumps to its maximum level, equal to 1, and stays there forever.[15] At which date does that happen? Denote by Δ the time it takes until the poor can purchase good $\overline{N}(t)$. Obviously, Δ is defined by the equation $N_P(t+\Delta) = \overline{N}(t)$. Along a balanced growth path, all variables grow at rate g, so also $N_P(t)$ will grow at rate g. The equation defining Δ can therefore be rewritten as $N_P(t)e^{g\Delta} = \overline{N}(t)$ from which it follows that $\Delta = -\ln[N_P(t)/\overline{N}(t)]/g = -\ln n_P/g$. Obviously, the duration Δ is long (i) if the poor are very poor (so the fraction of goods the poor can afford, n_P, is small); and (ii) if the growth rate g is low. Using again equation (4.3), we can determine the prices the innovator of $\overline{N}(t)$ charges after the poor have started to purchase. Denote by $\overline{N}(s'')$ the good introduced by the most recent innovator at date $s'' \geq t+\Delta$. We know that the price for good $\overline{N}(s'')$ equals $\overline{p}$, whereas the price of the good $\overline{N}(t)$, which is now purchased by both the rich and the poor, equals $p(\overline{N}(t)) = [\beta n_P^{\gamma} + (1-\beta)\overline{p}]\;[\overline{N}(t)/\overline{N}(s'')]^{-\gamma} = [\beta n_P^{\gamma} + (1-\beta)\overline{p}]\, e^{g\gamma(s''-t)}$

Using the above discussion we may calculate the value of an innovation as

$$\begin{aligned} B &= \int_t^{\infty} (1-\beta)\left(\overline{p}e^{g\gamma(s-t)} - 1\right) e^{-r(s-t)} ds \\ &\quad + \int_{t+\Delta}^{\infty} \beta\left(n_P^{\gamma} e^{g\gamma(s-t)} - 1\right) e^{-r(s-t)} ds \\ &= (1-\beta)\left(\overline{p}\frac{1}{\phi} - \frac{1}{\phi+g\gamma}\right) + \beta n_P{}^{\gamma}\left(\frac{(n_P)^{\phi/g}}{\phi} - \frac{(n_P)^{(\phi+g\gamma)/g}}{\phi+g\gamma}\right) \end{aligned} \tag{4.15}$$

where we used the definition $\phi = r - g\gamma$ and the fact that from (4.13) $r = \rho + g(\sigma(1-\gamma)+\gamma)$.

---

[15] That an innovator stays on the market forever is a simplifying assumption. We could introduce, for instance, finite patent protection and assume that the market become competitive once the patent has expired. Our main conclusions would remain unchanged, as long as patents expire before the poor can afford the good. If patents expire earlier, it is only the willingness to pay of the rich that counts for the incentive to innovate.

4.4 Distribution of Income and Wealth

Until now we have assumed that there are two types of consumers with population size β for the poor and $1-\beta$ for the rich. Furthermore, we have let the consumers' income out of labor and assets be different between households, leading to differences in the optimal budgets $E_i(t)$ between consumers. These differences, in turn, imply certain structures of consumption and prices, and determine the level of aggregate employment in sectors producing, respectively, the homogenous product and the hierarchical products in the economy.

Our analysis led us to conclude that the *personal* distribution of income affects the structure of prices. For instance, in the scenario we are focussing on, $N_P < N_R = \overline{N}$, we must have a sufficiently dispersed distribution of budgets, such that only the rich buy all goods, but the poor cannot afford all of these goods. On the other hand, the scenario, where $N_P = N_R = \overline{N}$ is obviously more likely if inequality in income and wealth is lower (and will be the outcome with perfect equality). We have also found that the structure of prices is determined by the *personal* distribution, which in turn implies that the profit level of each firm and hence also aggregate profits are determined by the personal distribution. Consequently, in this model the *personal* distribution of income affects the distribution of aggregate income between wages and profits, that is the personal distribution determines the *functional* distribution.

In general it is obvious, that the chain of causality also goes in the other way. A given distribution of aggregate income leads to a certain distribution of income between households, because in general, households differ in the relative importance of the two income sources. Hence a change in the functional distribution leads to a change in the personal distribution of income.

In order to keep the analysis tractable, we will henceforth assume, that each household has the same composition of income which means that the share of labor income is the same both for poor households and for rich households. The assumption of an identical income composition between the different types of households implies together with CRRA intertemporal utility that the savings rate is equal among individuals. Hence, the personal distribution of income does not change over time. Moreover, changes in the functional distribution do not feed back to the personal distribution, as this just means that the composition of income of each household changes and, in relative terms it changes equally within each household. Hence, the relative incomes are not affected, and the personal distribution is a really exogenous ingredient of the model.

We denote by θ the income level of the poor relative to the average. With constant savings rates we can directly write the expenditures of poor and rich in terms of average expenditures: $E_P(t) = \theta\ \bar{E}(t)$ and $E_R(t) = \frac{1-\beta\theta}{1-\beta}\ \bar{E}(t)$ where the latter expression follows from $\beta E_P + (1-\beta)E_R = \bar{E}$.

It should be clear that this assumption is a simplification that allows us to discuss the impact of income heterogeneity on growth and (the functional) distribution. Clearly, this assumption is not particularly realistic. (It implies, for instance, that the distribution of income and the distribution of wealth are identical, whereas in reality we have a situation where the distribution of wealth is more unequal than the distribution of income.) The main reason why we adopt this assumption is analytical convenience. However, the main mechanisms that drive the results in this model become clear when we use this simplifying assumption.

Using equations (4.6) and (4.7), and the fact that our distributional assumption implies $\frac{E_R(t)}{E_P(t)} = \frac{1-\beta\theta}{(1-\beta)\theta}$, we can write relative expenditures as

$$\frac{1-\beta\theta}{(1-\beta)\,\theta} = \frac{\left[\beta n_P^{\gamma} + (1-\beta)\overline{p}\right] \frac{n_P^{1-\gamma}}{1-\gamma} + \overline{p}\frac{1-n_P^{1-\gamma}}{1-\gamma} + \overline{p}\frac{\nu}{1-\gamma}}{\left[\beta n_P^{\gamma} + (1-\beta)\overline{p}\right] \frac{n_P^{1-\gamma}}{1-\gamma} + \left[\beta + (1-\beta)\overline{p} n_P^{-\gamma}\right] \frac{\nu n_P}{1-\gamma}}.$$

We note that this equation contains only two unknowns (this is where the distributional assumption makes things analytically tractable). We note that the above equation is linear in $\overline{p}$ which allows us to rewrite this equation as

$$\overline{p} = \frac{\nu\beta n_P + \frac{1-\theta}{(1-\beta)\theta}\beta n_P\,(1+\nu)}{1 - n_P^{1-\gamma} + \nu\left(1 - (1-\beta)n_P^{1-\gamma}\right) - \frac{1-\theta}{\theta} n_P^{1-\gamma}\,(1+\nu)}.$$

We note that, on the right-hand-side of the above equation, the numerator increases and the denominator decrease in n_P. This implies that $\overline{p}$ is monotonically increasing in n_P.

4.5 General Equilibrium

The discussion in Sections 3 to 6 has focused on the scenario where the rich, but not the poor buy the product that has least priority among all goods available in the market. In that case we have an equilibrium structure of consumption such that the poor buy all goods in the range $[0, N_P]$ whereas the rich buy the whole menu of goods that is available on the market $\left[0, \overline{N}\right]$. Clearly, these discussion is only relevant if the equilibrium outcome is such that $N_P < N_R = \overline{N}$. However, $N_P(t)$, $N_R(t)$, and $\overline{N}(t)$ are themselves endogenously determined. So, a comprehensive presentation of the general equilibrium of the model has to take account of all possible equilibria that the model may generate. We therefore have also to discuss the cases where the equilibrium outcome is such that no consumer can purchase all $\overline{N}(t)$ available goods (in which case we have $N_P < N_R < \overline{N}$); and the outcome where all consumers can buy all $\overline{N}(t)$ goods (in which case $N_P = N_R = \overline{N}$).

After having described the various possible equilibrium regimes, we proceed by discussing the conditions under which the various outcomes will be established.

4.5.1 The Three Possible Regimes

The regime $N_P < N_R = \overline{N}$.

In the regime when only the rich but not the poor purchase all the monopolistic goods that are supplied on the market we can characterized the equilibrium to the following three equations in the three unknowns $n_P, \overline{p}$, and g (we note that $\phi = \rho + g\sigma(1-\gamma)$).

$$\begin{aligned} 1 &= gF + b(\beta n_P + 1 - \beta) \\ &\quad + \frac{\nu b}{1-\gamma}\left[\beta^2 n_P + \beta(1-\beta)\overline{p} n_P^{1-\gamma} + (1-\beta)\overline{p}\right] \\ &\quad \text{(resource constraint)} \end{aligned} \tag{4.16}$$

$$\begin{aligned} \frac{F}{b} &= (1-\beta)\left(\overline{p}\frac{1}{\phi} - \frac{1}{\phi + g\gamma}\right) + \beta n_P{}^{\gamma}\left(\frac{(n_P)^{\phi/g}}{\phi} - \frac{(n_P)^{(\phi+g\gamma)/g}}{\phi + g\gamma}\right) \\ &\quad \text{(zero-profit condition)} \end{aligned} \tag{4.17}$$

$$\begin{aligned} \overline{p} &= \frac{\nu\beta n_P + \frac{1-\theta}{(1-\beta)\theta}\beta n_P(1+\nu)}{1 - n_P^{1-\gamma} + \nu\left(1 - (1-\beta)n_P^{1-\gamma}\right) - \frac{1-\theta}{\theta} n_P^{1-\gamma}(1+\nu)} \\ &\quad \text{(static equilibrium condition)} \end{aligned} \tag{4.18}$$

It is obvious that this system can easily be reduced to two equations in the two unknowns, by substituting the last equation into, respectively, the zero-profit condition and the resource constraint. Therefore, the most convenient presentation of the equilibrium in the regime $N_P < N_R = \overline{N}$ is in terms of the growth rate, g, and the fraction of monopolistic goods that the poor can afford, n_P.

The regime $N_P < N_R < \overline{N}$.

In this case where neither the poor nor the rich can afford all products that are available on the market, the general equilibrium differs form the above regime in two respects. First, in this scenario good $\overline{N}$ has no demand and hence the price of this good, $\overline{p}$, is not defined in this case. However, the structure of price can be expressed similarly as before in terms of the price of the good with least priority that is actually purchased. This good is now N_R and we can express all other prices in terms of $p(N_R)$. It is easy to see that the price of good N_R must equal the marginal cost, that is $p(N_R) = 1$. If $p(N_R) > 1$ it would be profitable for a firm $j > N_R$ to start production since the willingness to pay of the rich would be above marginal costs.

The second crucial difference between the regime $N_P < N_R < \overline{N}$ and the regime $N_P < N_R = \overline{N}$ is that fraction of goods that the rich can afford is now an additional endogenous variable. It turns out convenient to express the new endogenous variables in term of the *waiting time of the innovator.* Obviously, a new innovator has no demand at the date when the innovation takes place. The reason is that not even the rich can afford this product, and the innovator has to wait until the rich are willing to pay a price that covers the cost of production. Nevertheless, the firm has an incentive to make the innovation, and to patent it in order to prevent other innovators from capturing this market. How long is the waiting time? Suppose we are on a balanced growth path with rate g, and the rich can afford $N_R(t) < \bar{N}(t)$ products. The waiting time which we denote by δ is defined by the equation $N_R(t)e^{g\delta} = \overline{N}(t)$, or equivalently, $\delta = -\frac{1}{g}\ln\left(\frac{N_R(t)}{\overline{N}(t)}\right)$. Obviously, the waiting time δ is short when growth is high and/or when the rich can already afford a high fraction of the available products.

In the appendix we show that the general equilibrium in the regime $N_P < N_R < \overline{N}$ boils down to three equations in the three unknowns, n_P, δ, and g, where we now have $n_P \equiv N_P(t)/N_R(t)$ as the fraction of goods purchased by the rich, that the poor can afford. (Note that this is not a change in the definition of n_P, as in the regime $N_P < N_R = \overline{N}$, n_P is also the fraction of goods purchased by the rich that the poor can afford as we have $N_R = \overline{N}$; we also note that the mass of goods the poor consume at date t, $N_P(t)$, is now given by $N_P(t) = e^{-\delta g} n_P \overline{N}(t)$). The three equations are the resource constraint, the zero-profit condition, and the relation of the relative expenditures between the rich and the poor:

$$1 = gF + e^{-\delta g}\left(\begin{array}{c} b\left(\beta n_P + 1 - \beta\right) \\ +\frac{\nu}{1-\gamma} b\left[\beta^2 n_P + \beta(1-\beta) n_P^{1-\gamma} + 1 - \beta\right] \end{array}\right) \qquad (4.19)$$

(resource constraint)

$$\frac{F}{b} = \begin{pmatrix} (1-\beta)\left(\frac{1-n_P}{\phi} - \frac{1-(n_P)^{\frac{\phi+g\gamma}{g}}}{\phi+g\gamma}\right) \\ +\left([\beta n_P^{\gamma} + (1-\beta)]\frac{(n_P)^{\frac{\phi}{g}}}{\phi} - \frac{(n_P)^{\frac{\phi+g\gamma}{g}}}{\phi+g\gamma}\right) \end{pmatrix} \cdot e^{-\delta[\phi+g\gamma]} \tag{4.20}$$

(zero-profit condition)

$$\frac{1-\theta}{(1-\beta)\,\theta} = \frac{\left(1+\nu-n_P^{1-\gamma}\right) - \nu\left(\beta n_P + (1-\beta)n_P^{1-\gamma}\right)}{\left(\beta n_P + (1-\beta)n_P^{1-\gamma}\right)(1+\nu)} \tag{4.21}$$

(static equilibrium condition)

This system of equations reduces conveniently to two equations in two unknowns, the growth rate g and the waiting time δ. To see this, note that the only endogenous variable that shows up in the third equation is n_P. The numerator on the right-hand-side of this equation is decreasing and the denominator is increasing in n_P, meaning there is a unique value[16] of $n_P \equiv \tilde{n}_P$ that satisfies the third equation. $\tilde{n}_P$ depends on the primitive parameters of the model γ, β, θ, and ν.[17] Once n_P is determined, we are left with the resource constraint and the zero-profit condition as the remaining equations and with g and δ as the remaining endogenous variables.

We also note that at the point where the switch from the regime $N_P < N_R = \overline{N}$ to the regime $N_P < N_R < \overline{N}$ takes place we have $\overline{p} = 1$ and $\delta = 0$. It is straightforward to check from the resource constraints and the zero-profit conditions in both regimes, that these two respective equations become identical for $\overline{p} = 1$ (in regime $N_P < N_R = \overline{N}$) and $\delta = 0$ (in regime $N_P < N_R < \overline{N}$). This means that at the switch of the regimes there is no discrete jump in the growth rate g.

The regime $N_P = N_R = \overline{N}$.

Finally, it remains to describe the static equilibrium when we have a situation where both types of consumers purchase all differentiated goods that are available on the market, the case $N_P = N_R = \overline{N}$. There is one crucial difference to the former two cases: until now we had a situation such that the good that has least priority for consumer i, N_i had a price that was equal to consumer i's willingness to pay for that good, $q_i(N_i)$. Now, as N_i is identical for both types of consumers, the good that has least priority for the rich, is priced at the willingness to pay for the poor. This means the rich' willingness to pay for good $\overline{N}$ is higher than

[16] Note that this value is strictly smaller than 1, since $n_P = 1$ implies the right hand side of the static equilibrium condition to be zero.

[17] In particular, $\frac{\partial \tilde{n}_P}{\partial \theta} > 0$ and $\frac{\partial \tilde{n}_P}{\partial \beta} < 0$.

the price $\overline{p}$. Consequently, the rich spend relatively more of their budget on the homogeneous good.

The system becomes easier than in the former two cases as we have now a situation where all consumers buy all goods, so $n_P = 1$ and $\delta = 0$. Compared to the previous regime ($N_P < N_R < \overline{N}$) we now get rid of two variables, but have only one additional variable, the price of good $\overline{N}$, which, just like before, we denote by $\overline{p}$. In the Appendix we solve the system step by step, and show that the general equilibrium can be reduced to two equations, the resource constraint and the zero-profit condition in two unknowns: the growth rate g, and the price of the good with least priority $\overline{p}$. These equations are

$$1 = gF + b + b\overline{p}\frac{1+v-\theta}{\theta(1-\gamma)} \quad \text{(resource constraint)} \tag{4.22}$$

$$\frac{F}{b} = \overline{p}\frac{1}{\phi} - \frac{1}{\phi + g\gamma} \quad \text{(zero-profit condition)} \tag{4.23}$$

Also here we consider the point where the switch from the regime $N_P < N_R = \overline{N}$ to the regime $N_P = N_R = \overline{N}$ takes place. From the general equilibrium conditions for regime $N_P < N_R = \overline{N}$ above we immediately see that, when $n_P = 1$, the resource constraint and the zero-profit condition become identical to the above two equilibrium conditions for the regime $N_P = N_R = \overline{N}$.

4.5.2 A Graphical Representation of the Equilibrium

In the following we will show under which conditions an equilibrium exists and when it is unique. Furthermore, we will discuss when either of the three regimes actually occurs. In particular, the analysis will allow us to discuss parameter constellations that make certain regimes more likely. The discussion of the general equilibrium of the model will be done by using a graphical representation. From the discussion in the last subsection it has become clear that the equilibrium conditions in each regime can be conveniently reduced to two equations in two unknowns. In all three regimes, one of the endogenous variables is the growth rate g. However, the second relevant endogenous variable is different across regimes: it is the fraction of goods purchased by the poor n_P in regime $N_p < N_R = \bar{N}$; it is the innovator's waiting time δ in regime $N_P < N_R < \bar{N}$; and it is price charged by the most recent innovator $\overline{p}$ in regime $N_p = N_R = \bar{N}$.

In what follows we will represent the general equilibrium by looking at the zero-profit condition and the resource constraint (substituting out the static equilibrium condition) for all three regimes (Figures 2 and 3). In (g, δ) space for the regime $N_P < N_R < \bar{N}$; in (g, n_P)-space for the regime $N_P < N_R = \bar{N}$; and in $(g, \overline{p})$ space for the regime $N_P = N_R = \bar{N}$.

To separate the different regimes, we have to identify the relevant ranges of the endogenous variables and how they depend on the exogenous parameters of the model. First, consider a switch from the regime $N_p < N_R < \bar{N}$ to the regime $N_p < N_R = \bar{N}$. At the switch the most recent innovator charges price $\bar{p} = 1$ and has no waiting time, so $\delta = 0$. The switch occurs at consumption level of the poor $n_P = \tilde{n}_P$ where $\tilde{n}_P$ is the value of n_P that satisfies equation (4.21). The regime $N_p < N_R = \bar{N}$ therefore starts at $n_P = \tilde{n}_P$ and ends as $n_P = 1$.

Second, consider a switch from the regime $N_p < N_R = \bar{N}$ to the regime $N_p = N_R = \bar{N}$. In that case we have $n_P = 1$ and the most recent innovator is indifferent between selling only to rich at a high price and serving the entire market charging the price that the poor are willing to pay. When this firm sells to only to the rich, it charges a price equal to $\bar{p} = \hat{p} = \frac{\nu\beta + \frac{1-\theta}{(1-\beta)\theta}\beta(1+\nu)}{\nu\beta - \frac{1-\theta}{\theta}(1+\nu)}$ (insert $n_P = 1$ into (4.18) to get $\hat{p}$). When this firm sells to the entire market, the price is $\frac{\hat{p}-\beta}{1-\beta}$. Consequently, when we are in the regime $N_p = N_R = \bar{N}$, the lower limit for the price of the most recent innovator becomes $\frac{\hat{p}-\beta}{1-\beta}$ (see Figure 4.2).

We proceed by discussing the general equilibrium of the model by looking at the resource constraint R and the zero-profit condition Z. We will again discuss the general equilibrium graphically using Figure 2 and 3 below. Before doing so we study the shape of the two curves in more detail. This is done in the following two Lemmas.

Lemma 5 *(zero profit condition Z)*

a) The value of innovation monotonically falls in the growth rate if $\gamma \leq \frac{\sigma\frac{F\rho}{b}}{1+\sigma\frac{F\rho}{b}}$ *("flat hierarchy").*

b) The zero profit condition crosses the n_p-axis at n_p^Z where $\bar{p} = 1 + \frac{1}{1-\beta}\frac{F\rho}{b}$ given that $1 + \frac{1}{1-\beta}\frac{F\rho}{b} \leq \hat{p}$.

c) If $1 + \frac{1}{1-\beta}\frac{F\rho}{b} > \hat{p}$ the zero profit condition crosses the $\bar{p}$-axis at $\bar{p}^Z = 1 + \frac{F\rho}{b}$

Proof. see Appendix. ■

To determine the slope of the Z-curve, it suffices to check the signs of the partial derivatives with respect to the endogenous variables. First, the value of innovations increases in n_P, in the $N_p < N_R = \bar{N}$ regime, as can be seen by direct inspection of (4.15). If n_P is higher, the poor' willingness to pay is higher (note that (4.18) implies $\partial\bar{p}/\partial n_P > 0$) and the time until the poor buy is shorter. Second, according to Lemma 5a, flat hierarchy (γ low enough) is a sufficient and necessary condition for the value of innovations to be monotonically decreasing in the growth rate g. The reason for ambiguity is this: On the one hand, a higher growth rates goes hand in hand with a higher real interest rate. This means that future profits are discounted more strongly which reduces the value of an innovation. On the other hand, with a higher economy-wide growth rate the willingness to pay rises faster. This the demand effect of economic growth, and the size of this effect depends the steepness of the hierarchy. Lemma 5a says that, when the hierarchy is flat enough, the interest rate effect always dominates the demand effect and the zero-profit curve has a positive slope in (g, n_P)-space. In the regime $N_P = N_R = \bar{N}$ the value of an innovation is monotonically increasing in the price of the most recent innovator $\bar{p}$, and falls in the growth rate g (again under the conditions of Lemma 5). Hence in this regime the zero-profit curve increases monotonically in $(g, \bar{p})$-space. We conclude that, with a flat hierarchy, the zero profit curve is monotonically increasing, starting in the regime $N_P < N_R = \bar{N}$ at $n_P^z > \tilde{n}_P$ and switching to the regime $N_P = N_R = \bar{N}$ at $p = \frac{\hat{p}-\beta}{1-\beta}$. The regime $N_P < N_R < \bar{N}$ is never reached. Hence, with flat hierarchy, the zero-profit locus looks like in Figure 4.2.

Lemma 6 *(resource constraint* **RC***)*

a. The **RC***-curve crosses the* n_P*-axis at* $n_P^{RC} \geq \tilde{n}_P$ *if* $1 \geq b\left(\beta\tilde{n}_P + 1 - \beta\right) + \frac{\nu}{1-\gamma} b[\beta^2 \tilde{n}_P + \beta(1-\beta)\tilde{n}_P^{1-\gamma} + 1 - \beta]$.

b. The **RC***-curve crosses the* n_P*-axis at* $n_P^{RC} \leq 1$ *if* $\left(\theta - \frac{1-\theta}{\beta}\frac{1+\nu}{\nu}\right)\frac{1-b}{b}(1-\gamma) \leq 1 + \nu - \theta$.

c. If $\left(\theta - \frac{1-\theta}{\beta}\frac{1+\nu}{\nu}\right)\frac{1-b}{b}(1-\gamma) > 1 + \nu - \theta$*, the RC-curve crosses the p-axis at* $\bar{p}^{RC} = \frac{1-b}{b}\frac{\theta(1-\gamma)}{1+\nu-\theta}$

Proof. Part a. The right hand side of the resource constraint (4.16) increases in n_P. We get the condition directly by inserting $g = 0$ into (4.16).

Part b. If $n_P^{RC} \leq 1$, the right hand side of (4.16) at $n_P = 1$ and $g = 0$ would exceed one: $1 \leq b + \frac{\nu}{1-\gamma} b\left(\beta^2 + \beta(1-\beta)\hat{p} + (1-\beta)\hat{p}\right)$. Inserting the value of $\hat{p}$ and rearranging terms, gives us the required result.

Part c. Solve (4.22) for $\bar{p}$ at $g = 0$. ∎

Lemma 6a gives a necessary condition for existence of regime $N_p < N_R = \bar{N}$. If this condition does not hold, the resource constraint can never be fulfilled in that regime and the $N_p < N_R < \bar{N}$ case is the only possible equilibrium. On the other hand, the condition of Lemma 6c is necessary such that the $N_P = N_R = \bar{N}$ regime is possible. Intuitively, that latter condition guarantees that the differentiated sector is sufficiently productive, such that a situation where *all* consumers buy *all* available differentiated products is feasible.

Following the procedure above, we determine the slope of the RC-curve. In the $N_p < N_R = \bar{N}$ regime the resource constraint (4.16) is falling in the (g, n_P)-space. We see this from (4.16): more resources are needed when the growth rate g is higher because there are more researchers, and when the share of the products consumed by all consumers n_P is higher (note that (4.18) implies $\partial\bar{p}/\partial n_P > 0$). The curve crosses the n_P-axis at n_P^{RC} which is implicitly defined by (4.16) and $g = 0$. But Lemma 6 above exactly states the conditions on the parameter values such that $\tilde{n}_P < n_P^{RC} < 1$.

In the $N_p = N_R = \bar{N}$ regime the resource constraint is a linear function in g and $\bar{p}$. The first order conditions of consumer optimization suggest the expenditures on traditional goods to rise if $\bar{p}$ rises, thus more resources are needed when $\bar{p}$ increases. Finally, as a higher growth rate needs more researchers, we conclude that the resource constraint is a falling line in the $(g, \bar{p})$-space.

In the $N_p < N_R < \bar{N}$ regime the resource constraint (4.19) is a function of the growth rate g and the waiting time δ. (Recall that the relative consumption of the poor $\tilde{n}_P$ is independent of g and δ). Looking at (4.19) we see directly that, if δ rises, less resources are needed for the production of innovative and traditional goods. With a larger growth rate g there is a direct effect: more researchers are needed to sustain a higher growth rate. However, a higher g also reduces consumption demand. The reason is that, given the waiting time δ a larger fraction of monopolistic sector is still in the waiting period. Thus less resources needed in final output production. However, if the condition in Lemma 6a. is satisfied, the first effect dominates: higher g leads to an increase in the demand for labor resources and the resource constraint is a falling curve in (g, δ)-space.

Having discussed that shape of the zero profit conditions and the resource constraint we can turn to the problem of existence and uniqueness of the general equilibrium. We have seen that, if the hierarchy is flat enough, the zero-profit condition is monotonic, and that the resource constraint is monotonic, irrespective of the steepness of the hierarchy. We can therefore state the following proposition.

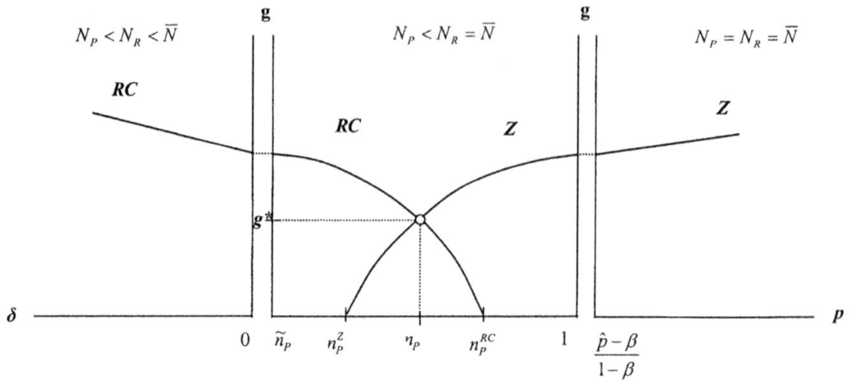

Fig. 4.2. A Unique Positive Equilibrium with Flat Hierarchy

Proposition 10 *(existence and uniqueness of equilibrium).*

a. If hierarchy is flat and $n_p^Z < n_P^{RC}$ or $\bar{p}^Z < \bar{p}^{RC}$, there exists a unique general equilibrium with a positive growth rate.

b. If hierarchy is flat and $n_p^Z \geq n_P^{RC}$ or $\bar{p}^Z \geq \bar{p}^{RC}$, the unique equilibrium is stagnation.

c. If the hierarchy is flat, both the regimes $N_P < N_R = \bar{N}$ and the regime $N_P < N_R < \bar{N}$ can be equilibrium outcomes. A positive growth rate equilibrium with $N_P < N_R < \bar{N}$ can only arise, if the hierarchy is steep enough.

4.5.3 Steeper Hierarchy

We finally discuss shortly the case when $\gamma > \frac{\frac{\sigma}{1-\beta}\frac{F\rho}{b}}{1+\frac{\sigma}{1-\beta}\frac{F\rho}{b}}$. Note first, that the whole discussion concerning the behavior of the resource constraint still holds because Lemma 5 was not needed there. Thus, the shape of the *RC*-curve does not change significantly. Instead, the zero profit constraint now looks different. With steep hierarchy the zero-profit condition is not monotonic. It still starts at n_P^z but then has a negative slope, and may reach the regime $N_P < N_R < \bar{N}$. As the growth rate g becomes larger, the slope becomes positive again and reaches again the regime $N_P < N_R = \bar{N}$. This pattern is due to fact that the interest rate effect is weaker (stronger) than the demand effect at low (high) g. In addition, it is straightforward to verify that a longer waiting time δ reduces the value of innovations. Figure 4.3 below shows a case where a positive growth equilibrium with waiting time exists.

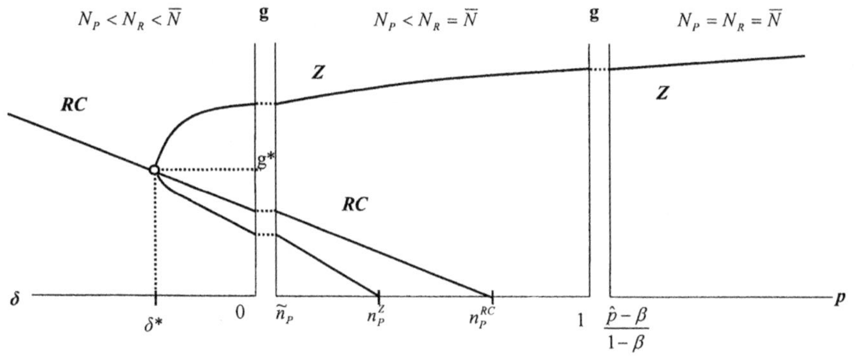

Fig. 4.3. An Equilibrium with Positive Waiting Time δ (Steep Hierarchy)

4.6 The Impact of Inequality on Growth

We have developed a model which allows us to discuss the effects inequality has on the demand structure and, in particular, on the demand for innovators. Thus, it is natural to ask how the growth rate g, the relative consumption level of the poor n_P,and the share of the traditional sector x are affected if the inequality parameters β and θ change.

4.6.1 No Traditional Sector ($\nu = 0$)

To gain intuition, it is instructive to look at the baseline case where $\nu = 0$, i.e. no traditional sector exists. From Lemma 6b we know that in this case the regime $N_P = N_R = \bar{N}$ can not exist. We are able to state the following proposition

Proposition 11 *If $\nu = 0$ and hierarchy is flat, the growth rate g increases and the share of the poor n_P/n_R decreases if θ decreases or β increases.*

Proof. see Appendix. ■

The proposition states that increases in inequality in the Lorenz-sense (as captured by an increase in θ or a decrease in β) unambiguously increase growth. The intuition can be grasped by looking either at the allocation of labor or at the resulting incentives for innovations.

With a higher θ the poor become relatively richer, thus their consumption share increases, but this needs more labor in final good production what means that less researchers can be employed, this reduces growth. On the other hand, if β

increases there are less people in the economy who consume all goods, hence more labor is left for research and growth rises. To get some intuition by looking at the innovation incentives note that the research expenditures equal profits in this economy. Since higher inequality rises growth, as is suggested by the proposition, it is equivalent to say that the profit share increases with inequality. But this simply means that the average markups are higher in this economy. The reason is that monopolists may charge higher markups from the rich and more product are sold at higher markups (since the consumption of the poor falls). The lower markups on products which both buy cannot dominate the first two effects.

4.6.2 The General Case $\nu > 0$

With $\nu > 0$, we have to refer to simulations. However, we can draw general conclusions for the regime $N_P = N_R = \bar{N}$, which is now possible to arise in equilibrium.

Proposition 12 *In the $N_P = N_R = \bar{N}$ regime a rise in θ, i.e. decreasing inequality, unambiguously increases growth. A change in β leaves the growth rate unaffected.*

Proof. The equilibrium is characterized by equations (4.22) and (4.23). A rise in θ decreases the right hand side of (4.22), hence higher growth for given $\bar{p}$ is feasible (RC-curve shifts up). The parameter β does not appear in (4.22) and (4.23). ■

Since the monopolists always sell to both groups, the prices they can set are determined only by the marginal willingness to pay of the poor, as θ increases, the poor want to pay more what allows the innovators to raise prices and increase profits. These increases in innovation incentives raise the growth rate. On the other hand, a change in the groups size β can have no effect on the growth. With θ held constant the marginal willingness to pay of the relevant consumers is unaffected and innovation incentives are unchanged.

In the $N_p < N_R = \bar{N}$ regime we have to refer to simulations. We got the result, as can be seen from Figure 4.4 below, that increases in θ (decreasing inequality) always decreases growth, i.e. the result from the $\nu = 0$ case still holds. The figure shows further that for $\theta > 0.926$ decreasing inequality raises the growth rate, because for $\theta > 0.926$ the $N_P = N_R = \bar{N}$ regime arises in equilibrium.

Default values:
$\theta = 0.8$, $\beta = 0.5$, $F = 5$, $b = 0.3$, $\sigma = 2$, $\rho = 0.02$, $\gamma = 0.3$, $\nu = 0.8$

The growth rate in dependence of θ

The regime switch, where $n_p = 1$, arises at $\theta = 0.926$

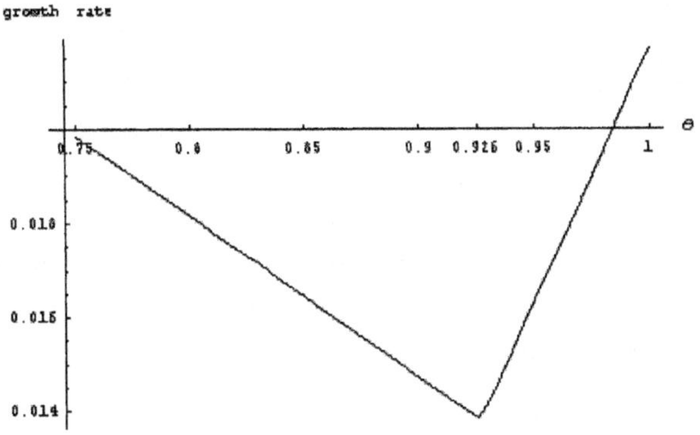

The growth rate in dependence of β

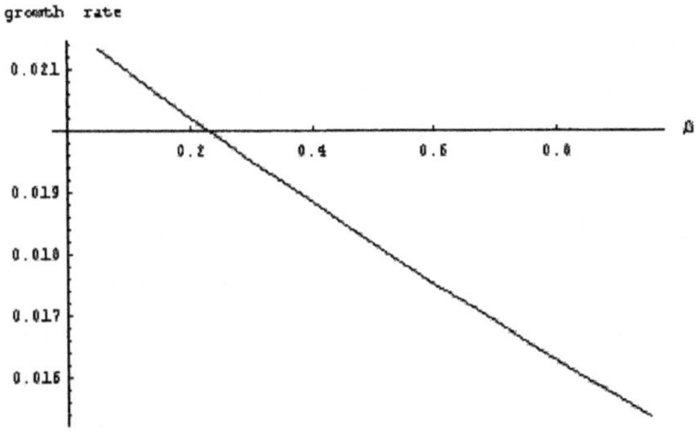

Fig. 4.4. Growth Simulations

Instead, for parameter constellations where ν is high and inequality is low (θ high), we found that an increase in β (which increases inequality since θ is fixed) decreases the growth rate. An example is plotted in the second graph of Figure 4.4. This is an important result: "higher inequality" per se is a too crude statement to judge whether and how the demand structure is affected. Loosely speaking, changes in θ affect the willingness to pay, whereas changes in β affect the market size. What is the exact mechanism which leads to the different effects of higher inequality induced by a higher β or a lower θ, respectively? Similar to lower θ, a higher β increases inequality, but this increase will be small when θ is high.[18] This increases growth due to the implied higher profit share described above. But unlike to a lower θ, a higher β directly increases the price distortion in the monopolistic sector because the products' prices which only the rich buy must be higher as their market size $1-\beta$ is smaller than before. The increases price distortion shifts demand away from the innovative sector to the traditional x-sector, which decreases growth. The size of the latter effect is determined by the value of ν, i.e. it will dominate the first effect when ν and θ are high which confirms the results of the simulations.

4.7 Summary

In this chapter we have explored the relationship between inequality and economic growth when the structure of demand varies with income because consumers have non-homothetic preferences. We have shown that changes in inequality affect the aggregate price structure and, with sufficient inequality, the poor will be excluded from markets of recent innovators.

A central result of our analysis is that the relationship between inequality and growth is non-monotonic. Higher inequality, given the groups size of rich and poor, tends to increase growth, if there is exclusion of the poor. This is because the profit share increases. Higher inequality due to a bigger group of poor people (higher concentration of income among a smaller number of rich people) may reduce growth. Instead, if the innovators always sell to the whole population, inequality has an unambiguously negative impact on growth. These results suggest that one should be careful in empirical testing. A simple linear regression of an inequality

[18] Since θ is fixed, the relative income of the rich $\frac{1-\beta\theta}{1-\beta}$ must rise since their group size has become smaller. In addition, the rise in inequality will be more substantial, the lower θ is: $\frac{\partial}{\partial\beta}\frac{1-\beta\theta}{1-\beta}=\frac{1-\theta}{(1-\beta)^2}$. Obviously, this is larger when θ is smaller.

measure can cause misleading results. Inequality has an impact on growth through the demand channel but it depends on the nature of a change in inequality, as well as on the initial conditions, whether or not inequality increases or decreases growth.

4.8 Appendix

4.8.1 The Case With Preemptive Patenting

Maximized static utilities and expenditures ($N_P < N_R < \overline{N}$)

We have now an additional variable, $\delta = -\frac{1}{g}\ln(N_R/\overline{N})$ that says how long an innovator has to wait until his product has positive demand. At the same time the price of the good that has least priority among all goods that are actually sold, i.e. the price of good N_R must equal the marginal cost, that is $p(N_R) = 1$. (If $p(N_R) > 1$ it would be profitable for a firm $j > N_R$ to start production since the willingness to pay of the rich would be above marginal costs.) The prices of the goods $j > N_R$ are not defined. Using analogous arguments as in Section 3 (for the regime $N_P < N_R = \overline{N}$), in the case when we have $N_P < N_R < \overline{N}$ it is straightforward to calculate the equilibrium price structure as

$$p(j) = \begin{cases} [\beta n_P^{\gamma} + (1-\beta)] \left(\frac{j}{N_R}\right)^{-\gamma} & j \in [0, N_P], \\ \left(\frac{j}{N_R}\right)^{-\gamma} & j \in (N_P, N_R]. \end{cases} \tag{4.24}$$

where we note that now $n_P = N_P(t)/\overline{N}(t)$. The static equilibrium is then the solution to the following six equations in the six unknowns $n_P, n_R, x_P, x_R, \lambda_P$ and λ_R. (note that $N_P(t) = n_P e^{-\delta g}\overline{N}$ and $N_R(t) = e^{-\delta g}\overline{N}$).

$$\beta + (1-\beta) n_P^{-\gamma} = \frac{x_P^{\nu}\left(n_P e^{-\delta g}\overline{N}\right)^{-\gamma}}{\lambda_P} \tag{R1}$$

$$1 = \frac{x_R^{\nu}\left(e^{-\delta g}\overline{N}\right)^{-\gamma}}{\lambda_R} \tag{R2}$$

$$\nu x_P^{\nu-1}\frac{\left(n_P e^{-\delta g}\overline{N}\right)^{1-\gamma}}{1-\gamma} = \lambda_P p_x \tag{R3}$$

$$\nu x_R^{\nu-1}\frac{\left(e^{-\delta g}\overline{N}\right)^{1-\gamma}}{1-\gamma} = \lambda_R p_x \tag{R4}$$

$$\frac{E_P}{\overline{N}} = [\beta n_P^{\gamma} + (1-\beta)]\frac{n_P^{1-\gamma}}{1-\gamma} + \frac{p_x x_P}{\overline{N}} \tag{R5}$$

$$\frac{E_R}{\overline{N}} = [\beta n_P^{\gamma} + (1-\beta)]\frac{n_P^{1-\gamma}}{1-\gamma} + \frac{1-n_P^{1-\gamma}}{1-\gamma} + \frac{p_x x_R}{\overline{N}}. \tag{R6}$$

Again the first two equations equate the willingnesses to pay to the respective good with least priority for both types of consumers, the equations (R3) and (R4) determine the equilibrium amount of the homogeneous good and the final two equations (R5) and (R6) say that the budget constraints have to be satisfied for both types of consumers.

We proceed similarly as before and reduce this system to two equations in the two unknowns n_P and n_R. Combining, respectively, equations (R1) and (R3), and equations (R2) and (R4), we can write

$$p_x x_P = \frac{\nu \overline{N}}{1-\gamma} \left[\beta + (1-\beta) n_P^{-\gamma}\right] n_P \tag{4.25}$$

and

$$p_x x_R = \frac{\nu \overline{N}}{1-\gamma} n_R, \tag{4.26}$$

and substitute these relations into equations (R5) and (R6) of the above system. This yields

$$\frac{E_P}{\overline{N}} = \left[\beta n_P^{\gamma} + (1-\beta)\right] \frac{n_P^{1-\gamma}}{1-\gamma} + \left[\beta + (1-\beta) n_P^{-\gamma}\right] \frac{\nu n_P}{1-\gamma}, \tag{4.27}$$

and

$$\frac{E_R}{\overline{N}} = \left[\beta n_P^{\gamma} + (1-\beta)\right] \frac{n_P^{1-\gamma}}{1-\gamma} + \frac{1-n_P^{1-\gamma}}{1-\gamma} + \frac{\nu}{1-\gamma}, \tag{4.28}$$

and we note that both E_P and $\overline{N}$ as well as E_R and $\overline{N}$ are proportional when n_P is fixed.

Finally, we calculate the maximized static utilities in terms of the endogenous variables n_P and n_R. Substituting the relations (4.25) and (4.26) into the utility flow function (4.1). This yields for the rich

$$u_R(n_R < 1,\ n_P < 1) = \left(\frac{\nu}{1-\gamma} \frac{1}{w b_x}\right)^{\nu} e^{-\delta g (1+\nu-\gamma)} \frac{\overline{N}^{1-\gamma}}{1-\gamma} \tag{4.29}$$

and for the poor

$$u_P(n_R < 1,\ n_P < 1) = \left(\left[\beta n_P^{\gamma} + (1-\beta)\right] \frac{\nu}{1-\gamma} \frac{1}{w b_x}\right)^{\nu} \left(n_P e^{-\delta g}\right)^{1+\nu-\gamma} \frac{\overline{N}^{1-\gamma}}{1-\gamma} \tag{4.30}$$

¿From (4.6) and (4.7) we know that, for given values of n_P and $\overline{p}$, the range of available goods $\overline{N}$ and the expenditure levels E_i are proportional for both types of consumers. Moreover, we will see in the next section that also $\frac{\overline{N}}{p_x}$ is a constant. It follows that the instantaneous utilities can be written as

$$u_i(n_P, \delta) = \mu_i(n_P, \delta) \frac{E_i^{1-\gamma}}{1-\gamma}. \tag{4.31}$$

Equation (4.10) confirms that important result we derived in chapter 2, namely that instantaneous utility is of the CRRA-type with hierarchy-parameter γ as the relevant parameter.[19]

The resource constraint ($N_P < N_R < \overline{N}$)

The resource constraint when $N_P < N_R < \overline{N}$ is given by the sum of employment in R&D L_R, manufacturing of the differentiated hierarchical products L_N; and production of the homogenous good L_x. Just like before, we have again a level of R&D employment equal to $L_R = gF$; a level of employment to produce output in the monopolistic sector given by $L_N = (1-\beta)\widetilde{b}(t)N_R(t) + \beta\widetilde{b}(t)N_P(t) = b\left[(1-\beta)e^{-\delta g} + \beta n_P\right]$; and using (4.25) and (4.26), employment necessary to produce the homogeneous good, $L_x = \frac{v}{1-\gamma}b\left(\beta\left[\beta n_P^{-\gamma} + (1-\beta)\right]n_P + (1-\beta)e^{-\delta g}\right)$. The resource constraint is therefore given by

$$1 = gF + b\left(\beta n_P + (1-\beta)e^{-\delta g}\right) + \frac{\nu}{1-\gamma}b\left[[\beta^2 + \beta(1-\beta)n_P^{-\gamma}]n_P + (1-\beta)e^{-\delta g}\right]$$

The zero-profit condition ($N_P < N_R < \overline{N}$)

In equilibrium we must have that the innovation cost equals the value of an innovation. In the equilibrium where $N_P < N_R < \overline{N}$ no household can afford good $\overline{N}$ when the innovator incurs the fixed cost so that good $\overline{N}$ is actually available on the market. This means that innovator have a waiting time δ during which nobody will buy the new product. At date $t+\delta$, the waiting time ends, and the rich consumers start to buy the good $\overline{N}(t)$ (which has been invented at date t). From date $t+\delta$ until date $t+\delta+\Delta$ only the rich can afford this good, as monopolists set prices equal to the willingness to pay of the rich. But at date $t+\delta+\Delta$ also the poor have a sufficiently high willingness to pay so the monopolist will cut prices and charge the willingness to pay of the poor, so the monopolistic firm gets the entire market. The waiting time δ until the rich start to buy consumers in the economy is given by $N_R(t+\delta) = \overline{N}(t)$ and using the fact that both $\overline{N}(t)$ and $N_R(t)$ grow at the same rate, δ can be calculated as

[19] An important observation can be made here though the utilities of the rich and the poor are CRRA in their expenditures over time, the ratio of utility between the poor and the rich at a given point of time does not exhibit a CRRA relationship, even if $v = 0$, i.e. $\frac{u(x_R(t),n_R(t))}{u(x_P(t),n_P(t))} \neq \left(\frac{E_R}{E_P}\right)^{1-\gamma}$ in general. The reason is that the expenditure share of a single good is not the same for the rich and the poor, they even do not consume the same goods. Since prices of the various goods are different, rich and poor face a different average price level.

$\delta = -(1/g)\ln n_R$. Moreover, the additional waiting period Δ until also the poor buy (i.e. until it becomes profitable to cut prices and sell to the entire market) is given by $\Delta = -(1/g)\ln \frac{n_P}{n_R}$.

By these arguments, we can calculate the zero-profit condition in the case Proceeding similarly as in the case $N_P < N_R < \overline{N}$ as (we proceed similarly as in the case $N_P < N_R < \overline{N}$ described in detail in the main text)

$$\begin{aligned}\frac{F}{b} &= \int_{t+\delta}^{t+\delta+\Delta}(1-\beta)\left(\left(\frac{\overline{N}(s)}{\overline{N}(t)}\right)^{\gamma}-1\right)e^{-r(s-t)}ds \\ &+\int_{t+\delta+\Delta}^{\infty}\left([\beta n_P^{\gamma}+(1-\beta)]\left(\frac{\overline{N}(s)}{\overline{N}(t)}\right)^{\gamma}-1\right)e^{-r(s-t)}ds \\ &= \left(\begin{array}{c}(1-\beta)\left(\frac{1-n_P}{\phi}-\frac{1-(n_P)^{\frac{\phi+g\gamma}{g}}}{\phi+g\gamma}\right)\\ +[\beta n_P^{\gamma}+(1-\beta)]\frac{(n_P)^{\frac{\phi}{g}}}{\phi}-\frac{(n_P)^{\frac{\phi+g\gamma}{g}}}{\phi+g\gamma}\end{array}\right)\cdot e^{-\delta[\phi+g\gamma]}\end{aligned}$$

where we have again used the definition $\phi = r - g\gamma = \rho + g\sigma(1-\gamma)$ where the latter equality follows from (4.13).

The equilibrium conditions ($N_P < N_R < \overline{N}$)

The general equilibrium consists of the following 3 equations in the 3 unknowns n_P, n_R, and g: (i) the zero-profit conditions, (ii) the resource constraint, and (iii) the condition on relative expenditures

$$\frac{F}{b} = \left(\begin{array}{c}(1-\beta)\left(\frac{1-\left(\frac{n_P}{n_R}\right)^{\frac{\phi}{g}}}{\phi}-\frac{1-\left(\frac{n_P}{n_R}\right)^{\frac{\phi+g\gamma}{g}}}{\phi+g\gamma}\right)\\ +\left[\beta\left(\frac{n_P}{n_R}\right)^{\gamma}+(1-\beta)\right]\frac{\left(\frac{n_P}{n_R}\right)^{\frac{\phi}{g}}}{\phi}-\frac{\left(\frac{n_P}{n_R}\right)^{\frac{\phi+g\gamma}{g}}}{\phi+g\gamma}\end{array}\right)\cdot n_R^{\frac{\phi+g\gamma}{g}} \qquad (E'a)$$

$$\begin{aligned}1 &= gF + b(\beta n_P + (1-\beta)n_R) \qquad (E'b)\\ &+\frac{\nu}{1-\gamma}b\left[[\beta^2+\beta(1-\beta)\left(\frac{n_P}{n_R}\right)^{-\gamma}]n_P+(1-\beta)n_R\right]\end{aligned}$$

and, by dividing both sides of equation (4.28) by equation (4.27), using $E_R/E_P - 1 = \frac{1-\theta}{(1-\beta)\theta}$, we get

$$\frac{1-\theta}{(1-\beta)\theta} = \frac{\left(1+\nu-n_P^{1-\gamma}\right)-\nu\left(\beta n_P+(1-\beta)n_P^{1-\gamma}\right)}{\left(\beta n_P+(1-\beta)n_P^{1-\gamma}\right)(1+\nu)}. \qquad (E'c)$$

4.8.2 The Case Where All Individuals Buy All Products

Maximized static utilities and expenditures ($N_P = N_R = \overline{N}$)

Finally, it remains to describe the static equilibrium when we have a situation where both types of consumers purchase all differentiated goods that are available on the market, the case $N_P = N_R = \overline{N}$. There is one crucial difference to the former two cases: in both of those cases we had a situation such that the good that has least priority for consumer i, N_i has a price that is equal to consumer i's willingness to pay for that good, $q_i(N_i)$. Now, as N_i is identical for both types of consumers, we have a situation where the good that has least priority for the rich, is priced at the willingness to pay for the poor. But this means that we have a situation where the rich' willingness to pay for good $\overline{N}$ is higher than the price $\overline{p}$. This is important as it implies that the rich spend relatively more of their budget on the homogeneous good than they would if the firm could get the willingness to pay from the rich. It terms of our equilibrium equations, it implies that we have only five equations (plus one inequality) in the following five variables, $\overline{p}, x_P, x_R, \lambda_P$ and λ_R

$$\overline{p} = \frac{x_P^{\nu}\overline{N}^{-\gamma}}{\lambda_P} \tag{Q1}$$

$$\overline{p} < \frac{x_R^{\nu}\overline{N}^{-\gamma}}{\lambda_R} \tag{Q2}$$

$$\nu x_P^{\nu-1}\frac{\overline{N}^{1-\gamma}}{1-\gamma} = \lambda_P p_x \tag{Q3}$$

$$\nu x_R^{\nu-1}\frac{\overline{N}^{1-\gamma}}{1-\gamma} = \lambda_R p_x \tag{Q4}$$

$$\frac{E_P}{\overline{N}} = \frac{\overline{p}}{1-\gamma} + \frac{p_x x_P}{\overline{N}} \tag{Q5}$$

$$\frac{E_R}{\overline{N}} = \frac{\overline{p}}{1-\gamma} + \frac{p_x x_R}{\overline{N}}. \tag{Q6}$$

Relations (Q1) and (Q2) say that the price of good $\overline{N}$, $\overline{p}$, is equal to the willingness to pay of the poor, but lower than the willingness to pay of the rich. The remaining equations are the conditions for the equilibrium quantities of the homogeneous good x_i ((Q3) and (Q4)) and the budget constraints for both types of consumers ((Q5) and (Q6)).

We can reduce this system to one equation in $\overline{p}$. Using (Q1) and (Q3), solving for $p_x x_P$ yields

$$p_x x_P = \frac{\nu\overline{N}}{1-\gamma}\overline{p}, \tag{4.32}$$

and substituting this into (Q5) yields the expenditure function for the poor (which solves for $\overline{p}$)

$$\frac{E_P}{\overline{N}} = \overline{p}\frac{1+\nu}{1-\gamma}. \tag{4.33}$$

The expenditure function of the rich can now be easily expressed in terms of the endogenous variables $\overline{p}$ and x_R as From the budget constraint $E_R = \frac{\overline{p}\overline{N}}{1-\gamma} + p_x x_R$ and the previous equation (4.33) it is straightforward to calculate

$$\frac{E_R}{\overline{N}} = \frac{\overline{p}}{1-\gamma} + \frac{p_x x_R}{\overline{N}} \tag{4.34}$$

The maximized static utility for the poor can be using that x_P is given by (4.32). Substituting this into the static utility (4.1) yields

$$u_P(n_R = n_P = 1,\ \overline{p} > 1) = \left(\overline{p}\frac{\nu}{1-\gamma}\frac{\overline{N}}{p_x}\right)^{\nu} \frac{\overline{N}(t)^{1-\gamma}}{1-\gamma} \tag{4.35}$$

To get the utility value of the rich, we use (4.33) and (4.34) to calculate $x_R = \frac{N}{p_x}\left(\frac{E_R - E_P}{N} + \frac{\overline{p}\nu}{1-\gamma}\right)$ and substitute this into the utility function (4.1) to get

$$u_R(n_R = n_P = 1,\ \overline{p} > 1) = \left(\frac{N}{p_x}\left(\frac{E_R - E_N}{N} + \frac{\overline{p}\nu}{1-\gamma}\right)\right)^{\nu} \frac{\overline{N}(t)^{1-\gamma}}{1-\gamma}.$$

Provided that $\frac{N}{p_x}$ and $\frac{E_R - E_N}{N}$ are constants (which will be the case along the balanced growth path), we can write the maximized static utilities as

$$u_i(n_P,\ \overline{p}) = \mu_i(n_P, \overline{p}, \frac{\overline{N}}{p_x})\ \frac{E_i^{1-\gamma}}{1-\gamma}.$$

The resource constraint ($N_P = N_R = \overline{N}$)

The resource constraint in the case when $N_P = N_R = \overline{N}$ is given by the sum of employment in R&D L_R, manufacturing of the differentiated hierarchical products L_N; and production of the homogenous good L_x. Just like before, we have again a level of R&D employment equal to $L_R = gF$; a level of employment to produce output in the monopolistic sector given by $L_N = (1-\beta)\widetilde{b}(t)N_R(t) + \beta\widetilde{b}(t)N_P(t) = b$; and using (4.32) and (4.34), a level of employment necessary to produce the output of the homogeneous good, $L_x = b_x\left[\beta\frac{\overline{N}}{p_x}\frac{\nu\overline{p}}{1-\gamma} + (1-\beta)\frac{\overline{N}}{p_x}\left(\frac{E_R - E_P}{\overline{N}} + \frac{\overline{p}\nu}{1-\gamma}\right)\right] = \frac{1}{w}\left[\beta\frac{\nu\overline{p}}{1-\gamma} + (1-\beta)\left(\frac{E_R - E_P}{\overline{N}} + \frac{\overline{p}\nu}{1-\gamma}\right)\right]$ (because $b_x\frac{\overline{N}}{p_x} = b_x\frac{\overline{N}(t)}{w(t)b_x} = \frac{1}{w}$). Now we use $\frac{E_P}{\overline{N}} = \overline{p}\frac{1+\nu}{1-\gamma}$ and $E_R - E_P = E_P\left[\frac{1-\beta\theta}{(1-\beta)\theta} - 1\right] = \frac{1-\theta}{(1-\beta)\theta}$. So we get $\frac{E_R - E_P}{\overline{N}} =$

$\frac{E_P}{\overline{N}}\frac{1-\theta}{(1-\beta)\theta} = \overline{p}\frac{1+\nu}{1-\gamma}\frac{1-\theta}{(1-\beta)\theta}$ and $L_x = b\left[\beta\frac{\nu\overline{p}}{1-\gamma} + (1-\beta)\frac{\overline{p}}{1-\gamma}\left(\frac{(1+\nu)(1-\theta)}{(1-\beta)\theta} + \nu\right)\right] = b\overline{p}\frac{1+\nu-\theta}{(1-\gamma)\theta}$. The resource constraint is therefore given by

$$1 = gF + b + b\overline{p}\frac{1+\nu-\theta}{\theta\,(1-\gamma)}.$$

The zero-profit condition ($N_P = N_R = \overline{N}$)

In equilibrium we must have that the innovation cost equals the value of an innovation. In the equilibrium where $N_P = N_R = \overline{N}$ all households buy all $\overline{N}$ goods already from the point of time when the innovator incurs the fixed cost and enters the market. The price the firm charges equals the willingness to pay of the poor already from the beginning. Hence the zero-profit condition in this case simplifies to

$$\begin{aligned} \frac{F}{b} &= \int_t^{\infty}\left(\overline{p}e^{g\gamma(s-t)} - 1\right)e^{-r(s-t)}ds \qquad (4.36) \\ &= \overline{p}\frac{1}{\phi} - \frac{1}{\phi + g\gamma}. \end{aligned}$$

The equilibrium conditions ($N_P = N_R = \overline{N}$)

When $N_P = N_R = \overline{N}$ the equilibrium conditions consist of two equations in the two unknowns g and $\overline{p}$

$$\frac{F}{b} = \overline{p}\frac{1}{\phi} - \frac{1}{\phi + g\gamma} \qquad (E''a)$$

and

$$1 = gF + b + b\overline{p}\frac{1+\nu-\theta}{\theta\,(1-\gamma)}. \qquad (E''b)$$

(We observe that the 'third' condition, relative budgets, is now redundant, as $n_P = n_R = 1$.)

4.8.3 Proof of Lemma 5

We first prove part b. and c. of the Lemma. To calculate the value of $\overline{p}$ where Z crosses the horizontal axis, we have to solve the zero profit condition for $\overline{p}$ where $g = 0$.

Proof. In the $N_P < N_R = \overline{N}$ regime we get, using formula (4.15) and noting that $\Delta \to \infty$ as $g \to 0$.

$$B|_{g=0} = \int_t^{\infty}(1-\beta)(\overline{p}-1)\,e^{-\rho(s-t)}ds = \frac{1-\beta}{\rho}(\overline{p}-1) = \frac{F}{b}$$

We solve for $\overline{p}$ and Lemma 2b. follows immediately. ■

Proof. In the $N_P = N_R = \overline{N}$ regime we use (4.23) and get

$$\frac{1}{\rho}(\overline{p}-1) = \frac{F}{b}$$

Solving again for $\overline{p}$ yields Lemma 2c. ■

Proof. We derive the value of an innovation in the $N_P < N_R = \overline{N}$ regime (4.15) with respect to g and we get

$$\begin{aligned}\frac{\partial B}{\partial g} &= \int_t^{t+\Delta}(1-\beta)\left[(\sigma(1-\gamma)+\gamma)-\sigma(1-\gamma)\overline{p}e^{g\gamma(s-t)}\right]e^{-r(s-t)}(s-t)ds \\ &\quad -\frac{\ln n_P}{g^2}\Pi_R(\bar{N}(t+\Delta))+\frac{\ln n_P}{g^2}\Pi_{tot}(\bar{N}(t+\Delta)) \\ &\quad +\int_{t+\Delta}^{\infty}\left[\begin{array}{c}(\sigma(1-\gamma)+\gamma) \\ -\sigma(1-\gamma)\left[\beta n_P^{\gamma}+(1-\beta)\overline{p}\right]e^{g\gamma(s-t)}\end{array}\right]e^{-r(s-t)}(s-t)ds\end{aligned}$$

Note that $\Pi_R(\bar{N}(t+\Delta)) = \Pi_{tot}(\bar{N}(t+\Delta))$. We give first a sufficient condition for the second integral above to be negative. The integral starts at $t+\Delta$, this implies that $e^{g\gamma(s-t)} \geq e^{g\Delta\gamma} = n_P^{-\gamma}$. We note that

$$\begin{aligned}&\left[\sigma(1-\gamma)+\gamma-\sigma(1-\gamma)\left[\beta n_P^{\gamma}+(1-\beta)\overline{p}\right]e^{g\gamma(s-t)}\right] \\ &\leq\ \sigma(1-\gamma)+\gamma-\sigma(1-\gamma)\left[\beta+(1-\beta)\overline{p}n_P^{-\gamma}\right]\leq 0\end{aligned}$$

if $\overline{p}n_P^{-\gamma} > \overline{p} \geq 1+\frac{\gamma}{\sigma(1-\gamma)(1-\beta)}$. This condition also implies the first integral to be negative. We directly see that $\sigma(1-\gamma)+\gamma-\sigma(1-\gamma)\overline{p}e^{g\gamma(s-t)} \leq 0$ if $\overline{p} \geq 1+\frac{\gamma}{\sigma(1-\gamma)}$, which is a weaker condition.

If $\frac{\partial B}{\partial g} < 0$ the zero profit condition has to be positively sloped. Together with Lemma 3b. this implies that $\overline{p} \geq 1+\frac{1}{1-\beta}\frac{F\rho}{b}$. Combining we get the final condition

$$\frac{1}{1-\beta}\frac{F\rho}{b} \geq \frac{\gamma}{\sigma(1-\gamma)(1-\beta)}$$

If we solve this expression for γ, Lemma 2a. follows for the $N_P < N_R = \overline{N}$ regime.

For the $N_P = N_R = \overline{N}$ regime the result is much easier to prove. In that regime, the derivative of the value of innovation with respect to g reads

$$\frac{\partial B}{\partial g} = \int_t^{\infty}\left[(\sigma(1-\gamma)+\gamma)-\sigma(1-\gamma)\overline{p}e^{g\gamma(s-t)}\right]e^{-r(s-t)}(s-t)ds$$

Using the same argument as above, the integral is negative if $\overline{p} \geq 1+\frac{\gamma}{\sigma(1-\gamma)}$. Again, the zero profit condition has a positive slope under the conditions of the Lemma. From Lemma 2c. we hence note that $\overline{p} \geq 1+\frac{F\rho}{b}$. Combining we get the same final condition and the same solution for γ as above. ■

4.8.4 Proof of Proposition 11

Proof. With flat hierarchy the $N_P < N_R = \overline{N}$ regime is the only outcome in equilibrium. The static equilibrium condition (4.18) reads, when $\nu = 0$.

$$\bar{p} = \frac{\beta}{1-\beta}\frac{(1-\theta)\, n_P}{\theta - n_P^{1-\gamma}}$$

This implies directly that $\frac{\partial \bar{p}}{\partial \theta} < 0$ and $\frac{\partial \bar{p}}{\partial \beta} > 0$.

How are the equilibrium curves defined by (5.2) and (4.17) affected? A rise in θ does not affect RC, since this parameter does not appear if $\nu = 0$. A rise in β, however, implies that less resources are needed, RC shifts up. To discuss the shifts of Z note that $\Pi_{tot}(j) = [\beta n_P^{\gamma} + (1-\beta)\overline{p}] \left(\frac{j}{N}\right)^{-\gamma} - 1$ and $\Pi_R(j) = \left[\overline{p}\left(\frac{j}{N}\right)^{-\gamma} - 1\right](1-\beta) = \overline{p}(1-\beta)\left(\frac{j}{N}\right)^{-\gamma} + \beta$. Using the formula for $\bar{p}$ above we get the expression $\overline{p}(1-\beta) = \beta\frac{(1-\theta)n_P}{\theta - n_P^{1-\gamma}}$. Hence, $\overline{p}(1-\beta)$ falls in θ and increases in β. With n_P fixed, we directly get the result that $\frac{\partial \Pi_{tot}(j)}{\partial \theta} < 0$, $\frac{\partial \Pi_R(j)}{\partial \theta} < 0$ and $\frac{\partial \Pi_{tot}(j)}{\partial \beta} > 0$, $\frac{\partial \Pi_{tot}(j)}{\partial \beta} > 0$. Obviously, the Z-curve shifts to the right when θ increases and it shifts to left when β increases. ■

5

Markups and Exclusion

5.1 Introduction

In this last chapter we want to take a step back and analyze the effects of non-homothetic preferences on monopolistic competition in a static framework. This allows us to follow closely the standard macroeconomic literature on monopolistic competition, originated by Dixit and Stiglitz (1977). We are interested in the effects of economic inequality when firms have market power, and we want to explore its macroeconomic consequences. Which prices will monopolistic producers charge in view of different demands by rich and poor consumers? How does such pricing behavior affect the industry structure of an economy? Does the interaction between inequality and market power affect the demand for labor and, if so, may an increase in inequality even aggravate the unemployment problem?

While these questions are at the heart of macroeconomics, they are not easily accessible with the standard tools of macroeconomic analysis. Macroeconomic models of monopolistic competition - building upon work of Dixit and Stiglitz (1977)[1] - have a bias against any impact of consumer heterogeneity. The reason

[1]The original work of Dixit and Stiglitz (1977) was focused on the determinants of excess capacity and product diversity in a monopolistically competitive industry, a question central to industrial organization rather than macroeconomics. Due to its simplicity and tractability, these tools have become central to macroeconomics (see e.g. the influential textbook by Romer (2000, Chapter 6).

is the assumption of homothetic preferences which implies that consumer heterogeneity is irrelevant for macroeconomic outcomes. Such outcomes can be viewed as if they were generated by decisions of a "representative consumer".

The recent macroeconomic literature has paid increasing attention to issues of income distribution. This literature has extensively dealt with the imperfections on the *capital market* for investment decisions.[2] The literature has also extensively focused on mechanisms that generate inequalities in the *labor market*. However, the interaction of inequality and the *product market* has largely been ignored by the literature. Such interaction, however, is economically relevant. For instance, we deliberately use terms like 'mass consumption goods', 'exclusive goods', 'luxuries', and the like descriptive to suggest that individual consumption behavior varies by income levels and therefore different firms serve different consumer groups. Furthermore, we argued repeatedly in this book that the empirical evidence clearly rejects the assumption of homothetic preferences.

The interaction between economic inequality and product market imperfections is not only economically relevant, but is also theoretically interesting. The standard monopolistic competition model has been applied to important macroeconomic issues, like economic development, growth, business cycles, and trade. These are questions that are inextricably connected with issues of income distribution. The approach introduced in the following chapter attempts to provide an analytical framework that should allow us to address such distributional issues by introducing non-homothetic preferences into the monopolistic competition model.

Our analysis explores the interactions between market power and economic inequality within the following general framework. (i) Consumers are unequally endowed with factors of production (have unequal labor endowments and/or own unequal shares in the monopolistic firms). Instead, we rule out any differences in tastes between consumers so that differences in consumption behavior are entirely due to differences in incomes between households. (ii) Firms have a monopoly position on the market of their particular product, but the firms are infinitely small relative to the aggregate economy. This is the usual "monopolistic competition" assumption. (iii) We assume that technology and preferences are "symmetric". By this we mean that the various products that are supplied on the market have identical production technologies; and that also preferences are symmetric with respect to the various products. Hence, any differences in outcomes between the

[2]See Galor and Zeira (1993), Banerjee and Newman (1993), and Aghion and Bolton (1997) for important early papers in this literature.

various markets are entirely due to inequality in endowments, but are not due to preferences and technology.

The central result of our analysis is that a change in distribution of resources across the population may lead to different equilibria in the economy. When the distribution is rather even, the likely outcome is a symmetric one in which all firms charge the same prices and the economic resources are evenly distributed across sector of production. Hence, the production structure and the markups are unaffected by inequality. However, with a more polarized distribution, the outcome may be completely different. It may pay for some monopolists to set high prices, and sell their product only to the rich. The poor are excluded from the market in the sense that their willingness to pay would be above marginal cost. Further, a more unequal distribution leads to more exclusion and to higher markups. Hence, the production and the price structure are affected by inequality.

Secondly, under certain conditions the equilibrium outcome is unemployment. This is the case even though the labor market is competitive, so that wages are fully downward flexible. The reason for unemployment is that, under our assumptions, the revenues of a monopolist are bounded, and no monopolist will ever produce more output than the one that maximizes revenues. Hence, even when wages go to zero, labor demand will be limited. We show that the conditions under which unemployment arises depend crucially on the distribution of income. When incomes are very polarized, more monopolists will choose the strategy of exclusion, that is, charge high prices and produce low quantities that are sold only for the rich. Hence the aggregate labor demand in such a situation is lower with higher inequality.

Our analysis is restricted to a special case - quadratic preferences and two types of consumers. Analyzing this specific example is valuable for several reasons. First of all, it allows us to shed light on the importance of assumptions made in standard monopolistic competition models. Second, our analysis proves by example that an equilibrium exists that excludes poor individuals from markets. More generally, the structure of industry (that is, the allocation of productive resources across sectors) is determined by the distribution of income. Third, while our results are derived under special assumptions, it is easy to imagine that equilibria with a similar structure may arise under many different specifications of preferences and distributions. Finally, the example is simple and tractable. From a methodological point of view, the model presented below may be an interesting tool to study macro-issues in which both consumer heterogeneity and market power are important.

There are several related strands of the macroeconomic literature. Our analysis is related to Saint-Paul (2005) who analyzes distribution and growth when consumers have "limited needs". Saint-Paul (2005) implicitly assumes that income distribution is sufficiently even so that the macroeconomic equilibrium is always symmetric and an exclusion regime can never arise. In contrast, we show under which conditions asymmetric outcomes arise and how these outcome are affect by the distribution of income.

Gabszewicz and Thisse (1979) discuss the importance of consumer heterogeneity for the distribution of output across sectors in a vertical differentiation framework. They analyze a situation where firms offer different qualities. When the distribution is sufficiently unequal, we may have a situation where the highest quality is sold to the rich and the lower quality is sold to the poor. (See also Gabszewicz and Thisse, 1980, and Shaked and Sutton, 1982, 1984). Our equilibrium outcome is similar in the sense the income distribution affects the industry structure. However, in our model products are horizontally (instead of vertically) differentiated. More importantly, our analysis focuses on the general equilibrium, whereas those papers are interested in issues of competition in a partial equilibrium framework. As a consequence, they do not address the possibility of unemployment and implications for aggregate welfare.

A different strand of the related literature deals with the importance of inequality for the industry structure in the context of economic development and growth. Murphy, Shleifer, and Vishny (1989) analyze how income inequality affects the size of markets and determines for how many sectors adopt a modern technology. In Murphy, Shleifer, and Vishny (1989) prices and mark-ups are exogenous and inequality affects the size of the various industries because consumers have asymmetric (hierarchic) preferences. A similar approach is followed in Falkinger (1994) who studies growth along a hierarchy of wants in which the demand for new products is affected by the distribution of income. In that paper, as in Zweimueller (2000), distribution only affects income and shapes the industry structure prices via preferences that are asymmetric across products. Prices and mark-ups are exogenously given. In contrast, income distribution in the present model shapes the industry structure despite the fact that goods are symmetric with respect to preferences.

Finally, our analysis is related to a literature that addresses the question whether imperfections in the product market *per se* may be relevant for unemployment (Hart, 1982, Silvestre, 1990, d'Aspremont et al., 1990, and others). When there is upper bound on the firm's revenues, the maximum level of output (and hence employment) that a firm is willing to produce is also finite, even if the costs of production, that is the wage rate, becomes zero. In other words, downward flexibility of wages does not necessarily eliminate the unemployment problem. While these papers have been concerned with the existence of unemployment equilibria in a representative agents environment, our model shows that the more uneven the distribution of income the more an unemployment regime is likely. Moreover, we point to the possibility that higher inequality may aggravate the unemployment problem.

The chapter is organized as follows. In the next Section we describe the general set-up and derive equilibrium conditions for general specifications of preferences and distribution. Section 3 studies symmetric and asymmetric equilibria of this model and puts particular emphasis on the role of income distribution for the respective outcome. In Section 4 we analyze the possibility of unemployment and look at the role of income distribution in that regime. Section 5 discusses our results in light of the assumptions and draws some conclusions.[3]

5.2 Monopolistic Competition With Non-Homothetic Preferences

Preferences and Technology

There is a population of consumers of mass 1 and all consumers have identical preferences. Their objective function is defined over a continuous range of differentiated products $j \in [0, N]$. We assume *symmetry* and *separability* of the various products. We denote by $v(c(j))$ the utility gained from consuming good j in quantity $c(j)$ and normalize the utility from not consuming a good to zero, $v(0) = 0$. The consumer's objective function is specified as

$$u(\{c(j)\}) = \int_0^N v(c(j))dj. \tag{5.1}$$

We make two assumptions that are crucial for the analysis below. First, we assume that $v'(0) < \infty$. This implies it may or may not be beneficial to consume a certain good. (This can never occur with CES-preferences as in Dixit and Stiglitz, 1978, where and $v'(0) = \infty$). Second, we assume that $-cv''(c)/v'(c)$ is increasing in c and that $\lim_{c\to 0} -cv''(c)/v'(c) < 1$. (This also different from the Dixit-Stiglitz formulation, where $-cv''(c)/v'(c)$ is independent of c). We will see below that these assumptions have implications for the price elasticity of demand.

[3]The chapter follows Foellmi and Zweimueller (2003).

All goods are produced with the same technology. Production takes place with labor as the only production factor and we assume a simple linear technology $x(j) = al(j)$ where $x(j)$ is output of good j and $l(j)$ is the labor input. The productivity parameter $a > 0$ is an exogenously given constant. The labor market is competitive and the wage rate equals w. Hence the marginal cost of production are w/a, the same for all goods.

Endowments

Consumers are heterogenous with respect to their incomes. As the income level is endogenously determined in the model, the distribution we take is given is that of labor endowments, and that of shares in the profits of monopolistic profits. We make a further assumption that greatly simplifies the analysis, namely that the *composition* of endowments is identical across households.[4] A household that has twice as many shares in monopolistic profits also supplies twice as many labor units on the market. Hence the distribution of firm shares and the distribution of labor endowments is identical and can be described by a cumulative density function $F(\theta)$. The distribution has support over the interval $\left[\underline{\theta}, \overline{\theta}\right]$, with $0 < \underline{\theta} < \overline{\theta} < \infty$. Average endowments are normalized to unity, $E(\theta) = 1$. Hence households with $\theta >$ ($<$)1 are endowed above (below) average. This assumption gives us a unique ordering of individuals by income, irrespective of the (endogenously determined) distribution of income between wages and profits.

Resource constraint

Labor is the only factor of production. We assume that each household supplies labor of amount θ. On average, households supply $E(\theta) = 1$ units of labor, and the population has mass 1. Hence labor supply is equal to unity. Labor demand comes from the production sector. The resource constraint is

$$a \geq \int_0^N x(j)dj. \tag{5.2}$$

[4]If one assumed for example that profit shares are distributed more unequally than labor endowments, we would still get the result that more inequality makes exclusion more likely. However, there might arise multiple equilibria because - as we will see below - more inequality leads to a higher profit share.

5.2.1 Consumers and Firms

An equilibrium is characterized by a set of quantities $\{c(\theta, j)\}_{\theta \in [\underline{\theta}, \bar{\theta}],\, j \in [0,N]}$ and a set of prices $\{p(j)\}_{j \in [0,N]}$ such that consumers maximize utility, firms maximize profits and the resource constraint is met.

Consumer demand

The individuals maximize their utility (5.1) subject to the budget constraint $y(\theta) = \int_0^N p(j)c(j)dj$ and the non-negativity constraints $c(j) \geq 0$. The individual demand function $c(p(j), \theta)$ is implicitly given by the first order conditions

$$\begin{aligned} v'(c(p(j), \theta)) &= \lambda(\theta)p(j) \qquad \text{if } p(j) \leq v'(0)/\lambda(\theta) \\ c(p(j), \theta) &= 0 \qquad \text{if } p(j) > v'(0)/\lambda(\theta) \end{aligned} \tag{5.3}$$

where $\lambda(\theta)$ denotes the Lagrangian multiplier (i.e. the marginal utility of income of an agent with relative income θ). The above first order conditions yield the demand for each good $j \in [0, N]$ by an agent with endowment level θ. We note that, in general, nonnegativity constraints may become binding because we have assumed that $v'(0)$ is finite. If $v'(0) \leq \lambda(\theta)p(j)$, consumer θ does not want to consume good j because the price $p(j)$ is too high.

As long as agent θ is consuming good j, the individual reaction to a price change can be found by differentiating equation (5.3) (we suppress the j-index) $\partial c/\partial p = \lambda/v''(c) = \frac{1}{p}v'(c)/v''(c)$. The price elasticity of the individual demand curve varies with across consumers with different endowment levels

$$\eta(\theta) \equiv -\frac{\partial c(\theta)}{\partial p}\frac{p}{c(\theta)} = -\frac{v'(c(\theta))}{c(\theta)\, v''(c(\theta))}.$$

Pricing decisions of firms.

The market for each good is monopolistic. There is a mass of N monopolists who are unique suppliers for their respective product and who set prices to maximize profits. The market demand curve that monopolistic producer for good j faces, it given by horizontal aggregation of individual demand curves for this product. Obviously, the market demand function $x(p(j))$ depends on the price $p(j)$ and on the distribution of income, $F(\theta)$

$$x(p(j)) = \int_{\hat{\theta}(p(j))}^{\bar{\theta}} c(p(j), \theta)dF(\theta).$$

The slope of the market demand function can then be written as (for ease of notation we will suppress the j-index and those arguments of the $c(\cdot)$- and $x(\cdot)$-

functions that are not directly relevant)[5]

$$\frac{dx}{dp} = \frac{1}{p}\int_{\hat{\theta}(p(j))}^{\bar{\theta}} \frac{v'(c(\theta))}{v''(c(\theta))} dF(\theta),$$

where individuals with endowment $\theta < \hat{\theta}$ do not consume this good as in that case $v'(0) < \lambda(\theta)p$.

Monopolist j chooses the price that maximizes profits taking the prices of all other firms as given. Formally, monopolist j solves the problem

$$\max_{p(j)} \; p(j)\, x(p(j)) - \frac{w}{a}\, x(p(j)).$$

The solution to this problem is given by the familiar Lerner index (again, for ease of notation, we suppress the j-index)

$$\frac{p - w/a}{p} = \frac{1}{\varepsilon(p)} \qquad \text{where} \qquad \varepsilon(p) = \int_{\hat{\theta}(p)}^{\bar{\theta}} \frac{c(p,\theta)}{x(p)} \frac{-v'(c(\theta,p))}{c(\theta,p)v''(c(\theta,p))} dF(\theta). \quad (5.4)$$

Formula (5.4) tells us that the monopoly price depends on a weighted average of individual price elasticities of demand $[-v'(c)/(cv''(c))]$, taking the consumption shares $c(\theta)/x$ as weights.

5.2.2 *Restrictions on Preferences and Distribution*

It is obvious that, without putting more structure both on preferences and distribution, not much can be said about the general equilibrium of this model. The main problem is that we cannot explicitly solve for the monopoly price which makes the model intractable. Hence we proceed by putting more structure on both the subutility function $v(\cdot)$ as well as the distribution function $F(\cdot)$. We make the following assumptions:

(i) *Inequality* only consists of two groups. There is a group of poor households, indexed by P, of size β, and a group of rich households, indexed by R, of size $1-\beta$. The relative income of the poor household is denoted by θ_P whereas the relative income level of the rich group is denoted by θ_R. The wealth shares of both groups must sum up to unity so we must have

$$\beta\theta_P + (1-\beta)\theta_R = 1.$$

For ease of notation we take $\vartheta \equiv \theta_P$ as an exogenous constant. The group share of the rich is then implicitly given by $\theta_R = (1-\beta\vartheta)/(1-\beta)$

[5] To get this equation note that, by definition, we have $c(\hat{\theta}(p)) = 0$.

(ii) The *subutility* $v(\cdot)$ is quadratic and given by

$$v(\cdot) = -\frac{1}{2}\left[s - c(j)\right]^2,$$

where $s > 0$ denotes the saturation level. Note that $v'(0) = s < \infty$, and that the elasticity of substitution $-v'(c)/\left[cv''(c)\right] = (s-c)/c$ is decreasing in c for $c < s$.

In the next sections, we will analyze the equilibria of this model and fully characterize these equilibria in terms of exogenous parameters, in particular, the parameters characterizing the distribution of income. At the end of the chapter, we take stock and assess the robustness of our results with respect to the particular assumption on preferences and distribution.

Demand functions and monopoly prices.

For further use, it is convenient to describe the individual and market demand functions that arise from our specification of preferences and the distribution of endowments. We denote by λ_P and λ_R the marginal utility of income of the poor and the rich, respectively. The first order conditions form utility maximization yields the individual demand curves

$$c_i(j) = s - \lambda_i p(j), \qquad i = R, P. \tag{5.5}$$

The market demand curve results from horizontal aggregation of individual demand curves and can be written as

$$x(j) = \begin{cases} 0 & \text{if} \quad p(j) \in [s/\lambda_R, \infty), \\ (1-\beta)\left[s - \lambda_R p(j)\right] & \text{if} \quad p(j) \in [s/\lambda_P, s/\lambda_R), \\ s - \left[\beta\lambda_P + (1-\beta)\lambda_R\right] p(j) & \text{if} \quad p(j) \in [0, s/\lambda_P). \end{cases} \tag{5.6}$$

When the price exceeds the prohibitive price of the rich, $p(j) \geq s/\lambda_R$, market demand is zero. When the price is between the prohibitive price of the rich and the poor, $p(j) \in (s/\lambda_P, s/\lambda_R]$, only rich consumers purchase the good in positive amounts, but poor consumers do not buy. When the price is sufficiently low, so that it also falls short of the prohibitive price of the poor, $p(j) < s/\lambda_P$, both rich and poor consumers purchase the monopolist's product. (Figure 5.1).

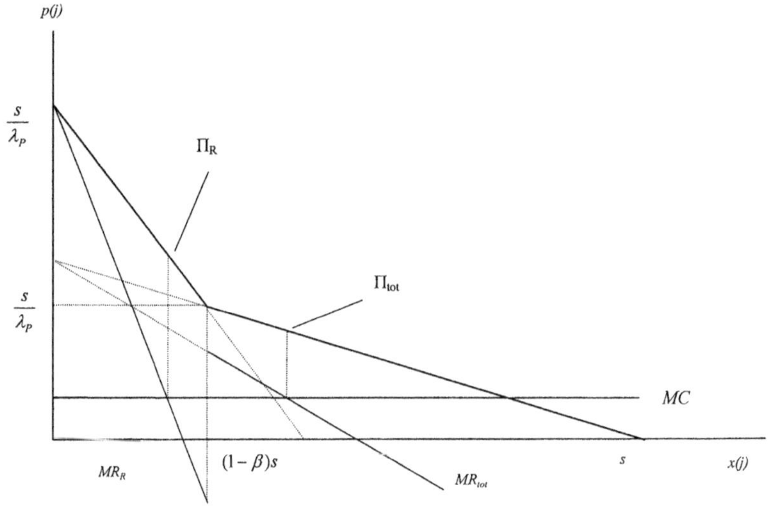

Fig. 5.1. Aggregate Demand and Monopolistic Pricing Decision

We can easily derive the monopoly prices along the above demand curve. As the demand curve is piecewise linear, there are two candidates for the monopoly price. Taking each of the two segments of the demand function (5.6) separately, it is straightforward to calculate the respective monopoly prices for these two demand curves as

$$p(j) = \begin{cases} \frac{1}{2}\left[\frac{w}{a} + \frac{s}{\lambda_R}\right] & \text{if only the rich buy,} \\ \frac{1}{2}\left[\frac{w}{a} + \frac{s}{\beta\lambda_P + (1-\beta)\lambda_R}\right] & \text{if all consumers buy.} \end{cases} \tag{5.7}$$

Obviously, selling only to the rich is only an option for the monopolist when the prohibitive price of the poor $v'(0)/\lambda_P$ is smaller than $\frac{1}{2}\left[\frac{w}{a} + \frac{s}{\lambda_R}\right]$. This is the case if λ_R and λ_P are sufficiently unequal. (In Figure 1, the monopoly price when selling only to the rich must lie on the relevant range of the steep segment of the demand curve). We also note that the two prices in equation (5.7) are local maxima, and it depends on the values of the endogenous variables λ_R and λ_P which strategy yields the (globally) higher profit.

5.3 Symmetric versus Asymmetric Equilibria

5.3.1 Symmetric Equilibrium

We now study the general equilibrium of this model. The first, and obvious, candidate for an equilibrium is a symmetric outcome. Because all goods enter the utility function in the same manner, and because the production of all goods takes place with the same technology, a situation where each consumer consumes the same amount of each product demand, and where all firms charge the same prices, sells the same quantity, and earn the same profit appears to be a likely outcome.

Such an outcome, however, will only prevail in equilibrium if the distribution of income is sufficiently even. When the distribution is very polarized, however, the outcome will be one where not all firms sell their product to both rich and poor consumers. There will be some firms that find it profitable to set a high price (above the prohibitive price of poor individuals) and sell only to rich consumers. Hence there are "exclusive" goods, that only rich people can afford. Poor individuals are "excluded" in the sense that they have a willingness to pay that is above the marginal cost of production (and hence, in the absence of market power on the side of producers, they would purchase the product in positive amounts). Since all firms are alike, (have the same market demand curves and the same marginal cost of production), the general equilibrium is a situation where a monopolistic producer is indifferent between selling only to the rich or serving the entire market. In other words, the equilibrium can be characterized by an arbitrage condition that guarantees the same profits for each firm.

We note at this point that an exclusion equilibrium can never arise when the marginal loss in utility from not consuming a good in positive amounts is infinitely large, i.e. when we have $v'(0) = \infty$. This is the assumption that monopolistic competition models based upon preferences suggested by Dixit and Stiglitz (1978) adopt. Hence our assumption $v'(0) < \infty$ is crucial in this respect.[6]

When the equilibrium is symmetric, all consumers spend the same amount on each variety; and market demand, prices, and profits are the same in each sector. This means that only the flat segment along the piecewise linear demand function (5.6) is relevant.

The equilibrium is easily calculated in this case. We can substitute $x(j) = x$ into the resource constraint (5.2). Hence we have

$$x = \frac{a}{N}.$$

[6]We note that, with a general $v(\cdot)$ function, and $v'(0) = \infty$ it is possible that there is more than one global maximum for the monopolists' choice. This would mean some firms may find it profitable to set a high price with (perhaps very) little demand from poor consumers, or a low price and a larger market. However, such an equilibrium can only arise as a a knife-edge case, and will not robust to exogenous changes in parameters.

¿From equation (5.7) it is also straightforward to calculate the monopoly price as $p = \frac{1}{2}\left[w/a + s/\left(\beta\lambda_P + (1-\beta)\lambda_R\right)\right]$. This expression still contains the two endogenous variables λ_P and λ_R. To solve for p in terms of exogenous parameters we use the budget constraint to express λ_i as a function of p. First, we make use of the fact that utility maximization requires that $s - c_i = \lambda_i p$, $i = R, P$. Second, we note that the income level of consumer i is simply a fraction θ_i of average (=aggregate) income. Aggregate income consists of aggregate wages and aggregate profits, so $y_i = \theta_i\left[w + (p - w/a)N\right]$.[7] Using these relations we can rewrite the budget constraint of consumer i as $pN\left(s - \lambda_i p\right) = \theta_i\left[w + (p - w/a)N\right]$. This latter equation gives us the λ_i's as functions of p. We use these to calculate the monopoly price as a function of the exogenous parameters of the model

$$p = \frac{w}{a}\frac{sN - a}{sN - 2a}. \tag{5.8}$$

There are several interesting points worth mentioning. First, we see from equation (5.8) that p does not depend on the distribution parameters β and ϑ. This means that, when the equilibrium is symmetric, the monopoly price, and hence mark-ups and the real wage, do not depend on the distribution of endowments. This is not surprising, because the quadratic utility function exhibits HARA. Equation (5.4) implies that distribution does not affect markups as long as $v'(c)/v''(c)$ is affine linear, i.e. if $v(\cdot)$ belongs to the class of quasi-homothetic preferences (the HARA-class) which are characterized by linear income expansion paths. As long as non-negativity constraints do not become binding, the market demand function (5.6) is independent of the distribution of income.[8] Second, the monopoly price increases in the range of supplied varieties N and in the saturation level s. This is a result of our assumption that the elasticity of demand decreases along the demand curve. (In terms of our initial assumptions, the quadratic utility function features the condition $-v'(c)/cv''(c) = (s - c)/c$ decreases in c.) When the saturation level s is larger, consumers have a higher elasticity of demand, hence mark-ups and prices are lower. A larger range of supplied products N means that consumption per variety is lower, as consumers spread their expenditures across more varieties. This leads to a higher price elasticity, a lower mark-up and a lower price. Finally, and interestingly, the effect of productivity a is not a priori clear. On the one hand, an increase in a directly decreases the cost of production and hence tends to reduce the price at a given mark-up. On the other hand, an increase in a raises

[7] Average and aggregate income are the same as we have normalized population size to unity.

[8] Foellmi and Zweimueller (2004) study the inequality effects on product diversity and mark-ups for a general class of preferences. That analysis, however, is restricted to symmetric equilibria.

equilibrium consumption level which decreases the price elasticity of demand, and increases the mark-up. (This has been pointed out in Saint-Paul (2002).) The latter demand effect may dominate the productivity effect when a is already large relative to the potential market size sN. More precisely, real wages *decreases* in response to a productivity *increase* when $a > sN(1 - \frac{\sqrt{2}}{2})$. When a falls short of this critical level, the cost effect dominates and real wages increase in response to a productivity increase.

We summarize our discussion in the following

Proposition 13 *a) Income inequality does not affect prices, mark-ups, and the real wage. b) An increase in the number of competitors N, or an increase in the maximum size of a market s leads to lower prices and mark-ups, and increases the real wage. c) An increase in productivity a increases (decreases) prices and decreases (increases) real wages when $a > (<)sN(1 - \frac{\sqrt{2}}{2})$.*

5.3.2 A Condition Whether Symmetry Constitutes an Equilibrium

So far, we have not discussed in detail under which conditions a symmetric equilibrium exists. It is intuitively clear, however, that such a situation become more unlikely when the endowment distribution is more unequal. In other words, the borderline between a symmetric and an asymmetric equilibrium is determined by a critical degree of endowment inequality. We now discuss this condition in more detail.

For the symmetric outcome to be an equilibrium it must be that no monopolist has an incentive to set a very high price and sell only to rich customers. In order to assess whether the symmetric equilibrium exists, we have to work out the conditions under which the "exclusive good" strategy is not option for *any* firm on the market. To see the profits a firm could earn by adopting this strategy, we have to focus on the steep segment of the piecewise linear market demand function (5.6). Along this segment, market demand is $(1-\beta)(s - \lambda_R p)$, and the profit maximizing price equals $\frac{1}{2}\left[\frac{w}{a} + \frac{s}{\lambda_R}\right]$. Hence the maximum profit a firm can obtain from selling only to rich customers equals $\Pi_R = \frac{1}{4}(1-\beta)\left(s - \lambda_R \frac{w}{a}\right)^2 / \lambda_R$. Alternatively, if the firm sets the profit-maximizing price that attracts all customers, the flat segment is relevant, and from (5.6) and (5.7), we know that demand along this segment is $s - [\beta\lambda_P + (1-\beta)\lambda_R]\,p$ and the profit-maximizing price is $\frac{1}{2}\left[w/a + s/\left(\beta\lambda_P + (1-\beta)\lambda_R\right)\right]$. Hence, the maximum profit one can obtain from setting a low price and selling to all customers is given by $\Pi_{tot} = \frac{1}{4}\left[s - (\beta\lambda_P + (1-\beta)\lambda_R)\frac{w}{a}\right]^2 / \left[\beta\lambda_P + (1-\beta)\lambda_R\right]$. The exclusive strategy is *no option for any firm* if Π_R is strictly smaller than Π_{tot}. The expression for these two profit levels still contain the endogenous variables λ_R and λ_P and, in order to make progress, we have to express them in terms of exogenous parameters. Recall that in a symmetric equilibrium, $c_i = s - \lambda_i p$, and $c_i = \theta_i a/N$, $i \in \{P, R\}$ holds. Using equation (5.8) to replace p, we can express the marginal utility of income for customer $i \in \{P, R\}$ as $\lambda_i = (s - \theta_i a/N)(a/w)(sN - 2a)/(sN - a)$. This allows us to express the critical profits levels Π_R and Π_{tot} in terms of the exogenous parameters of the model. After some manipulations we get

$$\Pi_R = \frac{(1-\beta)}{4}\frac{wa}{N}\frac{((1+\theta_R)sN - 2\theta_R a)^2}{(sN-a)(sN-2a)(sN-\theta_R a)}, \quad \text{and} \quad \Pi_{tot} = \frac{wa}{N(sN-2a)} \tag{5.9}$$

The symmetric outcome is an equilibrium if, starting from a situation where *all* firms charge a price that attracts the whole customer base, no single firm has an incentive to deviate and adopt the exclusive good strategy. In other words, the strict inequality $\Pi_R < \Pi_{tot}$ must hold strictly. Using equations (5.9), we can express this condition as

$$\frac{1-\beta}{4}\frac{(1+\theta_R - 2\theta_R z)^2}{(1-z)(1-\theta_R z)} < 1 \text{ where } z = a/sN < 1/2.$$

(The condition $a/sN < 1/2$ is necessary to guarantee a full employment equilibrium. For an unemployment outcome, see Section 4). We can solve this condition for β, noting that $\theta_R = (1-\beta\vartheta)/(1-\beta)$, and get

$$\beta < \frac{4\vartheta(1-z)^2}{(1+\vartheta)^2 + 4\vartheta z(\vartheta z - (1+\vartheta))}. \tag{5.10}$$

It is easy to see that this condition will eventually be violated if ϑ decreases (note that $z < 1/2$) and/or β increases. Recall that a decrease in ϑ and an increase in β implies an increase in endowment inequality. Hence the result corresponds to our previous intuitive reasoning: more inequality makes the exclusion regime more likely. Furthermore, condition (5.10) is more easily violated the higher z is. If a increases or N decreases, consumption per good $c = x = a/N = sz$ of both groups increases, marginal utilities fall, and therefore the consumers are willing to pay at the margin. However, the willingness to pay of the rich rises more strongly because they are now relatively closer to the saturation point s than the poor. As a result the symmetric equilibrium is less likely, the higher z. Therefore, if we evaluate expression (5.10) at $z = 1/2$ (the lowest level of z compatible with full employment), we get a *necessary* condition for the existence of an exclusion regime

$$\beta > \vartheta$$

With the same reasoning we get a *sufficient* condition if we evaluate the condition (5.10) at $z = 0$.

$$\beta > \frac{4\vartheta}{(1+\vartheta)^2}$$

Obviously, this condition is stronger since $\vartheta < 4\vartheta/(1+\vartheta)^2$.

5.3.3 The Asymmetric Case ('Exclusion')

To get an intuition for an asymmetric equilibrium consider a distribution function with a small fraction of very poor agents. These are consumers who have a very high λ_P, and hence a rather high prohibitive price $v'(0)/\lambda_P$. As we have $v'(0) < 0$, the prohibitive price is finite, and small for poor consumers. Thus it could well be profitable for a monopolist to set a price larger than $v'(0)/\lambda_P$. The monopolist would earn higher unit profits $p - w/a$ but his output would not drop dramatically. Market demand is not strongly affected when the poor do not buy, both because the demand per capita is low and because the group share of the poor is small. In such an equilibrium the outcome is asymmetric: in some markets, the poor will be excluded from consumption as monopolists set prices that exceed the prohibitive price of the poor, i.e. the poor are "excluded" from certain markets.

How does such an "exclusion" equilibrium look like? Trivially, it *cannot* be an equilibrium that *all* monopolists only serve the market of rich households. In that case, poor people would consume nothing and would not exhaust their budget constraint. This implies they are willing to buy every product at any price. Therefore, the general equilibrium must be characterized by a situation where a fraction of firms sets low prices and sells to all consumers, whereas other firms serve only (a smaller or larger) subgroup of the population. However, since firms are symmetric ex ante, the profits of all firms must be equal in equilibrium. Otherwise, a firm would not have chosen a profit-maximizing price.

In this equilibrium, there are $N - n$ firms selling only to the rich at a high price; and n firms serving the entire population at a low price. We can order the goods in such a way, that $j \in [0, n]$ are those firms that sell to all agents and set a price $\underline{p}$, whereas firms supplying goods in the range $j \in (n, N]$ sell only to the rich consumers and set the high price $\bar{p}$. Note that the variable n is now an additional variable. Within the range $[0, n]$ all firms are alike and also within the range $(n, N]$.

Now consider the monopoly prices for the two types of firms. Take the first segment of the demand function (5.6). Along this segment only the rich consumers buy and the demand curve is given by $x(j) = (1-\beta)\left[s - \lambda_R p(j)\right]$. The price that maximizes profits along this demand function is equal to $p = \frac{1}{2}\left[w/a + s/\lambda_R\right]$. Now take the second segment where all consumers buy. Along this segment demand is $x(j) = s - \left[\beta\lambda_P + (1-\beta)\lambda_R\right] p(j)$ and the price that maximizes profits along this demand function is given by $\frac{1}{2}\left[w/a + s/\left(\beta\lambda_P + (1-\beta)\lambda_R\right)\right]$. Hence the monopoly price can be written as

$$p(j) = \begin{cases} \frac{1}{2}\left[\frac{w}{a} + \frac{s}{\lambda_R}\right] \equiv \bar{p} & \text{if } j \in [0,n], \\ \frac{1}{2}\left[\frac{w}{a} + \frac{s}{\beta\lambda_P + (1-\beta)\lambda_R}\right] \equiv \underline{p} & \text{if } j \in (n,N]. \end{cases} \tag{5.11}$$

When, in equilibrium, the poor are excluded from certain markets the outcome is asymmetric. In that case it is convenient to focus on the two monopoly prices $\bar{p}$ and $\underline{p}$ as the main endogenous variables, and write all other endogenous variables as functions of $\bar{p}$ and $\underline{p}$. We start by replacing the marginal utilities of income of both poor and rich, λ_P and λ_R. From equation (5.11) we can write $\lambda_R = s/\left(2\bar{p} - w/a\right)$ and $\lambda_P = (s/\beta)\left[1/\left(2\underline{p} - w/a\right) - (1-\beta)/(2\bar{p} - w/a)\right]$. Similarly, we can express the quantities purchased by rich and poor consumers c_R and c_P in terms of the monopoly prices $\bar{p}$ and $\underline{p}$. We get for the consumption levels of the rich $c_R = s - s/\left(2\bar{p} - w/a\right)\underline{p}$ for $j \in [0,n]$ and $c_R = s - s/\left(2\bar{p} - w/a\right)\bar{p}$ for $j \in (n,N]$. The consumption levels of the poor read $c_P = s - (s/\beta)\left[1/\left(2\underline{p} - w/a\right) - (1-\beta)/(2\bar{p} - w/a)\right]\underline{p}$ for $j \in [0,n]$ and $c_P = 0$ for $j \in (n,N]$. Finally, the equilibrium quantities can then be written as $x(\underline{p}) = s\left(\underline{p} - w/a\right)/\left(2\underline{p} - w/a\right)$ for $j \in [0,n]$ where all buy, and for $j \in (n,N]$ where only the rich purchase the good we get $x(\bar{p}) = (1-\beta)\,s\left(\bar{p} - w/a\right)/\left(2\bar{p} - w/a\right)$

Using these expression, it is straightforward to can calculate the profit Π_{tot} of a firm that serves the entire market; and the profit Π_R for a firm that sells only to the rich. Obviously, in an equilibrium with exclusion, firms must be indifferent between selling to the rich at the high price $\bar{p}$ and selling to all consumers at the low price $\underline{p}$. This is because all firms are identical ex ante (they have the same cost and demand functions). Any situation where the two profit levels differ, would lead lower-profit firms to change prices and switch the customer base. We note also that, a situation where all firms charge high prices and sell only to the rich, cannot be an equilibrium either. This is because poor consumers would have resources to spend and willing to pay very high prices. This means that, in equilibrium, we have either no exclusion of poor consumers (in which case $\Pi_R < \Pi_{tot}$) or we have exclusion of poor consumers from some but not all markets (in which case $\Pi_R = \Pi_{tot}$). We can use the expressions in the last paragraph to write the arbitrage condition in the exclusion equilibrium as

$$\Pi_R = \Pi_{tot} \quad \Leftrightarrow \quad s(1-\beta)\frac{\left(\bar{p} - w/a\right)^2}{2\bar{p} - w/a} = s\frac{\left(\underline{p} - w/a\right)^2}{2\underline{p} - w/a} \tag{5.12}$$

Note that we can solve the latter equation for $\bar{p}$ and we get the following monotonically increasing relationship between $\bar{p}$ and $\underline{p}$

$$\bar{p}-\frac{w}{a}=\frac{\left(\underline{p}-w/a\right)^2+\left(\underline{p}-w/a\right)\sqrt{\left(\underline{p}-w/a\right)^2+\left(1-\beta\right)\left(2\underline{p}-w/a\right)w/a}}{\left(1-\beta\right)\left(2\underline{p}-w/a\right)}\equiv g(\underline{p})$$

Equation (5.12) is the first equilibrium condition in $\bar{p}$ and $\underline{p}$ that a general equilibrium with exclusion has to satisfy. Combinations of $\bar{p}$ and $\underline{p}$ that satisfy equation (5.12) guarantee that (i) firms are indifferent between selling to only to the rich and selling to all customers, (ii) firms (locally) maximize profits, and (iii) consumers have made optimal choices of their consumption levels.

We get the second condition by looking at the resource constraint and at the household's budget constraint. When there is full employment, the resource constraint (5.2) has to be satisfied with equality and aggregate production equals a. Using the expressions derived above, we can express individual consumption levels in terms of $\bar{p}$ and $\underline{p}$ which allows us to write the resource constraint as

$$ns\frac{\underline{p}-w/a}{2\underline{p}-w/a}+(N-n)s(1-\beta)\frac{\bar{p}-w/a}{2\underline{p}-w/a}=a. \tag{5.13}$$

Finally, the individual budget constraints must hold in equilibrium. We get $y_R = ns\left[\left(2\bar{p}-\underline{p}-w/a\right)/\left(2\bar{p}-w/a\right)\right]\underline{p}+(N-n)s\left[\left(\bar{p}-w/a\right)/\left(2\bar{p}-w/a\right)\right]\bar{p}$ and $y_P = ns\left[1-\left(\underline{p}/\beta\right)\left\{1/\left(2\underline{p}-w/a\right)-\left(1-\beta\right)/\left(2\bar{p}-w/a\right)\right\}\right]\underline{p}$, using (5.6) and (5.11). We further note that $y_R=\theta_R y$ and $y_P=\theta_P y$ (y is aggregate income). Using $\theta_P=\vartheta$ and $\theta_R=(1-\beta\vartheta)/\left(1-\beta\right)$ allows us to write relative expenditures y_R/y_P as

$$\frac{1-\beta\vartheta}{\left(1-\beta\right)\vartheta}=\frac{\underline{p}ns\frac{2\bar{p}-\underline{p}-w/a}{2\bar{p}-w/a}+\bar{p}(N-n)s\frac{\bar{p}-w/a}{2\bar{p}-w/a}}{\underline{p}ns\left[1-\frac{\underline{p}}{\beta}\left(\frac{1}{2\underline{p}-w/a}-\frac{1-\beta}{2\bar{p}-w/a}\right)\right]}.$$

Solving the resource constraint (5.13) for n and replacing n in the latter equation, we may rewrite relative expenditures as where $z=a/(sN)$

$$\frac{1-\beta\vartheta}{\left(1-\beta\right)\vartheta}=\frac{\underline{p}\frac{2\bar{p}-\underline{p}-w/a}{2\bar{p}-w/a}-\bar{p}\frac{\bar{p}-w/a}{2\bar{p}-w/a}\left[\frac{\underline{p}-w/a}{2\underline{p}-w/a}-z\right]/\left[\left(1-\beta\right)\frac{\bar{p}-w/a}{2\underline{p}-w/a}-z\right]}{\underline{p}\left[1-\frac{\underline{p}}{\beta}\left(\frac{1}{2\underline{p}-w/a}-\frac{1-\beta}{2\bar{p}-w/a}\right)\right]}. \tag{5.14}$$

Equation (5.14) implicitly defines those combinations of $\underline{p}$ and $\bar{p}$ that ensure (i) there is full employment, (ii) consumers have made optimal choices of their consumption levels, and (iii) firms (locally) maximize profits.

Equations (5.12) and (5.14) represent two equations in the two unknowns $\underline{p}$ and $\bar{p}$. Once we know the solution to these two endogenous variables, all other variables of interest can be easily calculated. To show that a general equilibrium exists, and that it is unique, we proceed as follows. We know from equation (5.12) that $\bar{p} = g(\underline{p})$ with $g'(\underline{p}) > 0$. Hence we can replace $\underline{p}$ in equation (5.14) by $g(\cdot)$. This implies that the right-hand-side of equation (5.14) depends only on $\underline{p}$ (and exogenous parameters of the model), that is we get

$$\frac{1-\beta\vartheta}{(1-\beta)\,\vartheta} = h(\underline{p}, g(\underline{p})). \tag{5.15}$$

The following proposition shows that an exclusion equilibrium exists and that it is unique. In particular, $h(\underline{p}, g(\underline{p}))$ monotonically increases in $\underline{p}$ and equals $\frac{1-\beta\vartheta}{(1-\beta)\vartheta}$ for a finite value of $\underline{p}$ which is associated with $n < N$.

Proposition 14 *a) There exists a unique equilibrium. b) More inequality, in terms of a lower ϑ, increases markups and leads to more exclusion.*

Proof. a) See appendix.

b) Since $h(\underline{p}, g(\underline{p}))$ monotonically increases in $\underline{p}$, we directly see that a lower ϑ increases the equilibrium value of $\underline{p}$. This in turn implies a higher $\bar{p}$, since $\bar{p}$ is positively related to $\underline{p}$. Set marginal costs w/a as numéraire, hence, mark-ups will unambiguously rise as both $\underline{p}$ and $\bar{p}$ rise. Further, the production levels $c(\underline{p})$ and $c(\bar{p})$ increase in $\bar{p}$ and $\underline{p}$. Hence, the resource constraint (5.2) can only be fulfilled if n, the number of goods sold to all, is lower. ■

Part b. of the proposition states the central result of the model. More inequality affects the industry structure, because there will be more exclusion. Further, a more unequal distribution of endowments leads to a larger price distortion in terms of higher markups. Therefore, more inequality increases the profit share. What is the intuition behind these results? First note that more inequality leads to more exclusion, i.e. more products will be sold only to the rich. Aggregate output is constant and equal to a, as long as there is full employment. Since more products are sold at the lower quantity, the production levels of the other products must rise to keep aggregate output constant. In particular, both $x(\underline{p})$ and $x(\bar{p})$ must rise as to guarantee the firms' arbitrage condition (5.12). Since the demand becomes more inelastic when quantities are higher, the mark-ups must be higher. Hence, the mark-ups on all product markets are higher *and* more products are sold at higher prices $\bar{p}$ because there is more exclusion. Therefore, the mark-ups (and the profit share) rise due to more inequality.

5.4 Unemployment

Theoretical explanations for involuntary unemployment have typically looked at labor market imperfections that prevent real wages from falling to the full employment level. However, Silvestre (1990), D'Aspremont et al. (1990), and others, have mentioned the possibility that "involuntary" unemployment[9] may also arise due to product market imperfection. More precisely, even if the labor market is perfectly competitive and real wages are fully downward flexible, there is unemployment at *any* positive real wage. As pointed out by Silvestre (1990), involuntary unemployment corresponds to a situation where the real wage is (perhaps substantially) lower than the physical marginal product of labor, a situation that Robinson (1933) has defined as "exploitation".

In what follows we will discuss the determinants of unemployment in our model. In particular, we are interested in the role of endowment inequality and whether high inequality may aggravate the unemployment problem. While our thought experiment lets real wage go to zero, the reader may think that this is only an irrelevant theoretical possibility, at least in a developed economy. We note however, that our analysis is also relevant when real wages have a lower bound that is strictly larger than zero. The crucial point of our analysis is that, when firms have market power and their demand functions are affected by the distribution of income, labor demand is also affected by the distribution. When the real wage hits lower bound (which may either be zero or strictly positive), inequality affects the maximum amount of labor that firms are willing to employ.

5.4.1 Symmetric Equilibrium

Consider first a situation where the equilibrium is *symmetric*. In this case the flat segment of the piecewise linear demand function (5.6) is relevant. With full employment, output per firm equals a/N. The open question is whether firms are willing to supply such a quantity of output. They will do so provided that the price elasticity of demand at $x = a/N$ is sufficiently elastic. This is what we have implicitly assumed in Section 3. However, suppose that a is very large relative to N. Due to our assumptions on preferences, the market demand function does not depend on the distribution of income as long as there are no consumers for whom

[9] Without going into the semantics of "involutary" unemployment, we mention that the way we use the term involuntary here is consistent with the definition of Keynes (1936) for whom this is a situation "...without of any method available for labor as a whole to make revised money bargains with entreprenuers that lead to full employment."

non-negativity constraints become binding - that is, in a symmetric equilibrium. In such a situation, the price elasticity of *market* demand of each firm is given by $-v'(x)/(x)v''(x) = (s-x)/x$. Obviously, the price elasticity decreases in x and approaches unity when x approaches $s/2$. When output equals $s/2$ the monopolistic producer has reached *maximum revenues.* This is the maximum level of output that a monopolistic producer is willing to supply (and hence, a maximum level of labor demand). In that case, aggregate labor demand equals $sN/2a$. To produce the level of output that maximizes revenues requires $s/2a$ workers and there each of the N firms employs this amount of labor. Hence the unemployment rate and, using equation (5.8) real wages are given by

$$u = \max\left(0, 1 - \frac{sN}{2a}\right) \text{ and } \frac{w}{p} = \max\left(0, a\frac{sN - 2a}{sN - a}\right)$$

There are several points worth mentioning. First, when the real wage has reached its lowest possible level, there will be involuntary unemployment.[10] In a symmetric equilibrium, the distribution of income does not affect the level of unemployment. This reason is similar to the full employment case, where the distribution had no impact on prices and mark-ups. Larger markets s and a large number of competitors N lead to a reduction of unemployment or, respectively, make an unemployment regime less likely. The opposite is true for the productivity level a. Productivity increases aggravate the unemployment problem - or make the unemployment regime more likely.

5.4.2 Asymmetric Equilibrium

Unemployment due to product market power arises if the price elasticity of demand on all markets is equal to unity. In that case, all firms have maximized their revenues, and real wages have fallen to zero. In the asymmetric equilibrium, where the poor are excluded from some markets, unemployment will arise more easily. On markets $j \in [0, n]$ monopolistic producers will produce at most $s/2$, the same as in a symmetric equilibrium with unemployment. On markets for the exclusive goods $j \in (n, N]$ only rich households purchase and production does not exceed $(1-\beta)s/2$. Therefore, there will be unemployment if $a > ns/2+(N-n)(1-\beta)s/2$. Note that n is an endogenous variable that remains to be determined.

[10]This lowest possible level of the real wage equals zero when the labor market is Walrasian. We may, however, have labor market imperfections that prevent the real wage from falling below some strictly positive level. Our analysis remains relevant (though expressions become somwhat more complicated).

We have assumed that the labor market is competitive. When labor demand falls short of an inelastic labor supply, wages will to zero. (So far we have taken prices on product markets $\underline{p}$ and $\bar{p}$ and taken the price of labor w as fixed, the "numéraire". Note, however, that we are free to set a numeraire, so lets take $\underline{p} = 1$ and think of nominal wage w as the variable that adjusts endogenously.) With zero wages, a firm that serves the entire market makes a profit given by $\Pi_{tot} = (\underline{p} - 0)\, s/2 = s/2$, and a firm that sells only to the rich makes a profit $= (\bar{p} - 0)\,(1-\beta)s/2$. In the symmetric equilibrium we must have $\Pi_{tot} = \Pi_R$, from which we can calculate the price of exclusive goods $\bar{p} = 1/(1-\beta) > 1$. Aggregate profits Π are then equal to $Ns/2$.

We can now determine n, the range of firms that sell to all consumers by using the budget constraints of poor consumers. With zero wages, aggregate income is equal to aggregate profits $Ns/2$ and the income of a poor household is $\vartheta Ns/2$. The consumption level of a poor household is $c_P = s - \lambda_P$ for goods $j \in [0, n]$ and $c_P = 0$ for the remaining goods $j \in (n, N]$. We know from Section 3.3 above that, in an asymmetric equilibrium, the marginal utility of income of a poor household λ_P can be written as $\lambda_P = (s/\beta)\left[1/2\underline{p} - (1-\beta)/2\bar{p}\right]$. Inserting $\underline{p} = 1$ and $\bar{p} = 1/(1-\beta)$ gives $\lambda_P = (s/2)(2-\beta)$ and hence we have $c_P = s - (s/2)(2-\beta) = \beta s/2$. The expenditures of a poor household are then $nc_P = n\beta s/2$ and setting this equal to the income level $\vartheta Ns/2$ yields

$$\frac{n}{N} = \frac{\vartheta}{\beta}.$$

As $\vartheta < \beta$, which is a necessary condition for the exclusion regime to exist, the share n/N is indeed smaller than one. The result is very intuitive. If inequality increases, either because relative income of the poor ϑ goes down, or because the group size of the poor β increases, the fraction of goods purchased by both groups of consumers decreases and the fraction of exclusive goods increases.

We determine the unemployment rate. To calculate aggregate demand, recall that $n = (\vartheta/\beta)\, N$ sectors sell to all consumers with output $s/2$ and $N - n = (1-\vartheta/\beta)N$ sectors sell only to the rich with output $(1-\beta)s/2$. Hence the aggregate demand for labor is $\frac{1}{a}\frac{s}{2}(\vartheta/\beta)\, N + \frac{1}{a}\frac{(1-\beta)s}{2}(1-\vartheta/\beta)N = \frac{sN}{2a}(1+\vartheta-\beta)$. The unemployment rate u equals the difference between aggregate labor supply (which is equal to unity) and aggregate labor demand. Hence u is given by

$$u = 1 - \frac{sN}{2a}(1+\vartheta-\beta)\,. \tag{5.16}$$

Proposition 15 *If there is exclusion, more inequality leads to higher unemployment.*

Proof. If ϑ falls or β rises, inequality rises in a Lorenz sense. The proposition then follows directly from (5.16). ■

In the exclusion regime, the unemployment rate depends on distribution. It is easy to see that u is higher in an asymmetric equilibrium than in the symmetric regime when $\vartheta < \beta$. If inequality rises, because ϑ falls or β rises, the poor will be excluded from more markets, that is n/N falls. In that case more monopolists choose to set the high price $\bar{p} = 1/(1-\beta)$ and produce only $(1-\beta)s/2$ (for the rich), instead of setting the low price $\underline{p} = 1$ and producing the larger quantity $s/2$ (for both rich and poor). As a result, more inequality reduces aggregate real output and labor demand.

The results have striking welfare implications. The equilibrium with unemployment is not Pareto efficient. Consider a redistribution of endowments from the rich to the poor such that ϑ rises and β remains constant. This implies that $n/N = \vartheta/\beta$ increases and more products are sold to all consumers. The poor consume more goods in quantity $c_P(1) = \beta s/2$, so their welfare is higher after the redistribution. However, also the welfare of the rich increases. The consumption of the rich equals $c_R(\bar{p}) = s/2$ for $j \in (n, N]$ and $c_R(1) = (1+\beta)\, s/2$ for $j \in [0, n]$. As n rises, they consume more goods at quantity $(1+\beta)\, s/2 > s/2$, hence their welfare rises although their relative income $\theta_R = (1-\beta\vartheta)/(1-\beta)$ is lower after the redistribution. With more equality, more monopolists choose to set low prices and to produce more. Hence, exclusion falls, the endogenous price distortion is reduced, and aggregate employment and production rise. The increase in output benefits all groups in the population.

Figure 5.2 shows which regimes arises depending on inequality parameters. Panel a. is depicted for the case $z = a/(sN) < 1/2$. The separation between the symmetric and the asymmetric regime is given by equation (5.10). In that case, unemployment is only possible in the exclusion regime and it occurs if and only if $z > (1+\vartheta-\beta)/2$. If β rises and/or ϑ falls, unemployment rises. If $\beta = 1$ and $\vartheta = 0$, aggregate output diverges to zero and the unemployment rate equals one. In Panel b. the parameter z is higher than 1/2. Then, unemployment will arise already in the pooling case. However, in the exclusion regime (which arises if $\beta > \vartheta$) unemployment is higher and depends on distribution.

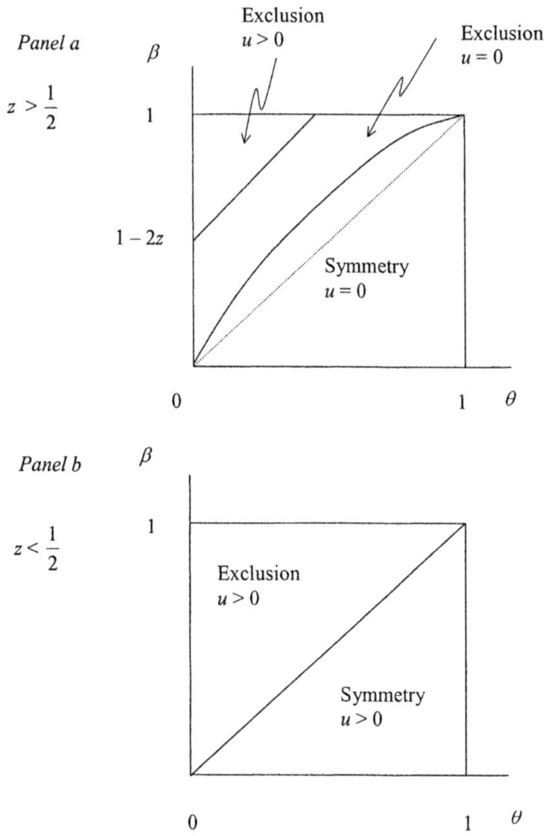

Fig. 5.2. Exclusion and Unemployment Depending on Inequality Parameters

5.5 Discussion

We have studied a model where firms have market power and consumers differ by income levels. We studied this model under the assumption that all goods are produced with the same technology and all goods enter the consumers' objective function in the same way.

We have seen that the general equilibrium of such an economy may be characterized by an asymmetric outcome if the distribution of endowments is sufficiently unequal. When consumers have non-homothetic preferences and when their endowments are sufficiently unequally distributed, an asymmetric outcome is possible and likely. In such a situation, some firms may find it profitable to sell their products only to rich people at very high prices. In other words, the products of these firms are "exclusive" goods, that are too expensive for poor households. The poor are excluded these markets in the sense that they would have a willingness to pay above the marginal cost of production, but the firms do not find it profitable to sell at this (low) price. While some firms sell exclusive goods, other firms sell "mass consumption" goods that both rich and poor individuals purchase. These goods have low prices and are sold at large quantities. Hence the general equilibrium is characterized by an asymmetric industry structure despite the fact that all goods symmetric with respect to technologies and preferences. In other words, income inequality affects the industry structure *and* the price structure of the economy.

Another interesting feature of our model is the possibility of unemployment. The reason for such unemployment that is entirely due to imperfections in the product market. No downward flexibility of wages in the labor market is needed. That such a possibility exists has been shown in previous papers, and the innovation of our model is that such a regime becomes more likely, the more unequal the distribution of income. Furthermore, we have shown that an increase in inequality may aggravate the unemployment problem.

How general are our results? We have assumed quadratic preferences and restricted the distribution to two types of consumers. (With respect to the assumption of quadratic preferences we note that this specific utility function belongs to the HARA class. This class has nice aggregation properties but these properties disappear as soon as non-negativity constraints do become binding.) However, our results do not hinge on the specific formulation of quadratic utility. Two important assumptions on preferences are needed to generate our results. The first assumption is that $v'(0)$ is finite, hence the prohibitive price is finite. The second assumption is that the elasticity of demand is falling in the consumption level. Hence richer individuals will also have the more inelastic demand, and monopolists are tempted to sell exclusively to the rich as mark-ups from such a strategy are higher. These two assumptions support an equilibrium (i) where some monopolists supply exclusive goods whereas other monopolists supply mass consumption goods, and (ii) where more inequality leads to more exclusion and higher markups. Many utility functions satisfy these properties and may generate equilibria that are of a similar type. It is in this sense that the quadratic utility function is an interesting example that highlights potentially important mechanisms relating inequality and market power.

Our focus on a distribution of endowments with only two groups is less essential. For instance, it is easy to imagine (though somewhat tedious to calculate) an equilibrium in which there are three (or more) different groups. If these groups are sufficiently different from each other, the asymmetric equilibrium will be characterized by a situation where a certain range of product is purchased only by the rich, another range also by the middle class, and the remaining goods will be mass consumption goods. Our result are robust to different assumptions about the distribution of income. What is essential to get an asymmetric equilibrium, however, is a sufficiently polarized income distribution.

Finally, our analysis has also pointed to the possibility of unemployment, that arises entirely from imperfections in the product market, whereas the labor market is Walrasian. We have shown that there is unemployment even if the wage rate falls to zero. The reader might think that this is only a theoretical possibility with no practical relevance. However, it should be noted that our analysis is relevant even if there is a lower bound to the real wage due to institutional reasons or due to other imperfections in the labor market. The important argument is that income inequality shapes the demand functions that monopolistic firms face and, in an asymmetric equilibrium, more inequality reduces the demand for labor and increases unemployment, given some given (rigid) real wage. It is in this sense, that an increase in inequality may aggravate the unemployment problem.

5.6 Appendix

Proof of Proposition 14

To show that the equilibrium exists it suffices to show that $h(\underline{p}, g(\underline{p}))$ is smaller than $\frac{1-\beta\vartheta}{(1-\beta)\vartheta}$ for small values of $\underline{p}$ and larger than $\frac{1-\beta\vartheta}{(1-\beta)\vartheta}$ for high $\underline{p}$ because $h(\cdot)$ is a continuous function. The minimum price $\underline{p}$ for which equation (5.15) is relevant, is the price $\hat{\underline{p}}$ which just implies $n = N$ in the resource constraint (5.13). For $\underline{p} > \hat{\underline{p}}$ the resource constraint can only be fulfilled for $n < N$. Inserting $n = N$ into (5.13) and solving for $\hat{\underline{p}}$ yields $\hat{\underline{p}} = \frac{w}{a}\frac{1-z}{1-2z}$ where $z = s/(aN)$. We calculate $h(\hat{\underline{p}}, g(\hat{\underline{p}}))$ (note that the formula greatly simplifies since $n = N$) and get after rearranging

$$\begin{aligned} h(\hat{\underline{p}}, g(\hat{\underline{p}})) &= \frac{2g(\hat{\underline{p}}) - \hat{\underline{p}} - w/a}{2g(\hat{\underline{p}}) - w/a - \frac{\hat{\underline{p}}}{\beta}\left(\frac{2g(\hat{\underline{p}}) - w/a}{2\hat{\underline{p}} - w/a} - (1-\beta)\right)} \\ &= \frac{1-\beta\vartheta}{(1-\beta)\,\beta\vartheta}\frac{4\vartheta\,(1-z)^2}{(1+\vartheta)^2 + 4\vartheta z\,(\vartheta z - (1+\vartheta))} \end{aligned}$$

Hence, $h(\hat{\underline{p}}, g(\hat{\underline{p}})) < \frac{1-\beta\vartheta}{(1-\beta)\vartheta}$ iff $\beta > \frac{4\vartheta(1-z)^2}{(1+\vartheta)^2+4\vartheta z(\vartheta z-(1+\vartheta))}$. This condition is equivalent to equation (5.10) which is necessary and sufficient that the exclusion regime exists.

We now show that $h(\underline{p}, g(\underline{p})) > \frac{1-\beta\vartheta}{(1-\beta)\vartheta}$ for high $\underline{p}$. First note that $h(\cdot)$ contains the term $-\left[\frac{\underline{p}-w/a}{2\underline{p}-w/a} - z\right] / \left[(1-\beta)\frac{\bar{p}-w/a}{2\bar{p}-w/a} - z\right]$ which goes to $+\infty$ when $\bar{p} = \frac{w}{a}\frac{1-z/(1-\beta)}{1-2z/(1-\beta)}$ (remember that $\frac{\underline{p}-w/a}{2\underline{p}-w/a} > (1-\beta)\frac{\bar{p}-w/a}{2\bar{p}-w/a}$ because (5.12) holds). Hence, if $z < (1-\beta)/2$, $h(\underline{p}, g(\underline{p}))$ goes to infinity as $\underline{p}$ and $\bar{p}$ grow and the claim is trivially satisfied. It remains to consider the case $z \geq (1-\beta)/2$. In that case we have to calculate $\lim_{\underline{p}\to\infty} h(\underline{p}, g(\underline{p}))$. Applying de l'Hôpital's Rule, we get

$$\lim_{\underline{p}\to\infty} h(\underline{p}, g(\underline{p})) = \frac{1+\beta-\beta^2-2\beta z}{(1-\beta)(2z+\beta-1)}$$

Remember that $z \leq 1/2$. Since the expression above is decreasing in z, we get a lower bound if it evaluated at $z = 1/2$

$$\lim_{\underline{p}\to\infty} h(\underline{p}, g(\underline{p})) > \frac{1-\beta^2}{(1-\beta)\beta} > \frac{1-\beta\vartheta}{(1-\beta)\vartheta}$$

where the latter inequality follows from $\beta > \frac{4\vartheta(1-z)^2}{(1+\vartheta)^2+4\vartheta z(\vartheta z-(1+\vartheta))} > \vartheta$.

The uniqueness of the equilibrium can be shown that the derivative of $h(\underline{p}, g(\underline{p}))$ with respect to $\underline{p}$ is positive whenever $h(\underline{p}, g(\underline{p})) = \frac{1-\beta\vartheta}{(1-\beta)\vartheta}$ holds.

6

Conclusions

It was the purpose of this book is to analyze how the consumption structure changes when (i) average income rises or (ii) incomes are redistributed across individuals holding aggregate income constant. In chapter 2 we offered a general formulation of non-homothetic and hierarchic preferences. With quite few assumptions, we found tractable functional forms that match the empirical facts.

Chapter 3 analyzed the interaction between endogenous growth and (demand driven) structural change. With hierarchic preferences, a rise in real income leads to a relative demand shift in the direction of the innovative goods. This implies that each industry will go (or has already gone) through a cycle of take-off, maturity and stagnation. In equilibrium, there are industries with an expanding and industries with a declining employment share. Nonetheless, we saw that macroeconomic aggregates grow pari passu at a constant rate. Thus, the model gives an intuitive explanation for structural change *and* it is able to explain structural change and balanced growth at the same time.

In chapter 4 we explored the relationship between inequality and demand structure in an endogenous growth model when consumers have hierarchic preferences. This enabled us to study the impact of inequality on demand for innovative products, on their prices, and hence on research incentives. As a result, changes in inequality affect the aggregate price structure and there may be market exclusion of the poor. With exclusion, higher inequality tends to increase growth because the profit share increases. However, higher inequality due to a bigger group of poor people may reduce growth. Instead, if the innovators always sell to all, inequality has an unambiguously negative impact on growth.

The impact of inequality on mark-ups and exclusion was discussed in chapter 5. We presented a macroeconomic model of monopolistic competition in which income distribution affects industry structure and (possibly) unemployment. High inequality may lead to a situation where the poor are excluded from certain markets because some firms set very high prices. Moreover, we indicated that there can be unemployment in such a case even if the labor market is competitive. We showed that such an unemployment regime is more likely with a more unequal distribution.

Our initial thoughts how the hierarchy of needs determines the consumption structure turned out to be very useful. It provided an intuitive framework to study structural change and growth and to analyze the ambiguous impact of inequality on the demand structure and growth. In addition, the gained know-how about non-homothetic preferences allowed us to gain important insights on aggregate price discrimination patterns.

We want to mention three applications of this approach which are worth further study.

First, the influence of inequality on *business cycles* can be analyzed. This is an interesting question since the influence of inequality on short-run phenomena has seldom been analyzed in the previous literature. With inequality affecting aggregate demand, the change in aggregate demand due to monetary or fiscal shocks is affected by inequality. In addition, if inequality affects price-setting (see chapter 5), the degree of nominal rigidity is affected by distribution.

Second, hierarchic preferences have clear implications about the *volatility of demand in different sectors.* In a business cycle where aggregate demand fluctuates, the demand for elementary goods exhibits a low volatility since the income elasticity of demand is below one. On the other hand, large fluctuations characterize the demand for new sectors, where income elasticities are high. This provides us an empirically testable hypothesis (which could be tested with time-series or cross-section data on equity stocks, for example): The relative volatility of sectors depends on the level of real income in a country. As incomes rise, the relative volatility of a given sector ought to be declining over time.

Third, hierarchic preferences in a world economy with rich and poor countries would imply interesting patterns of *international trade* and growth. On the one hand, it is a natural way of modelling the Linder-hypothesis (Linder, 1961) and/or the product-cycle hypothesis (Vernon, 1979). A rich country faces high home-demand and hence will innovate early. The poor country will first import new goods, but later on start to imitate. Hence rich countries will produce *new* goods with a high income elasticity and poor countries will produce *old* goods with a low elasticity. On the other hand, our set-up is also useful to shed light on the Prebisch/Singer-hypothesis (Prebisch, 1950, Singer, 1950) according to which the terms of trade for poor countries deteriorate as their exports are concentrated on goods with low income elasticities.

Macroeconomics so far has developed useful and powerful insights using representative-agent-models. Nonetheless such an analysis must always remain rather limited. This is due to at least two reasons. First, in analyzing a certain economic pattern, most (or even all) macroeconomic models are intended to give policy advice. However, the implementation of policy instruments is inextricably linked with its distribution implications. If there are important groups who lose due to this policy change, it is questionable whether the policy implementation will be a success or whether the policy will be implemented at all. Models with representative agents are simply useless to study such questions since it is excluded *per definitionem* that one group wins and the other loses. Second, the influence of inequality on aggregate variables is not well understood in macroeconomic theory. Chapter 4 and 5 of this book may have illustrated this claim. In a nutshell, even if we do not care about policy implementation, we are not even sure whether the results gained from these models are correct at all.

To overcome these theoretical challenges the present book has tried to derive a set-up which allows for consumer heterogeneity. The success of this approach will depend (i) on how easy the present set-up can be adapted to study more complex issues and (ii) whether the new theoretical predictions in this book can be found in the data. Whether this is the case will have to be judged. Anyhow, our know-how about aggregate phenomena can only rise if we take empirical or theoretical questions regarding inequality serious. Questions with heterogeneous agents will be among the major subjects of macroeconomics in the 21th century.

References

Alesina, Alberto and Dani Rodrik (1994); Distributive Politics and Growth, *Quarterly Journal of Economics* 109, 465-490.

Baland, Jean-Marie and Debraj Ray (1991); Why Does Asset Inequality Affect Unemployment? A Study of the Demand Composition Problem, *Journal of Development Economics* 35, 69-92.

Banerjee, Abhijit V. and Andrew F. Newman (1993); Occupational Choice and the Process of Development, *Journal of Political Economy* 101, 274-298.

Baumol, William J. (1967); Macroeconomics of Unbalanced Growth: The Anatomy of the Urban Crisis, *American Economic Review* 57, 415-426.

Baumol, William J., Sue Anne Batey Blackman, and Edward N. Wolff, (1985); Unbalanced Growth Revisited: Asymptotic Stagnancy and New Evidence, *American Economic Review* 75, 806-817.

Bertola, Giuseppe (1993); Factor Shares and Savings in Endogenous Growth, *American Economic Review* 83, 1184-1198.

Bertola, Giuseppe, Reto Foellmi and Josef Zweimueller (2005); *Distribution in Macroeconomic Models*, Princeton University Press, Princeton, forthcoming.

Bourguignon, François (1990); Growth and Inequality in the Dual Model of Development: the Role of Demand Factors, *Review of Economic Studies* 57, 215-228.

Carroll, Christopher D. (2000); Requiem for the Representative Consumer? Aggregate Implications of Microeconomic Consumption Behavior, *American Economic Review, Papers and Proceedings* 90(2), 110-115.

Chou, Chien-fu and Gabriel Talmain (1996); Redistribution and Growth: Pareto Improvements, *Journal of Economic Growth* 1, 505-523.

Clark, Colin (1940); *The Conditions of Economic Progress*, Macmillan, London.

Clarke, George R.G. (1995); More Evidence on Income Distribution and Growth, *Journal of Development Economics* 47, 403-427.

D'Aspremont, Claude, Rodolphe Dos Santos Ferreira, and Louis-André Gérard-Varet (1990); On Monopolistic Competition and Involuntary Unemployment, *Quarterly Journal of Economics* 105, 895-919.

David, Paul A. and Trond E. Olsen (1992); Optimal Duration of Patent-Based Monopolies, *International Journal of Industrial Organization* 10, 517-543.

Deaton, Angus and John Muellbauer (1980); *Economics and Consumer Behavior*, Cambridge MA, CUP.

De Janvry, Alain and Elisabeth Sadoulet (1983); Social Articulation as a Condition for Equitable Growth, *Journal of Development Economics* 13, 275-303.

Dixit, Avinash and Joseph Stiglitz (1977); Monopolistic Competition and Optimum Product Diversity, *American Economic Review* 67, 297-308.

Echevarria, Cristina (1997); Changes in Sectoral Composition Associated with Economic Growth, *International Economic Review* 38, 431-452.

Engel, Ernst (1857); Die Productions- und Consumptionsverhältnisse des Königreichs Sachsen, *Zeitschrift des Statistischen Büreaus des Königlich Sächsischen Ministeriums des Inneren*, No. 8 und 9.

Eswaran, Mukesh and Ashok Kotwal (1993); A Theory of Real Wage Growth in LDCs, *Journal of Development Economics* 42, 243-269.

Falkinger, Josef (1986); *Sättigung, Moralische und psychologische Grenzen des Wachstums*, Mohr Siebeck, Tübingen.

Falkinger, Josef (1990); On Growth Along a Hierarchy of Wants, *Metroeconomica* 41, 209-223.

Falkinger, Josef (1994); An Engelian Model of Growth and Innovation with Hierarchic Demand and Unequal Incomes, *Ricerche Economiche* 48, 123-139.

Foellmi, Reto (1999); *Monopolistische Preissetzung bei hierarchischen Präferenzen*, Diploma Thesis, University of Zurich.

Foellmi, Reto (2003); CRRA and Changes in the Composite Commodity, mimeo, University of Zurich.

Foellmi, Reto and Manuel Oechslin (2003); Who Gains From Non-Collusive Corruption?, IEW Working Paper No. 142, University of Zurich.

Foellmi, Reto and Josef Zweimueller (2001); Structural Change and Balanced Growth With A Hierarchy of Needs, mimeo, University of Zurich.

Foellmi, Reto and Josef Zweimueller (2002a); Structural Change and the Kaldor Facts of Economic Growth, CEPR Discussion Paper No. 3300, IEW Working Paper No. 111, University of Zurich.

Foellmi, Reto and Josef Zweimueller (2002b); Heterogeneous Mark-Ups, Demand Composition, and the Inequality-Growth Relation, mimeo, University of Zurich.

Foellmi, Reto and Josef Zweimueller (2003); Inequality and Macroeconomics: The Role of Product Market Power, mimeo, University of Zurich.

Foellmi, Reto and Josef Zweimueller (2004); Inequality, Market Power, and Equilibrium Product Diversity, *Economics Letters* 82, 139-145.

Friedman, Milton (1957); *A Theory of the Consumption Function*, Princeton University Press, Princeton.

Friend, Irwin and Blume, Marshall E. (1975); The Demand for Risky Assets, *American Economic Review* 65, 900-922.

Gabszewicz, Jaskold and Jacques-François Thisse (1979); Price Competition, Quality and Income Disparities, *Journal of Economic Theory* 20, 340 - 359.

Gabszewicz, Jaskold and Jacques-François Thisse (1980); Entry (and Exit) in a Differentiated Industry, *Journal of Economic Theory* 22, 327 - 338.

Galor, Oded and Omer Moav (2002); Das Human Kapital, mimeo, Brown University.

Galor, Oded and Joseph Zeira (1993); Income Distribution and Macroeconomics, *Review of Economic Studies* 60, 35-52.

Georgescu-Roegen, Nicholas (1966); *Analytical Economics: Issues and Problems*, Harvard University Press, Cambridge MA.

Glass, Amy J. (1996); Income Distribution and Quality Improvement, mimeo, Ohio State University.

Glass, Amy J. (2001); Price Discrimination and Quality Improvement, *Canadian Journal of Economics* 34, 549-569.

Hart, Oliver (1982); A Model of Imperfect Competition with Keynesian Features, *Quarterly Journal of Economics* 97, 109-138.

Hornstein, Andreas and Per Krusell (1996); Can Technology Improvements Cause Productivity Slowdowns?, in: Bernanke B. and J. Rotemberg (eds.), *NBER Macroeconomics Annual*, pp. 209-259.

Houthakker, Hendrick S. (1987); Engel Curve, in: J. Eatwell, M. Milgate, and P. Newman (eds.), *The New Palgrave Dictionary of Economics*, London, Macmillan, pp. 142-143.

Jackson, L. Fraser (1984); Hierarchic Demand and the Engel Curve for Variety, *Review of Economics and Statistics* 66, 8-15.

Jones, Charles I. (1995); Time Series Tests of Endogenous Growth Models, *Quarterly Journal of Economics* 110, 495-525.

Jones, Charles I. (1999); Growth With or Without Scale Effects, *American Economic Review, Papers and Proceedings* 89(2), 139-144.

Kaldor, Nicholas (1961); Capital Accumulation and Economic Growth, in: F. Lutz and D.C. Hague (eds.), *The Theory of Capital*, New York: St. Martin's Press, pp. 177-222.

King, Robert G. and Sergio Rebelo (1999); Resuscitating Real Business Cycles, in: J.B. Taylor and M. Woodford (eds.), *Handbook of Macroeconomics*, Vol. 1, North Holland.

Kindleberger, Charles (1989); *Economic Laws and Economic History*, Cambridge University Press, Cambridge.

Kirman, Alan P. (1992); Whom or What Does the Representative Agent Represent?, *Journal of Economic Perspectives* 6, 117-36.

Kocher, David (2001); *Structural Change and Balanced Growth With A Hierarchy of Needs: The Impact of Saturation Preferences*, Semesterarbeit, Universität Zürich.

Kongsamut, Piyabha, Sergio Rebelo, and Danyang Xie (2001); Beyond Balanced Growth, *Review of Economic Studies* 68, 869-882.

Laitner, John (2000); Structural Change and Economic Growth, *Review of Economic Studies* 67, 545-561.

Laussel, Didier and Jules Nyssen (1999); Endogenous Growth and Multiplicity due to Finite Patents' Lifetime, *Economics Letters* 63, 167-173.

Li, Chol-Won (1996); Inequality and Growth: a Schumpeterian Perspective, mimeo, University of Glasgow.

Linder, Staffan B. (1961); *An Essay on Trade and Transformation*, Stockholm, Almqvist & Wicksell.

Maddison, Angus (1987); Growth and Slowdown in Advanced Capitalist Economies: Techniques of Quantitative Assessment, *Journal of Economic Literature* 25, 649-698.

Malthus, Thomas (1798); *First Essay on Population*, Macmillan, London, 1966.

Mani, Anandi (2001); Income Distribution and the Demand Constraint, *Journal of Economic Growth* 6, 107-133.

Maslow, Abraham H. (1943); A Theory of Human Motivation, *Psychological Review* 50, 370-396.

Matsuyama, Kiminori (1992); Agricultural Productivity, Comparative Advantage, and Economic Growth, *Journal of Economic Theory* 58, 317-334.

Matsuyama, Kiminori (2000); A Ricardian Model with a Continuum of Goods under Nonhomothetic Preferences: Demand Complementarities, Income Distribution, and North-South Trade, *Journal of Political Economy* 108, 1093-1120.

Matsuyama, Kiminori (2002); The Rise of Mass Consumption Societies, *Journal of Political Economy* 110, 1035-1070.

Murphy, Kevin M., Andrei Shleifer, and Robert Vishny (1989); Income Distribution, Market Size, and Industrialization, *Quarterly Journal of Economics* 104, 537-564.

O'Donoghue, Ted and Josef Zweimueller (2004); Patents in a Model of Endogenous Growth, *Journal of Economic Growth* 9, 81-123.

Pasinetti, Luigi (1981); *Structural Change and Economic Growth*, Cambridge University Press, Cambridge.

Perotti, Roberto (1996); Growth, Income Distribution, and Democracy: What the Data Say, *Journal of Economic Growth* 1, 149-187.

Persson, Torsten and Guido Tabellini (1994); Is Inequality Harmful for Growth?, *American Economic Review* 84, 600-621.

Plato (360 BC); *Der Staat*, translated into German by R. Rufener, Artemis und Winkler, Düsseldorf, 2000.

Prebisch, Raul (1950); *The Economic Development of Latin America and Its Principal Problems*, New York: UN.

Ricardo, David (1810ff); *Letters 1810 - 1823, The Works and Correspondence of David Ricardo*, vol. VI - IX, Piero Sraffa (ed.), Cambridge, 1951.

Robinson, Joan (1933); *The Economics of Imperfect Competition*, MacMillan, London.

Romer, David (2000); *Advanced Macroeconomics*, 2nd edition, McGrawHill.

Romer, Paul (1990); Endogenous Technological Change, *Journal of Political Economy* 98, S71-S102.

Saint-Paul, Gilles (2005); Distribution and Growth in an Economy With Limited Needs, *Economic Journal*, forthcoming. Previous version: mimeo, University of Toulouse (2002).

Shaked, Avner and John Sutton (1982); Relaxing Price Competition Through Product Differentiation, *Review of Economic Studies* 49, 3 - 13.

Shaked, Avner and John Sutton (1983); Natural Oligopolies, *Econometrica* 51, 1469-1483.

Shapiro Matthew D. and David W. Wilcox (1996); Mismeasurement in the Consumer Price Index, in: Bernanke B. and J. Rotemberg (eds.), *NBER Macroeconomics Annual*, pp. 93-142.

Silvestre, Joaquim (1990); There May Be Unemployment When the Labour Market Is Competitive and the Output Market Is Not, *Economic Journal* 100, 899-913.

Singer, Hans W. (1950); The Distribution of Gains Between Borrowing and Investing Countries, *American Economic Review* 40, 473-485.

Smith, Adam (1776); *An Inquiry into the Nature and Causes of the Wealth of Nations*, R. H Campbell, A. S. Skinner and W. B. Todd (eds.) (The Glasgow Edition of the Works and Correspondence of Adam Smith, 2nd vol.), Oxford, 1976.

Stokey, Nancy L. (1988); Learning by Doing and the Introduction of New Goods, *Journal of Political Economy* 96, 701-717.

Stokey, Nancy L. (1991); The Volume and Composition of Trade Between Rich and Poor Countries, *Review of Economic Studies* 58, 63-80.

Vernon, Raymond S. (1966); International Investment and International Trade in the Product Cycle, *Quarterly Journal of Economics* 80, 190-207.

Walser, A. Victor (2002); *Konsumstrukturen in einer historischen Perspektive*, Semesterarbeit, University of Zurich.

Young, Alwin (1993); Substitution and Complementarity in Endogenous Innovation, *Quarterly Journal of Economics* 108, 775-807.

Zagler, Martin (2000); Economic Growth, Structural Change, and Search Unemployment, mimeo, EUI Florence and Vienna University of Economics.

Zweimueller, Josef and Johann K. Brunner (1996); Heterogeneous Consumers, Vertical Product Differentiation, and the Rate of Innovation, Working Paper No. 9604, Institute for Advanced Studies, Vienna.

Zweimueller, Josef and Johann K. Brunner (2005); Innovation and Growth with Rich and Poor Consumers, *Metroeconomica*, forthcoming. Previous version: CEPR Discussion Paper No. 1855 (1998).

Zweimueller, Josef (1996); Aggregate Demand, Non-Linear Engel-Curves, and R&D Investments, mimeo, Institute for Advanced Studies, Vienna.

Zweimueller, Josef (2000); Schumpeterian Entrepreneurs Meet Engel's Law: The Impact of Inequality on Innovation-Driven Growth, *Journal of Economic Growth* 5, 185-206.

Lecture Notes in Economics and Mathematical Systems

For information about Vols. 1–459
please contact your bookseller or Springer-Verlag

Vol. 460: B. Fleischmann, J. A. E. E. van Nunen, M. G. Speranza, P. Stähly, Advances in Distribution Logistic. XI, 535 pages. 1998.

Vol. 461: U. Schmidt, Axiomatic Utility Theory under Risk. XV, 201 pages. 1998.

Vol. 462: L. von Auer, Dynamic Preferences, Choice Mechanisms, and Welfare. XII, 226 pages. 1998.

Vol. 463: G. Abraham-Frois (Ed.), Non-Linear Dynamics and Endogenous Cycles. VI, 204 pages. 1998.

Vol. 464: A. Aulin, The Impact of Science on Economic Growth and its Cycles. IX, 204 pages. 1998.

Vol. 465: T. J. Stewart, R. C. van den Honert (Eds.), Trends in Multicriteria Decision Making. X, 448 pages. 1998.

Vol. 466: A. Sadrieh, The Alternating Double Auction Market. VII, 350 pages. 1998.

Vol. 467: H. Hennig-Schmidt, Bargaining in a Video Experiment. Determinants of Boundedly Rational Behavior. XII, 221 pages. 1999.

Vol. 468: A. Ziegler, A Game Theory Analysis of Options. XIV, 145 pages. 1999.

Vol. 469: M. P. Vogel, Environmental Kuznets Curves. XIII, 197 pages. 1999.

Vol. 470: M. Ammann, Pricing Derivative Credit Risk. XII, 228 pages. 1999.

Vol. 471: N. H. M. Wilson (Ed.), Computer-Aided Transit Scheduling. XI, 444 pages. 1999.

Vol. 472: J.-R. Tyran, Money Illusion and Strategic Complementarity as Causes of Monetary Non-Neutrality. X, 228 pages. 1999.

Vol. 473: S. Helber, Performance Analysis of Flow Lines with Non-Linear Flow of Material. IX, 280 pages. 1999.

Vol. 474: U. Schwalbe, The Core of Economies with Asymmetric Information. IX, 141 pages. 1999.

Vol. 475: L. Kaas, Dynamic Macroeconomics with Imperfect Competition. XI, 155 pages. 1999.

Vol. 476: R. Demel, Fiscal Policy, Public Debt and the Term Structure of Interest Rates. X, 279 pages. 1999.

Vol. 477: M. Théra, R. Tichatschke (Eds.), Ill-posed Variational Problems and Regularization Techniques. VIII, 274 pages. 1999.

Vol. 478: S. Hartmann, Project Scheduling under Limited Resources. XII, 221 pages. 1999.

Vol. 479: L. v. Thadden, Money, Inflation, and Capital Formation. IX, 192 pages. 1999.

Vol. 480: M. Grazia Speranza, P. Stähly (Eds.), New Trends in Distribution Logistics. X, 336 pages. 1999.

Vol. 481: V. H. Nguyen, J. J. Strodiot, P. Tossings (Eds.). Optimation. IX, 498 pages. 2000.

Vol. 482: W. B. Zhang, A Theory of International Trade. XI, 192 pages. 2000.

Vol. 483: M. Königstein, Equity, Efficiency and Evolutionary Stability in Bargaining Games with Joint Production. XII, 197 pages. 2000.

Vol. 484: D. D. Gatti, M. Gallegati, A. Kirman, Interaction and Market Structure. VI, 298 pages. 2000.

Vol. 485: A. Garnaev, Search Games and Other Applications of Game Theory. VIII, 145 pages. 2000.

Vol. 486: M. Neugart, Nonlinear Labor Market Dynamics. X, 175 pages. 2000.

Vol. 487: Y. Y. Haimes, R. E. Steuer (Eds.), Research and Practice in Multiple Criteria Decision Making. XVII, 553 pages. 2000.

Vol. 488: B. Schmolck, Ommitted Variable Tests and Dynamic Specification. X, 144 pages. 2000.

Vol. 489: T. Steger, Transitional Dynamics and Economic Growth in Developing Countries. VIII, 151 pages. 2000.

Vol. 490: S. Minner, Strategic Safety Stocks in Supply Chains. XI, 214 pages. 2000.

Vol. 491: M. Ehrgott, Multicriteria Optimization. VIII, 242 pages. 2000.

Vol. 492: T. Phan Huy, Constraint Propagation in Flexible Manufacturing. IX, 258 pages. 2000.

Vol. 493: J. Zhu, Modular Pricing of Options. X, 170 pages. 2000.

Vol. 494: D. Franzen, Design of Master Agreements for OTC Derivatives. VIII, 175 pages. 2001.

Vol. 495: I. Konnov, Combined Relaxation Methods for Variational Inequalities. XI, 181 pages. 2001.

Vol. 496: P. Weiß, Unemployment in Open Economies. XII, 226 pages. 2001.

Vol. 497: J. Inkmann, Conditional Moment Estimation of Nonlinear Equation Systems. VIII, 214 pages. 2001.

Vol. 498: M. Reutter, A Macroeconomic Model of West German Unemployment. X, 125 pages. 2001.

Vol. 499: A. Casajus, Focal Points in Framed Games. XI, 131 pages. 2001.

Vol. 500: F. Nardini, Technical Progress and Economic Growth. XVII, 191 pages. 2001.

Vol. 501: M. Fleischmann, Quantitative Models for Reverse Logistics. XI, 181 pages. 2001.

Vol. 502: N. Hadjisavvas, J. E. Martínez-Legaz, J.-P. Penot (Eds.), Generalized Convexity and Generalized Monotonicity. IX, 410 pages. 2001.

Vol. 503: A. Kirman, J.-B. Zimmermann (Eds.), Economics with Heterogenous Interacting Agents. VII, 343 pages. 2001.

Vol. 504: P.-Y. Moix (Ed.),The Measurement of Market Risk. XI, 272 pages. 2001.

Vol. 505: S. Voß, J. R. Daduna (Eds.), Computer-Aided Scheduling of Public Transport. XI, 466 pages. 2001.

Vol. 506: B. P. Kellerhals, Financial Pricing Models in Continuous Time and Kalman Filtering. XIV, 247 pages. 2001.

Vol. 507: M. Koksalan, S. Zionts, Multiple Criteria Decision Making in the New Millenium. XII, 481 pages. 2001.

Vol. 508: K. Neumann, C. Schwindt, J. Zimmermann, Project Scheduling with Time Windows and Scarce Resources. XI, 335 pages. 2002.

Vol. 509: D. Hornung, Investment, R&D, and Long-Run Growth. XVI, 194 pages. 2002.

Vol. 510: A. S. Tangian, Constructing and Applying Objective Functions. XII, 582 pages. 2002.

Vol. 511: M. Külpmann, Stock Market Overreaction and Fundamental Valuation. IX, 198 pages. 2002.

Vol. 512: W.-B. Zhang, An Economic Theory of Cities.XI, 220 pages. 2002.

Vol. 513: K. Marti, Stochastic Optimization Techniques. VIII, 364 pages. 2002.

Vol. 514: S. Wang, Y. Xia, Portfolio and Asset Pricing. XII, 200 pages. 2002.

Vol. 515: G. Heisig, Planning Stability in Material Requirements Planning System. XII, 264 pages. 2002.

Vol. 516: B. Schmid, Pricing Credit Linked Financial Instruments. X, 246 pages. 2002.

Vol. 517: H. I. Meinhardt, Cooperative Decision Making in Common Pool Situations. VIII, 205 pages. 2002.

Vol. 518: S. Napel, Bilateral Bargaining. VIII, 188 pages. 2002.

Vol. 519: A. Klose, G. Speranza, L. N. Van Wassenhove (Eds.), Quantitative Approaches to Distribution Logistics and Supply Chain Management. XIII, 421 pages. 2002.

Vol. 520: B. Glaser, Efficiency versus Sustainability in Dynamic Decision Making. IX, 252 pages. 2002.

Vol. 521: R. Cowan, N. Jonard (Eds.), Heterogenous Agents, Interactions and Economic Performance. XIV, 339 pages. 2003.

Vol. 522: C. Neff, Corporate Finance, Innovation, and Strategic Competition. IX, 218 pages. 2003.

Vol. 523: W.-B. Zhang, A Theory of Interregional Dynamics. XI, 231 pages. 2003.

Vol. 524: M. Frölich, Programme Evaluation and Treatment Choise. VIII, 191 pages. 2003.

Vol. 525: S. Spinler, Capacity Reservation for Capital-Intensive Technologies. XVI, 139 pages. 2003.

Vol. 526: C. F. Daganzo, A Theory of Supply Chains. VIII, 123 pages. 2003.

Vol. 527: C. E. Metz, Information Dissemination in Currency Crises. XI, 231 pages. 2003.

Vol. 528: R. Stolletz, Performance Analysis and Optimization of Inbound Call Centers. X, 219 pages. 2003.

Vol. 529: W. Krabs, S. W. Pickl, Analysis, Controllability and Optimization of Time-Discrete Systems and Dynamical Games. XII, 187 pages. 2003.

Vol. 530: R. Wapler, Unemployment, Market Structure and Growth. XXVII, 207 pages. 2003.

Vol. 531: M. Gallegati, A. Kirman, M. Marsili (Eds.), The Complex Dynamics of Economic Interaction. XV, 402 pages, 2004.

Vol. 532: K. Marti, Y. Ermoliev, G. Pflug (Eds.), Dynamic Stochastic Optimization. VIII, 336 pages. 2004.

Vol. 533: G. Dudek, Collaborative Planning in Supply Chains. X, 234 pages. 2004.

Vol. 534: M. Runkel, Environmental and Resource Policy for Consumer Durables. X, 197 pages. 2004.

Vol. 535: X. Gandibleux, M. Sevaux, K. Sörensen, V. T'kindt (Eds.), Metaheuristics for Multiobjective Optimisation. IX, 249 pages. 2004.

Vol. 536: R. Brüggemann, Model Reduction Methods for Vector Autoregressive Processes. X, 218 pages. 2004.

Vol. 537: A. Esser, Pricing in (In)Complete Markets. XI, 122 pages, 2004.

Vol. 538: S. Kokot, The Econometrics of Sequential Trade Models. XI, 193 pages. 2004.

Vol. 539: N. Hautsch, Modelling Irregularly Spaced Financial Data. XII, 291 pages. 2004.

Vol. 540: H. Kraft, Optimal Portfolios with Stochastic Interest Rates and Defaultable Assets. X, 173 pages. 2004.

Vol. 541: G.-y. Chen, X. Huang, X. Yang, Vector Optimization. X, 306 pages. 2005.

Vol. 542: J. Lingens, Union Wage Bargaining and Economic Growth. XIII, 199 pages. 2004.

Vol. 543: C. Benkert, Default Risk in Bond and Credit Derivatives Markets. IX, 135 pages. 2004.

Vol. 544: B. Fleischmann, A. Klose, Distribution Logistics. X, 284 pages. 2004.

Vol. 545: R. Hafner, Stochastic Implied Volatility. XI, 229 pages. 2004.

Vol. 546: D. Quadt, Lot-Sizing and Scheduling for Flexible Flow Lines. XVIII, 227 pages. 2004.

Vol. 547: M. Wildi, Signal Extraction. XI, 279 pages. 2005.

Vol. 548: D. Kuhn, Generalized Bounds for Convex Multistage Stochastic Programs. XI, 190 pages. 2005.

Vol. 549: G. N. Krieg, Kanban-Controlled Manufacturing Systems. IX, 236 pages. 2005.

Vol. 550: T. Lux, S. Reitz, E. Samanidou, Nonlinear Dynamics and Heterogeneous Interacting Agents. XIII, 327 pages. 2005.

Vol. 551: J. Leskow, M. Puchet Anyul, L. F. Punzo, New Tools of Economic Dynamics. XIX, 392 pages. 2005.

Vol. 552: C. Suerie, Time Continuity in Discrete Time Models. XVIII, 229 pages. 2005.

Vol. 553: B. Mönch, Strategic Trading in Illiquid Markets. XIII, 116 pages. 2005.

Vol. 554: R. Foellmi, Consumption Structure and Macroeconomics. IX, 152 pages. 2005.

GPSR Compliance

The European Union's (EU) General Product Safety Regulation (GPSR) is a set of rules that requires consumer products to be safe and our obligations to ensure this.

If you have any concerns about our products, you can contact us on ProductSafety@springernature.com

In case Publisher is established outside the EU, the EU authorized representative is:

Springer Nature Customer Service Center GmbH
Europaplatz 3
69115 Heidelberg, Germany

Batch number: 10844675

Printed by Printforce, the Netherlands